REPAIRING FURNITURE

Other Publications:

THE EPIC OF FLIGHT
THE GOOD COOK
THE SEAFARERS
THE ENCYCLOPEDIA OF COLLECTIBLES
THE GREAT CITIES
WORLD WAR II
THE WORLD'S WILD PLACES
THE TIME-LIFE LIBRARY OF BOATING
HUMAN BEHAVIOR
THE ART OF SEWING
THE OLD WEST
THE EMERGENCE OF MAN
THE AMERICAN WILDERNESS
THE TIME-LIFE ENCYCLOPEDIA OF GARDENING
LIFE LIBRARY OF PHOTOGRAPHY
THIS FABULOUS CENTURY
FOODS OF THE WORLD
TIME-LIFE LIBRARY OF AMERICA
TIME-LIFE LIBRARY OF ART
GREAT AGES OF MAN
LIFE SCIENCE LIBRARY
THE LIFE HISTORY OF THE UNITED STATES
TIME READING PROGRAM
LIFE NATURE LIBRARY
LIFE WORLD LIBRARY
FAMILY LIBRARY:
   HOW THINGS WORK IN YOUR HOME
   THE TIME-LIFE BOOK OF THE FAMILY CAR
   THE TIME-LIFE FAMILY LEGAL GUIDE
   THE TIME-LIFE BOOK OF FAMILY FINANCE

HOME REPAIR
AND IMPROVEMENT

REPAIRING FURNITURE

BY THE EDITORS OF
TIME-LIFE BOOKS

TIME-LIFE BOOKS
ALEXANDRIA, VIRGINIA

Time-Life Books Inc.
is a wholly owned subsidiary of
TIME INCORPORATED

Founder Henry R. Luce 1898-1967

Editor-in-Chief Henry Anatole Grunwald
President J. Richard Munro
Chairman of the Board Ralph P. Davidson
Executive Vice President Clifford J. Grum
Editorial Director Ralph Graves
Vice Chairman Arthur Temple

TIME-LIFE BOOKS INC.

Managing Editor Jerry Korn

Executive Editor David Maness
Assistant Managing Editors Dale M. Brown (planning), George Constable,
Thomas H. Flaherty Jr. (acting), Martin Mann,
John Paul Porter
Art Director Tom Suzuki
Chief of Research David L. Harrison
Director of Photography Robert G. Mason
Assistant Art Director Arnold C. Holeywell
Assistant Chief of Research Carolyn L. Sackett
Assistant Director of Photography Dolores A. Littles

Chairman Joan D. Manley
President John D. McSweeney
Executive Vice Presidents Carl G. Jaeger, John Steven Maxwell, David J. Walsh
Vice Presidents George Artandi (comptroller); Stephen L. Bair (legal
counsel); Peter G. Barnes; Nicholas Benton (public
relations); John L. Canova; Beatrice T. Dobie
(personnel); Carol Flaumenhaft (consumer affairs);
Nicholas J. C. Ingleton (Asia); James L. Mercer
(Europe/South Pacific); Herbert Sorkin (production);
Paul R. Stewart (marketing)

HOME REPAIR AND IMPROVEMENT

Editorial Staff for Repairing Furniture

Editor Robert M. Jones
Assistant Editors Robert A. Doyle, Betsy Frankel
Designer Edward Frank
Chief Researcher Oobie Gleysteen
Picture Editor Adrian Allen
Associate Designer Kenneth E. Hancock
Text Editors Leslie Marshall, Peter Pocock, Brooke Stoddard
Staff Writers Lynn R. Addison, Patricia C. Bangs, Jan Leslie Cook,
Steven J. Forbis, Kathleen M. Kiely,
Victoria W. Monks, Mary-Sherman Willis,
William Worsley
Researcher Kimberly K. Lewis
Art Associates George Bell, Fred Holz, Lorraine D. Rivard
Editorial Assistant Susan Larson

Editorial Production

Production Editor Douglas B. Graham
Operations Manager Gennaro C. Esposito, Gordon E. Buck (assistant)
Assistant Production Editor Feliciano Madrid
Quality Control Robert L. Young (director), James J. Cox (assistant),
Daniel J. McSweeney, Michael G. Wight (associates)
Art Coordinator Anne B. Landry
Copy Staff Susan B. Galloway (chief), Margery duMond,
Diane Ullius Jarrett, Brian Miller, Celia Beattie
Picture Department Greg Schaler
Traffic Jeanne Potter

Correspondents: Elisabeth Kraemer (Bonn); Margot
Hapgood, Dorothy Bacon, Lesley Coleman (London);
Susan Jonas, Lucy T. Voulgaris (New York); Maria
Vincenza Aloisi, Josephine du Brusle (Paris); Ann
Natanson (Rome). Valuable help was also given by:
Karin B. Pearce, Gail Ridgwell, Pat Stimpson
(London); Carolyn T. Chubet, Miriam Hsia, Christina
Lieberman (New York); Mimi Murphy (Rome).

THE CONSULTANTS: David Adamusko restores antiques professionally and is a consultant on restoration and cabinetwork. He teaches furniture restoration at the Smithsonian Institution in Washington, D.C., and woodworking technology in the Fairfax County, Virginia, public schools.

Roswell W. Ard is a consulting structural engineer and a professional home inspector in northern Michigan. He has written professionally on the structural uses of wood and on wood-frame construction techniques, and is experienced in finish carpentry.

Allen E. Cochran is senior conservator for the National Park Service in its furniture conservation laboratory at Harpers Ferry, West Virginia. He has restored furniture for more than 300 national parks, historic sites and monuments, including the White House.

Lawrence R. England Jr. works in L. R. England and Sons, the family cabinetmaking and woodworking business established by his grandfather in Boston in 1900. The firm specializes in the design and construction of custom-made furniture.

Aku Merali was born in Masaka, Uganda, and for several years owned a custom upholstery shop in Nairobi, Kenya. His custom workroom in Alexandria, Virginia, is noted for its innovative ideas in the use of fabrics for home decorating.

Harris Mitchell, special consultant for Canada, has worked in the field of home repair and improvement for more than two decades. He is Homes editor of *Today* magazine and author of a syndicated newspaper column, as well as of a number of books on home improvement.

Linwood C. Reynolds has been restoring antiques professionally since the 1940s in Ohio and the Washington, D.C., area. He deals in all types of restoration, from woodworking to metalworking and clock repair, with special emphasis on fine cabinetry and French finishing.

For information about any Time-Life book, please write:
Reader Information
Time-Life Books
541 North Fairbanks Court
Chicago, Illinois 60611

Library of Congress Cataloguing in Publication Data
Time-Life Books.
  Repairing furniture.
  (Home repair and improvement; 24)
  Includes index.
  1. Furniture—Repairing. 2. Furniture
finishing. 3. Upholstery. I. Title.
TT199.T49   1980   684.1'044   80-15452
ISBN 0-8094-2440-1
ISBN 0-8094-2439-8 (lib. bdg.)

Contents

Putting the Parts Back Together

A joint that endures. The dovetail joint—perhaps the most sophisticated version of the mortise-and-tenon joint used in fine furniture—is a sign of quality construction. Flared tongues fit snugly into matching dovetail-shaped sockets to increase strength; joints of this kind can be separated in only one direction. Dovetail joints are used in drawers and cabinets as a way of connecting two panels of wood at a right angle.

Good, solid, everyday furniture seldom lasts a lifetime. It gets sat upon, dined upon, leaned against, occasionally stood upon. Over the years, as one guest too many tilts backward on a dining-room chair, or the scuffs and glass marks become too numerous on a coffee table, or the springs on a favorite sofa finally give way, the piece gets tucked away in the attic or basement.

In days gone by, its life would have ended there. In the Middle Ages the chest, or coffer, that served as bench, bed and table as well as a trunk for storage or transport was discarded when its wooden panels split, warped or were otherwise damaged. It was too crudely made to be fixed. Today, thanks to modern materials and improved methods of joinery, most damaged furniture can be rescued. The repairs can range from simple tasks such as regluing loose joints, removing stains with special-purpose cleansers and conditioners, or re-covering cushions, to such complex and time-consuming projects as duplicating broken parts with a lathe, stripping and refinishing a cabinet, or reupholstering a sofa.

Deciding whether to do the job yourself or turn it over to a professional is only partly a matter of personal choice. The decision depends, of course, on how much you like the piece, the use you will get out of it when it is repaired and the nature of the work involved. However, if the piece is a true antique—defined by the U.S. Customs Service as anything made before 1830, and more loosely as anything more than 100 years old—it should be restored by a specialist, since any repair may reduce its value.

Whatever else is involved, restoring furniture to usefulness commonly begins with repairs to the joints and frame, which generally means regluing or replacing the parts of a joint. One basic joint of furniture making, the mortise and tenon, can be made with only a saw and chisel. Known to the ancient Egyptians and rediscovered by European craftsmen in the middle of the 14th Century, the mortise-and-tenon joint revolutionized furniture making. It was used in a new technique, paneled framing, in which thin panels of wood were set into grooves cut into thicker frames, making furniture lighter and less likely to split or warp.

Over the next 150 years, all well-made furniture came to be assembled by mortise and tenon, or with similar joints that used pegs or dowels rather than rectangular tenons. The furniture appeared on household inventories as "jointed" or "joined" furniture, and the guild of master craftsmen who made it were known as joiners. Sturdy and elegant, such hidden joints still hold together the frames of the best tables, chairs, sofas and beds—unchanged in concept although now, of course, the parts are cut with power tools.

Restoring Separated Joints in Wooden Chairs

Chairs have more joints than most other kinds of furniture, and they are joints that have to work hard. Even a lightweight ballerina puts stress on a chair's joints when she sits. If a man tilts the chair back and hooks his heels over a footrail, the stress is multiplied. Sooner or later, a joint works loose or separates altogether.

A weak joint should be strengthened, and the sooner the better. One bad joint puts increased stress on the remaining good joints, and if too many joints loosen, the entire chair will have to be disassembled. This is a prospect to be avoided if possible, because pulling joints apart can sometimes lead to further damage. You should, in fact, break down a chair into as few subassemblies as the repair permits and, if you can, correct loosened joints without separating them.

Although innumerable joints are used in chair construction, the two most commonly encountered are dowel joints and mortise-and-tenon joints. For a dowel joint, one end of a chair member is fitted with a separate dowel or is lathed into a dowel shape. The dowel fits into a socket in a second member.

A mortise-and-tenon joint is the rectangular equivalent of a dowel joint. Here, too, there are two basic styles. In one, the rectangular member is the tenon and fits into a mortise cut into a larger member. In the other, one end of the rectangular member is cut smaller to form a tenon that is said to be haunched—and the haunch can be cut into any one or all four sides of the member, depending on the design of the chair and the whim of the woodworker.

Both dowel joints and mortise-and-tenon joints must fit tightly for the joint to be strong. Although glue alone ordinarily holds joints together, sometimes a wedge has been added to fill a gap, and in some cases a brad or dowel has been driven into the side of the joint to reinforce it further. All these supports must be removed when the joint is repaired, a job that is not always easy. In fact, you may have to balance your wish for a solid chair against the risk of damage during disassembly. For a prized piece that is intact, albeit wobbly, it may be best to settle for stopgap repairs, then go easy on the chair, instead of restoring the joint.

Glue, wedges and dowels also figure prominently in the repertoire of techniques used to fix joints that have failed. Tools for these projects are, for the most part, simple. A wooden mallet or a hammer and a block of wood with sheet cork glued to one face are needed for disassembly. Straps that tighten like seat belts, called web clamps, hold repaired joints in place while the glue dries.

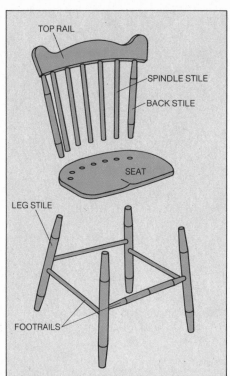

A platform chair. In chairs of this design—an elaboration of a simple stool—the seat is the nucleus of the structure, and the back and leg assemblies are attached to the seat and are completely independent of each other. The leg assembly ordinarily consists of four leg stiles, fitted into sockets on the bottom of the seat and reinforced with horizontal members called footrails. In the back assembly of a platform chair, a back stile supports each end of a top rail, and intermediary spindle stiles fill in the back and further reinforce the top rail.

Chairs of this type are often assembled entirely with dowel joints that have the dowels turned directly onto the ends of the members. The joints between the footrails and the leg stiles are generally the most vulnerable.

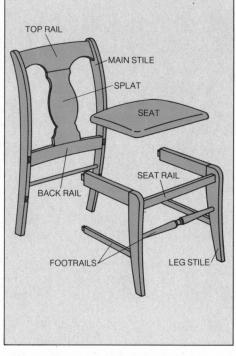

A frame chair. In chairs of this construction, the seat is in effect suspended in a wooden frame and is not a critical part of the support structure. Instead, the design centers on the two main stiles that run from the top to the bottom of the chair back, forming the rear legs and the back of the chair. Usually each of these stiles is a single piece of wood. The seat is commonly a separate element, resting on four seat rails. The front legs are joined to the side seat rails, and may be reinforced with footrails on all four sides. The main stiles are joined with a top rail and one or more back rails. When there is only a single back rail, a flat wood member, called a splat, may be inserted between the top and back rails. In many chairs of this design, the seat is upholstered or made of rush or cane.

In addition to dowel joints, frame chairs often have mortise-and-tenon joints where the seat rails meet the legs. On some, screws are used to hold the parts together. Generally the joints at the back of the seat, where the side seat rails meet the main stiles, are most vulnerable.

Choosing a Glue and Making It Stick

Wood furniture is made of solid parts, but one of the principal agents holding the parts together begins as a liquid. Scientists still do not completely understand the physical and chemical properties of glues, but furniture makers and repairers have attested to the powers of glue since 3000 B.C.

A proper glue joint has five layers, as illustrated below, and the weakest of them determines the strength of the joint. In earlier times the weakest layer was the glue, but modern glues are so strong that the surrounding wood usually breaks before the glue or the intermediate layers of glue-soaked fibers.

In order to make a well-bonded joint, you must clean the two abutting wood surfaces of old glue, dirt and finish. If the wood is smooth, roughen it by scoring with a knife. If the wood is moistened in the process of removing old glue, allow it to dry. Shape the joint so the fit is tight, leaving no gaps.

In addition, apply enough pressure to the joint to force the glue into the fibers of the wood. Usually you should pre-assemble the joint dry and clamp it, to make sure that the wood surfaces fit and that you have enough clamps. Then dismantle the joint and apply thin layers of glue to both adjoining surfaces—on end grain apply a slightly thicker layer than on side grain, which is less absorbent. Reassemble the joint, clamp it and wipe it clean—first with a damp cloth, then with a dry one. Immediately check the joint to make certain that the alignment is correct.

Choice of glue depends partly on the piece of furniture and where it will be used, and partly on preference—even professionals differ on which glues are best to use for furniture joinery. The following glues are most favored:

☐ WHITE GLUE, also known as polyvinyl acetate, is a good general adhesive for most indoor furniture. It comes ready to use and, once clamped, sets in 30 min-utes, although it should remain undisturbed until it reaches full strength in two days. It need be applied to only one surface of the adjoining pieces unless the joint has gaps, in which case it should be applied to both surfaces. White glue has low resistance to moisture and should not be used to glue outdoor furniture.

☐ YELLOW GLUE, also called aliphatic resin, is an improved offspring of the white variety. Slightly stronger and more resistant to moisture, it is also more viscous and dribbles less when applied. But it begins to dry faster than white glue and thus requires swifter clamping. The clamps can be removed after 30 minutes, but the joint should remain undisturbed until it reaches full strength 18 hours later. Yellow glue has good gap-filling properties and is especially good for ill-fitting joints.

☐ HIDE GLUE, made from animal hides, is the adhesive of purists because it was virtually the only glue available for use on furniture from early Egyptian times to about 1900. As restorers of antiques are quick to point out, the glue is reversible; steam and a sun lamp will undo the adhering properties of the glue, allowing a joint to be taken apart.

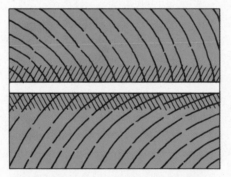

A proper glue joint. A glue joint has five layers: a thin film of glue, two areas (one on either side) consisting of wood fibers penetrated by glue, and the nearby wood that is unpenetrated. Chemical bonding between the wood fibers and the glue locks the wood pieces together.

In addition, liquid hide glue allows ample time—up to 20 minutes—for clamping before the glue begins to set. But it can be applied only at temperatures near 70° F.; it stiffens in temperatures lower than 50° and thins in temperatures higher than 90°. Joints assembled with hide glue must remain clamped for six to 12 hours, and it cannot be used for outdoor furniture.

☐ PLASTIC-RESIN GLUE, sometimes called urea-formaldehyde, is very strong and is used on joints subject to unusual stress. It comes as a powder that must be mixed with water, but once it has dried, the glue is highly resistant to moisture. Plastic-resin glue must be applied at temperatures higher than 70° F. It starts to set in five to 15 minutes and, once clamped, it must be kept under pressure for five to 12 hours, depending on the temperature. It does not fill gaps well, so the joints must be tight.

☐ RESORCINOL GLUE is prepared by mixing a powder with a liquid catalyst. it is very strong, has the highest resistance to heat and moisture—it is even used in boatbuilding—and is the best glue for repairing outdoor wood furniture. It should be applied at room temperature and left clamped for 10 to 12 hours.

☐ OTHER ADHESIVES. There are a number of other synthetic glues used in woodworking, and new ones are frequently introduced, but those listed above are favored by professionals for furniture repair. The familiar epoxy glues (there are a number of formulations, including some that harden very quickly) work chemically to form a strong bond between pieces of wood as well as such nonporous materials as metal or glass. However, epoxy is expensive; several less costly glues work at least as well in furniture repair. The contact cements, such as those used to laminate thin sheets of plastic to countertops, set almost instantly; they allow no time for adjustments when joints are glued.

Four Kinds of Joint Locks

Looking for obstacles. Before pulling a loose joint apart to make repairs, examine it to see if there is a fastener that you must first remove. Sometimes you must look for subtle clues. A dimple in the wood finish near the joint, for instance, may indicate that a brad is securing the end of a dowel *(near right, top)*. More obvious is a dowel that pins a mortise-and-tenon joint together *(far right, top)*, since its end is exposed.

Cracks around a joint often signal situations in which the joint should not be pulled apart. Hairline cracks on the sides of a dowel at the point where it emerges from its socket *(near right, bottom)* generally mean that the dowel has been wedged. Pulling such a joint apart may split the socket. In old furniture, cracks above and below a socket where a dowel enters an oval stile or rail are typical of a special joint called a shrink joint *(far right, bottom)*. In this older version of a dowel joint, a knobbed end of dry wood was fitted into a socket while the socketed member was still green. Since the socket then shrank around the knob as it dried, disassembling these joints probably will split the wood.

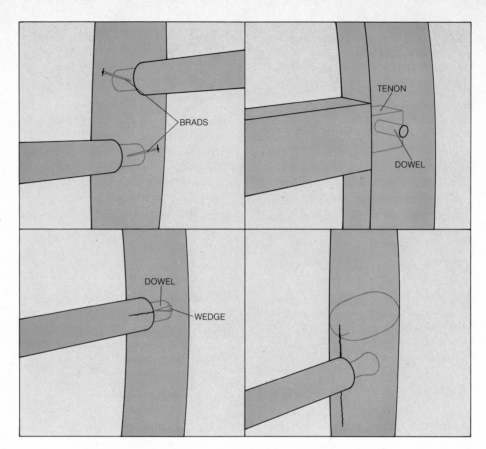

Regluing Loose Dowel Joints

1 Injecting glue. Pull the joint apart slightly and drill a perpendicular hole, slightly larger than the tip of a syringe-type glue injector, into the back of the dowel socket. Jam the tip of the injector into the hole, and squeeze the plunger until glue appears all around the dowel. You may have to drill and inject glue into a second hole if it is difficult to get glue into the first one or if the glue comes out on only one side of the dowel. Smear glue over the exposed section of the dowel, and press the joint back together again. Use wood filler to conceal the hole.

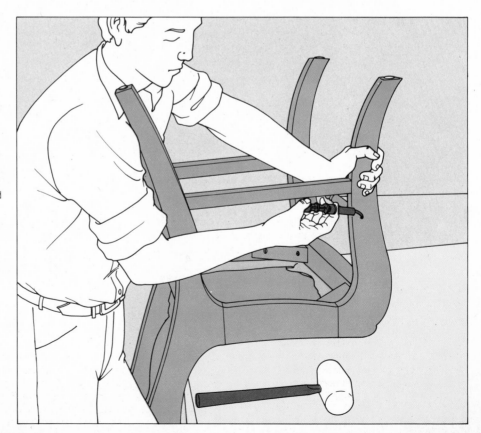

2 **Using a web clamp.** With the dowel in its socket, assemble a web clamp following the manufacturer's instructions, and loop it around the chair so that the loose joint will be forced together when the clamp is tightened. Rest sticks across rails or stiles as needed, to keep the web strap in place as the clamp is tightened (*inset*). Tighten the winch nut of the clamp with a screwdriver or a socket wrench; if you use a wrench, which is usually easier, tighten the nut only as much as you could if you were using a screwdriver. Tap the joint lightly with a mallet to make sure the dowel is completely seated. Let the glue dry before removing the clamp.

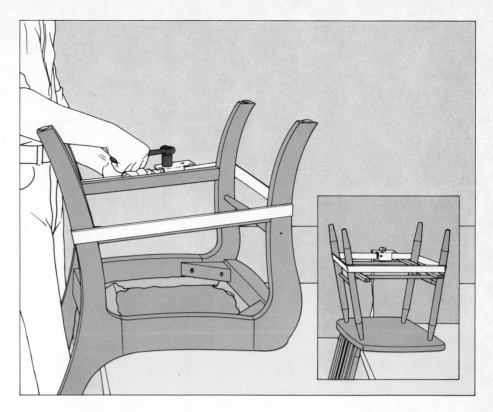

Wedging a Loose Mortise-and-Tenon Joint

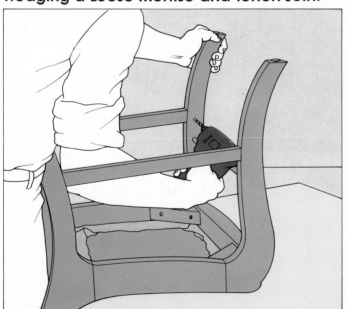

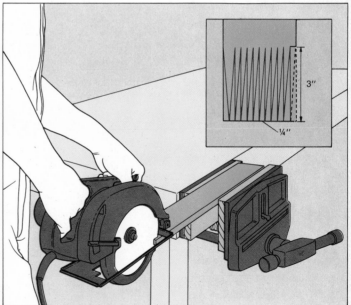

1 **Drilling out a dowel pin.** When a haunched tenon pinned with a dowel is loose, use an awl to make a starting hole for a drill bit in the center of the dowel. Then drill the dowel out, using a bit that has a diameter slightly greater than that of the dowel. If the tenon is not haunched, do not drill out the dowel; instead, fit wedges around the tenon to tighten it (*Steps 2 and 3*).

2 **Making wedges.** Use a table saw, radial-arm saw or portable circular saw to cut out hardwood wedges to fill the gaps around a loose tenon. If you use a circular saw, clamp the wood face up in a vise as shown here, and cut along the grain of the wood, not across it. Make wedges about 3 inches long, tapering from ¼ inch thick at the butt end to a sharp edge. For economical use of wood, alternate tapered cuts with straight cuts that square off the board again (*inset*).

3 **Wedging the tenon.** Pull the joint slightly apart, and trim thin wedges to fit the gap between the tenon and its mortise. For very loose joints, use wedges on all four sides to keep the mortise and tenon in alignment; for a joint only slightly loose, one wedge is sufficient. Inject glue into the back of the joint *(Step 1, page 10)*, and smear glue on the exposed part of the tenon. Coat both sides of each wedge with glue by sliding the wedge through a puddle of glue on a scrap of wood. Insert the wedges into the gaps around the tenon, and press the joint together to seat it. On a haunched tenon, as shown, the shoulders of wood will drive the wedges into place. On an unhaunched tenon, use a mallet and a small wood block to drive in the wedges. Clamp the joint *(Step 2, page 11)* until the glue dries.

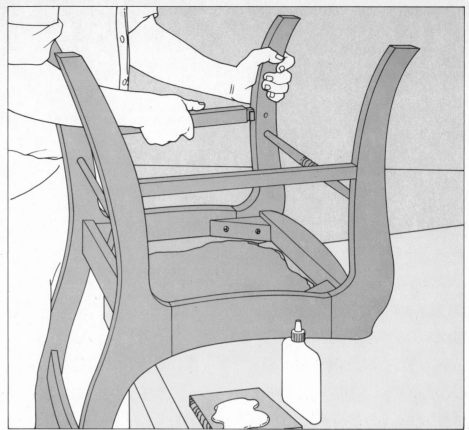

4 **Pinning the joint.** If you removed a dowel to release the joint *(Step 1, page 11)*, cut a new dowel of the same diameter as the drill bit you used but slightly longer than the depth of the hole. Bevel one end of the dowel to make it easier to insert. Use a stick to spread glue inside the hole; apply more glue to the dowel, and tap the dowel into the hole with a mallet. Let the glue dry, then sand the end of the dowel flush with the surrounding wood surface. Finish the end of the dowel to match the rest of the chair.

If necessary, use the same technique to add a dowel pin to a mortise-and-tenon joint that does not not already have one. Drill the hole for the dowel after the glue in the wedged joint is dry.

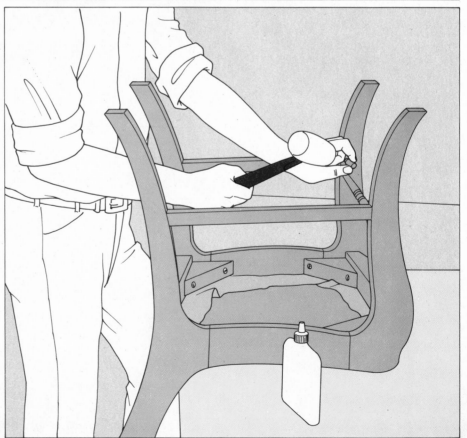

Techniques for Taking a Chair Apart

Using a mallet to loosen joints. With a mallet or hammer, break the bond of glue that holds the parts together. Label each part, as a guide for reassembly. Use a block faced with cork to protect the striking area, and lift that area of the chair slightly. Use blows of moderate force, then try levering (*below, right*) if necessary.

Separate the parts of a platform chair by first releasing the leg or back assembly from the seat, as shown below; then take apart the subassemblies as needed. On a frame chair, begin by separating the main stiles, as shown below, right, if they are loose; then proceed to the subassemblies. If the main stiles are not loose, separate only the parts with loose joints.

Using leverage to loosen joints. Cut two pieces of wood, the sum of whose lengths is slightly longer than the distance between the parts to be separated. Trim one end of each piece into a cup shape, to keep the pieces from slipping off the work, and cut a V and an inverted V in the other ends, to join the two pieces where they meet in the middle. Position this lever so that its outer ends are as close as possible to the joints that are to be opened, and place cork pads between the ends and the chair to protect the finish. Apply force gradually with your hand, to straighten the joint in the middle of the lever. To apply force over spans of other lengths, construct another two-part lever or recombine the halves of two different levers.

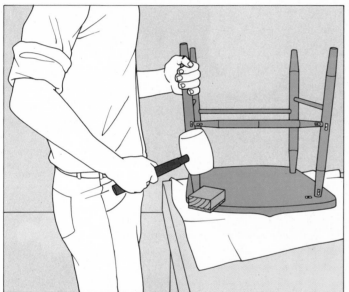

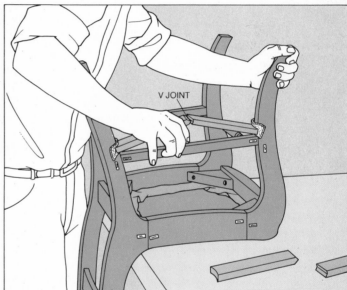

Refitting Dowels in a Disassembled Chair

1 **Scraping glue from the dowel.** Use a knife to scrape old glue from the surface of the doweled end. Hold the knife almost perpendicular to the wood, but tip the back of the knife slightly forward so that you will be dragging the blade across the surface of the wood. Use as much force as needed to remove the dried glue without digging into the wood.

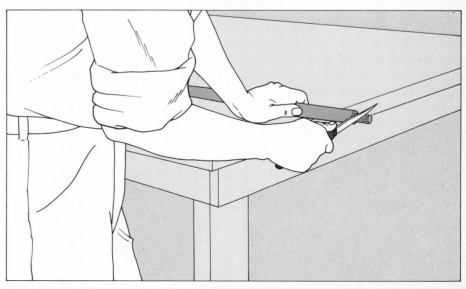

2 **Preparing the socket.** Wrap the socketed part of the chair in cork to protect its finish, and clamp it in a vise, socket up. Reach inside the socket with a ¼-inch chisel, held with the side of the blade against the side of the socket, and scrape out the old glue. Then enlarge the bottom of the socket slightly so that there will be enough room for the wedged dowel to expand.

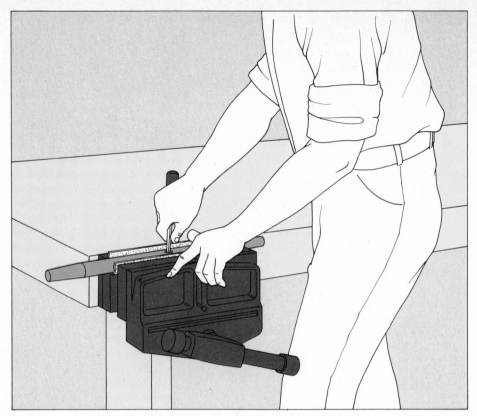

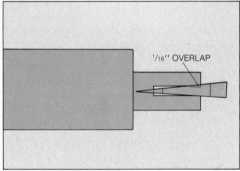

1/16" OVERLAP

4 **Wedging the dowel.** Cut a hardwood wedge (*page 11, bottom*), and fit it to the kerf in the dowel so that the end of the dowel will spread out slightly when the joint is assembled. First measure the depth of the socket and the length of the dowel to find the clearance between the end of the dowel and the bottom of the socket, usually about ⅛ inch. Then hold the wedge alongside the kerf, tapered end pointing toward the bottom of the kerf. Position the wedge so that its thickness where it passes the end of the dowel is ¹⁄₁₆ inch greater than the width of the kerf.

Mark the wedge at a distance, beyond the end of the dowel, equal to the clearance depth; mark the other end of the wedge just short of the bottom of the kerf. Cut the wedge at these two marks. Temporarily secure the wedge to the dowel with a rubber band until you have dry-fitted all the other joints and are ready to glue the entire chair back together (*pages 16-17*).

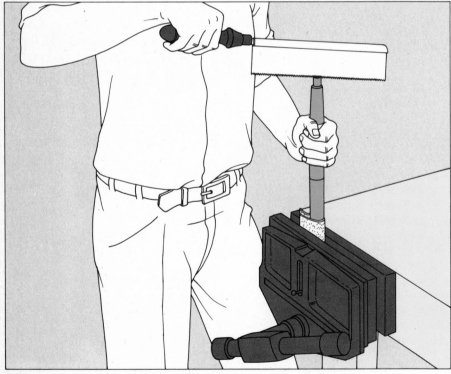

3 **Cutting a kerf in the dowel.** Use a dovetail saw or a small backsaw to cut a kerf in the end of the dowel, stopping just short of where the kerf would be visible. Orient the cut so that when the joint is assembled, the kerf will form a right angle with the grain of the socketed part.

Replacing a Broken Dowel

1 **Drilling a hole for a new dowel.** To replace a broken dowel, saw off the broken end and sand it flush with the dowel shoulder. Dimple its center with an awl, then drill a hole for a new dowel. To drill, clamp the chair part (wrapped in a protective sheet of cork) in a vise, and, with a helper, align a $1/16$-inch bit to enter the wood at the same angle as the old dowel, which in most cases is parallel to the chair part. Drill a pilot hole with the $1/16$-inch bit, then use a larger bit to drill the hole to the same depth and diameter as the adjoining socket. Bevel a new dowel so it fits easily into the hole, and trim its extension to three quarters of the depth of the socket.

To replace a dowel that has broken off inside the end of the doweled piece, drill it out with progressively larger bits, starting with a $1/16$-inch bit, until the hole is the required size. If the broken doweled end of a part is simply a tapered extension of that part, it will probably be necessary to replace the whole part.

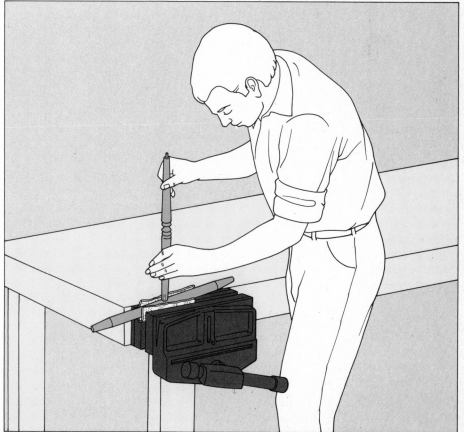

2 **Cleaning out the socket.** Saw, sand and drill out any broken dowel pieces left in the socket, using the same techniques and drill bits as in Step 1. Position the clamped chair part in the vise so that the socket is perpendicular to the top of the vise, regardless of the angle at which the dowel enters; to check the alignment, hold the joining piece—with its new dowel removed temporarily—in position against the socketed one.

Using Shims to Enlarge a Loosened Tenon

Applying veneer shims. To refit a loose mortise-and-tenon joint, disassemble the joint and cut veneer shims to fit any or all sides of the tenon, depending on where the gaps fall; cut each shim slightly larger than the side of the tenon it will cover. Smear glue on the tenon and shim, and join the two; place a layer of wax paper over the glued shim, and clamp tenon and shim between two wood blocks until the glue dries. When attaching shims to opposite sides of a tenon, glue and clamp both sides as a unit. Remove the clamp and wax paper when the glue has dried, and trim off the excess veneer. Repeat for the tenon's opposite sides if necessary.

Test-fit the tenon in the mortise. If you cannot seat the joint using manual force, pull the tenon out and look for shiny areas where it is too tight. Sand and test again. Repeat as needed.

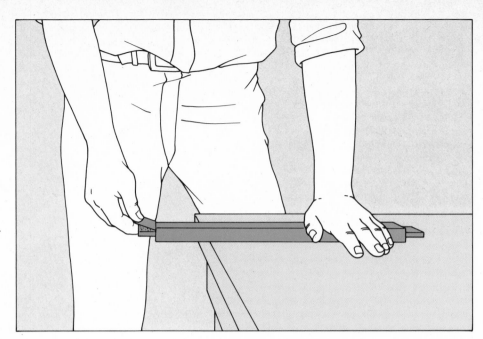

Reassembling a Platform Chair

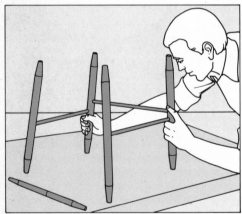

1 Assembling the legs and seat. Divide the reassembling of a platform chair into steps, and rehearse them first without glue or wedges, to prevent mishaps in the final assembly. If the chair has been completely disassembled, begin by reconstructing the legs and the seat. Make two H-shaped assemblies, each consisting of front and back leg stiles joined by a side footrail; then join the two Hs with front and back footrails. Next add the seat, and loop a web clamp around the assembly (*page 11*) to determine the best way to fit the clamp to the assembly.

Disassemble this portion of the chair and reassemble it in the same order, this time using glue and inserting wedges into any dowels that have been kerfed to receive them. Daub glue into sockets and mortises with a stick, smear it on dowels and tenons, and draw any wedges you are using through a puddle of glue poured onto a scrap of wood. Apply the web clamp, and proceed immediately to Step 2.

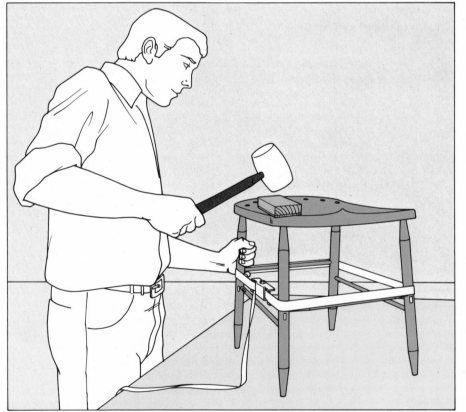

2 Leveling the chair. Place the assembled portion of the chair on a flat, level surface—such as the top of a desk or a table saw. To check that the surface is absolutely flat, draw a metal straightedge across it twice, the second time perpendicular to the first, and look for gaps beneath the straightedge; there should be no gap greater than $1/16$ inch. Apply glue and, using a cork-faced block to protect the finish, strike the top of the seat over each leg with a mallet, to firm the legs in the sockets. Do the same for the joints between the rails and the leg stiles, tightening the web clamp around the legs as you go. Let the glue dry.

3 **Attaching the back.** Rehearse the back assembly of the chair without wedges or glue, as in Step 1, fitting the main stiles and spindle stiles into their sockets. Wrap two web clamps around the back and under the seat so that the clamp winches are behind the back. Then disassemble the back and repeat the procedure with glue, adding dowel wedges, if any. Alternately tighten the winches and tap the top rail with a mallet until all the stiles are set firmly in their sockets.

If the chair has arms, fit the horizontal arm members into the back stiles and the vertical arm members into the seat before joining the back assembly to the seat assembly. When you rehearse this final procedure, cut a temporary brace to fit exactly between the two arms near their front ends *(inset)*. Wrap a web clamp under the seat and around the arms, just above where they join the seat, and use the brace to hold the arms apart while you tighten the clamp. For the back of the chair use a pair of web clamps, just as on an armless chair, but to avoid pulling the arms out of alignment position the winches in front of, not behind, the back.

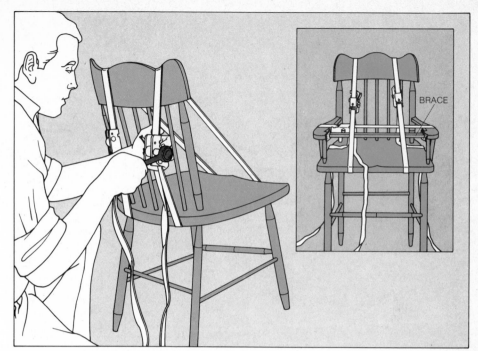

Reassembling a Frame Chair

Plotting the stages of reassembly. Rejoin the pieces of a frame chair into subassemblies, and test-fit them without glue or wedges; then repeat this procedure for the final assembly. Start gluing by joining the back stiles with their connecting rails, including the center splat, if there is one. Wrap one web clamp around this assembly just above the footrail and another just below the top rail. Alternately tighten the clamps and tap the joints with a mallet until they are firm. Lay the back assembly on a flat surface, and shift the parts until the back lies flat and the two diagonal measurements between the top of one main stile and the bottom of the opposite stile are the same. Allow the glue for this subassembly to dry before proceeding.

Assemble the front stiles and the rails that join them, then join the front and back assemblies with the side footrails and seat rails, and the arm parts if any. Position a web clamp around the legs of the chair halfway between the footrail and the seat rail. If the chair has arms, put a brace between the ends of the arms, and place a web clamp around the chair at arm level. If the arms consist of horizontal members joined to the vertical stiles with dowels or tenons, wrap another web clamp over the front ends of the arms and under the seat. Place the assembled chair on a flat, level work surface *(Step 2, opposite)*. Tap with a mallet and tighten the clamps until all of the joints are firmly in place and all the legs touch the work surface. Allow the glue to dry before you remove the clamps.

Taking the Waggle out of a Wobbly Table

Although a well-built table should last for many years, ordinary wear and tear frequently takes its toll, especially when the table is used for dining. The joints at the tops of legs are prime targets for trouble. Subjected to severe stress when the legs are kicked or the table is dragged across the floor, they may become loose or even break. Other commonly encountered problems are drop-leaf extensions that sag and sliding extension mechanisms that stick or break. Many of these flaws can be easily corrected.

Most tables intended for hard use are made with the top attached to an apron, a rectangular substructure of narrow boards permanently joined to the tops of the legs. In a few cases the apron is permanently joined to the top, and the legs are bolted to the apron. Simpler tables have legs attached directly to the underside of the top. These joints are held together by a variety of means, alone or in combination: glue, which may fail; tenons or dowels, which may break; clips, screws or bolts, which may loosen. Glue bonds that fail are easily reglued—use techniques shown for similar chair joints on pages 10-17—but in order to repair the more serious breaks in component parts, you may have to separate the joint and replace the broken parts. To complete the repair, you can reinforce joints by screwing on either metal corner plates or wood blocks.

Tables with moving parts that malfunction require other corrective measures. In most cases, you can treat a balky mechanism on an extension table by cleaning and lubricating the sliding parts, but if parts of the mechanism are broken, bent or missing, it may be necessary to replace them. The manufacturer or a hardware dealer can help you find new parts. For a sagging drop-leaf table, the simplest remedy is usually a wedge, which should be glued to the underside of the drop leaf to take up the slack.

For many of these repairs, it is helpful to have a glue injector to force glue into a confined area. Clamps of one sort or another are also very important. You will need C clamps to close splits, while a pipe clamp—a pair of clamping devices mounted on a length of common iron pipe—is required to maintain pressure on glued apron-to-leg joints. Whenever you use clamps, pad their jaws with thin pieces of cork or other soft wood to avoid marring the surface of the piece you are clamping. Use only the minimum pressure needed to close the glued sections, since too much pressure may force out so much of the glue that you end up with a weak joint.

When the repair involves a broken joint that you intend to fix with a doweled butt joint *(page 20),* you may want to invest in a doweling jig to guide the drill, and metal dowel centers; these tools, available at most hardware stores, ensure precise positioning and alignment of the dowel holes. Also helpful are specially grooved dowels, which make stronger glue bonds than smooth dowels.

Getting At a Damaged Substructure

Unscrewing the tabletop. To gain access to a broken joint, turn the table upside down atop several layers of cloth or a piece of rug, and remove the top. If the top is held in place with metal clips set into a groove, or kerf, in the apron *(right),* remove the screws and clips to detach the top. If the top is attached with screws or bolts to the apron or to corner blocks, remove these fasteners *(insets).* If the repair will require you to take the joints apart, use the disassembly techniques shown on page 13.

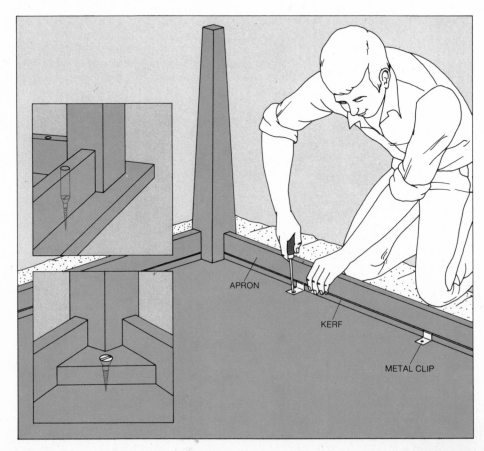

APRON

KERF

METAL CLIP

Analyzing the Leg-to-Apron Joints

Three types of joints. The most common permanent joint is a mortise and tenon, with a tenon (tongue) on the apron glued into a mortise (slot) on the leg *(left)*. Possible damage includes a split at the mortise or a broken tenon.

Also common is a butt joint, which is usually reinforced with dowels that are glued into matching holes in each of the two pieces *(center)*. These dowels may break; if they do, it will be nec-

essary to drill them out and replace them or to substitute a completely new dowel joint *(page 20, Step 2)*. Butt joints with dowels are sometimes further reinforced by the addition of a corner plate or block *(page 21)*; such a plate or block may also serve to strengthen a butt joint that is made without dowels.

If legs are connected to an apron by lap joints *(right)*, the apron is glued and screwed to the out-

er face of each leg. The screwheads are sunk below the surface of the apron in counterbored holes filled with wood plugs or buttons. If the screws pull out of a leg, drill the plugs out of the apron, remove the screws, reglue the joint and use new screws of the same length but the next larger diameter. You may have to enlarge the upper parts of the holes counterbored for the screwheads, but do not redrill the lower parts, which are sized to fit the screw threads.

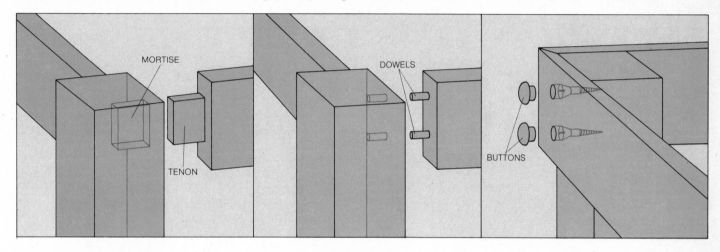

Closing a Split atop a Table Leg

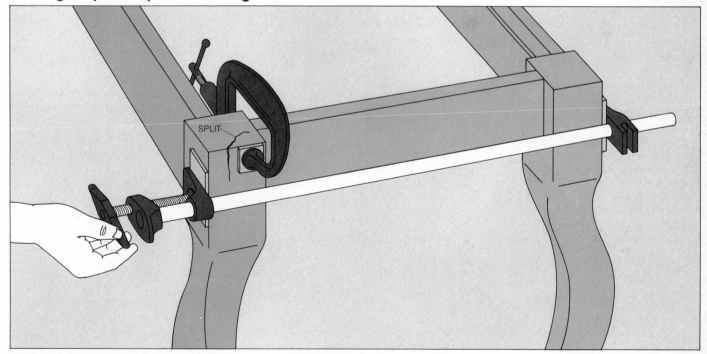

Gluing a split mortise. If a split occurs around the mortise at the top of a leg, inject yellow glue into the split as well as into the hairline opening between the mortise and tenon. Apply pressure with clamps. First put a C clamp across

the top of the leg to close the split; then put a pipe clamp across, extending from the outside of one leg to the outside of another, to hold the tenon in the mortise. Allow the glue to dry overnight before removing the clamps.

Repairs for a Broken Tenon

1 **Preparing for dowels.** When a tenon is badly cracked or broken, convert the joint to a doweled butt joint; first cut off the tenon and fill in the mortise. Use a fine-tooth crosscut saw—or better, a dovetail saw—to cut off the broken tenon flush with the end of the piece.

With a chisel, clear the mortise of glue and any pieces of broken tenon, then cut a wooden plug the same size as the mortise. Coat this plug with yellow glue and tap it into the mortise (inset). When the glue is dry, saw and sand away any wood protruding from the mortise.

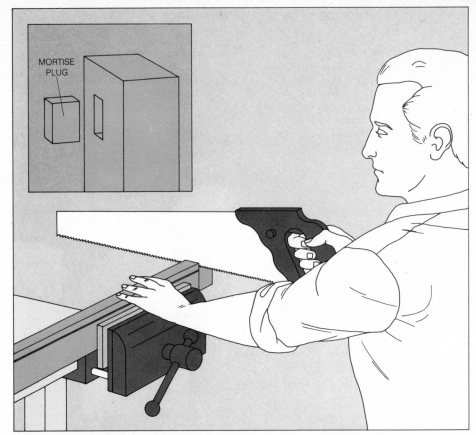

2 **Drilling and aligning dowel holes.** Mark two pencil lines across the end of the apron about one third of the way in from the top and the bottom. Center a dowel jig over one line and drill a $^5/_{16}$-inch hole 1⅛ inch into the end of the apron. Repeat at the other line.

Insert the dowel centers into the holes, align the apron carefully in position at the top of the leg, and tap the other end of the apron with a rubber mallet, using enough force to push the tips of the dowel centers against the leg (inset) to leave marks. Use these marks to position the dowel jig, and drill two $^5/_{16}$-inch holes 1⅛ inch into the side of the leg.

Spread a thin film of yellow glue on the end of the apron and on two $^5/_{16}$-inch dowels, each 2 inches long. Tap the dowels into the apron holes with the rubber mallet, then insert them into the leg holes and tap the apron into place. Apply pressure with a pipe clamp, as shown on page 19, until the glue dries.

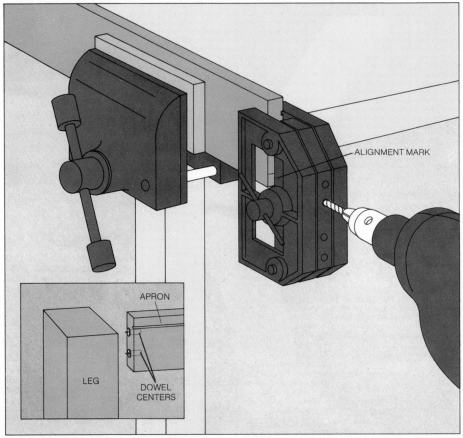

Two Joint Reinforcements

Bracing a corner. To attach a metal corner plate, *(below, top)*, position it across the leg and hold it temporarily in place against the apron by driving one screw on each side. Then drill a pilot hole into the leg through the center hole in the plate, using a drill bit slightly smaller than the diameter of the screw bolt. Remove the screws holding the plate and remove the plate. Screw the bolt into the leg, gripping the bolt in the center with pliers and turning it until all threads at the leg end are in the leg. Replace the plate, putting in all the end screws to fasten the plate to the apron. Then put a lock washer and wing nut onto the screw bolt and tighten.

To attach a wood corner brace *(bottom)*, cut a triangular block from hardwood, so that the grain runs from apron to apron, and notch it to fit around the leg. Attach the block to the apron with two No. 8 screws driven through the block and into the leg, perpendicular to the apron, one screw on each side of the leg.

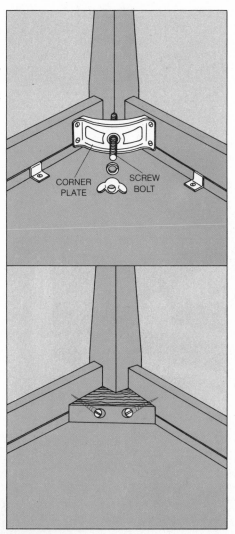

CORNER PLATE · SCREW BOLT

Leveling a Drop Leaf, Unsticking an Extension

Wedging a drop leaf. To level a drooping drop leaf, mark the outermost point where the supporting slide or gate leg touches the underside of the leaf, scrape away old glue or finish and attach a shallow wedge to the leaf. Cut the wedge from a scrap of hardwood, spread yellow glue on the upper face and push the wedge between the slide and the leaf, adjusting it until the leaf is level. Place a weight atop the leaf, to apply pressure until the glue dries.

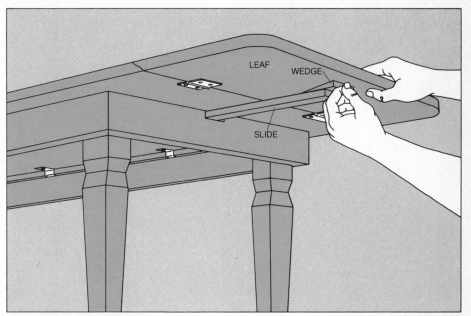

LEAF · WEDGE · SLIDE

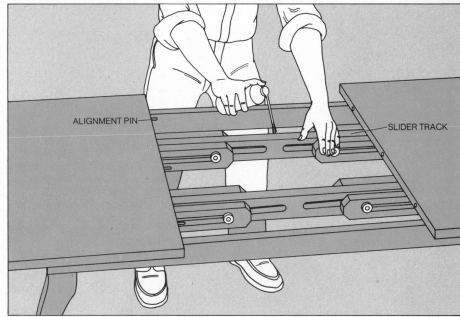

ALIGNMENT PIN · SLIDER TRACK

Rehabilitating an extension table. To unstick an extension table that refuses to slide on wooden tracks, open it until it is fully extended and use a chisel to scrape away deposits of dirt and hardened lubricant from the insides of the tracks. Apply fresh lubricant to all accessible moving parts, using either a silicone spray or beeswax. If you are working on an extension table that has metal tracks, use a tapered dowel or stick to clean out the sliding parts. Then sprinkle them with powdered graphite.

If a wooden alignment pin on the edge of an extension leaf breaks, drill out the stub and replace it with a hardwood dowel. Glue one end of the dowel into the cleared hole and taper the other end to fit loosely into the alignment hole, sanding to round its end and reduce its girth.

Joints for Beds: Strong but Easy to Take Apart

Beds appear to be massive and sturdy but they are in fact fairly fragile. If you take away the mattress and box spring, all that remains is a rectangle of relatively thin wood parts, some of them designed to shift slightly to accommodate the changing positions of sleepers, and others designed to separate at moving time. Small wonder, then, that these parts can begin to deteriorate.

Some problems with beds have much in common with other furniture ailments—breaks, splintering and warping—and can be repaired as described in Chapter 2. Unique to beds, however, are problems found in or near the side rails (the long pieces that connect a bed's head and foot). One particularly vulnerable spot is the joint between the side rails and the bedposts. Here, special hardware—used so that the joint can be dismantled—can eventually become a source of trouble.

Metal fasteners for these joints fall into three categories. On modern beds the commonest fastener is a pair of steel plates with interlocking parts; one plate is mounted on the rail, the other on the bedpost. The plates are sometimes set into the wood, sometimes mounted on the surface. Such fasteners seldom break, but the wood around them may weaken and split. You can usually correct the problem by moving the fastener.

Most older beds have pin-and-hook fasteners. Flat metal hooks, much like the hooks on a modern fastener, are set into the end of the side rail and enter a slot on the bedpost, where they latch over metal pins. In some cases the pins are set directly into the bedpost, and wooden plugs cover their ends. Or the pins are set into a wooden block, which is then inserted in a mortise cut into the bedpost.

When a pin-and-hook fastener fails, it is generally because the pins have weakened the wood around them. If pins inserted directly into the bedpost pose this problem, the old fastener must usually be abandoned and a new steel-plate fastener substituted. But with pins that are inserted in a wood block, it often is possible to salvage the fastener by replacing just the damaged block.

The last type of fastener, found on even older beds and on reproductions, is a long bolt that penetrates the thickness of the bedpost and extends several inches into the end of the rail; the bolt is fastened by a nut embedded in the rail. The bolthead is sometimes countersunk in the bedpost and covered with a small disk; the nut is locked into place with glue, and the access hole to it, in the side of the rail, is commonly filled with a wood plug. When one of these joints works loose, it usually is because the bolthead has eaten into the wood or because the nut has broken away from its caul of glue; both conditions are fixable.

Besides their joints with bedposts, side rails have other problem areas. They may bow outward under the weight of mattress and box springs. Or the narrow ledges attached to the rails, which support slats or box springs, may begin to sag. Mending a sagging ledge is a simple matter of refastening and reinforcing it, but straightening a bulging side rail calls for more elaborate techniques. A general rule to remember, however, is to avoid pulling in the side rails too much; allow ⅛ inch of space between slat and rail on each side to assure a proper fit.

Anatomy of a bed. A bedframe is a rectangle that can be taken apart for moving. The headboard and footboard are permanently fastened to bedposts with glued mortise-and-tenon joints, but special hardware used at side-rail and bedpost joints allow them to be separated. To support box springs or the slats that hold a mattress, there is a wood strip (*the ledge*) on the inside of each rail and sometimes also on the inside face of the headboard and of the footboard.

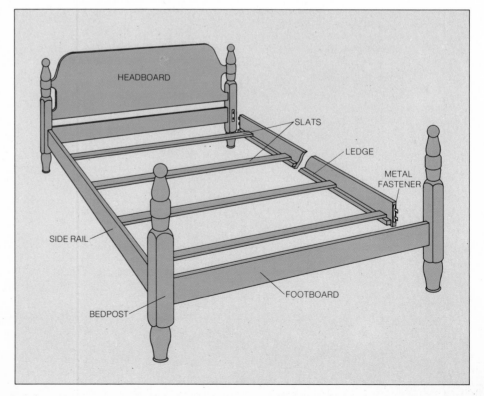

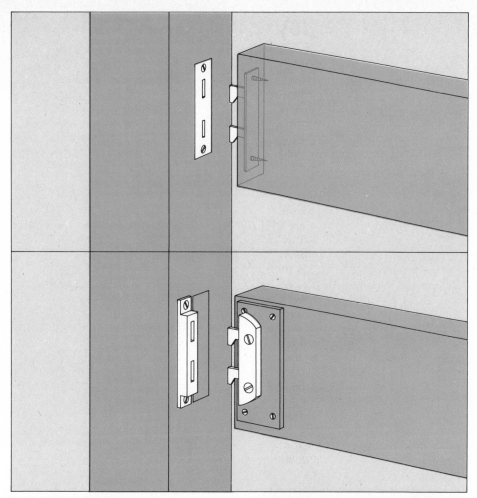

Mending the Detachable Post-and-Rail Joints

Repositioning a steel-plate fastener. Disassemble a worn interlocking steel-plate joint (*top left*) and remove the fastener from the bedpost and the rail. Repair the damaged wood if possible; you can strengthen the end of the rail with a piece of plywood or hardboard, glued and screwed to the inside. Then remount the fastener parts in new positions on both the bedpost and the rail. To establish these positions, have a helper align the bedpost and rail while you hold the closed fastener against them, marking the new positions. Then separate bedpost and rail, and screw the fastener parts in place.

If the existing fastener parts are of the recessed type, replace them with a surface-mounted fastener (*bottom left*). Fill in the mortises with blocks of wood (*page 20*).

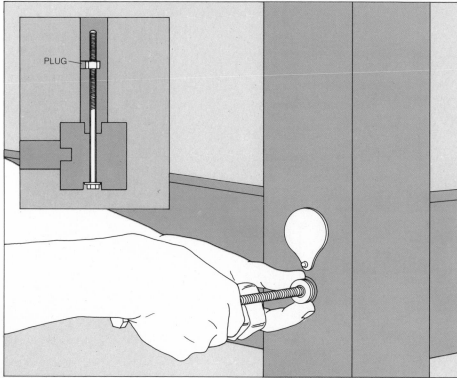

PLUG

Tightening old-fashioned bolt joints. To tighten a bolthead that has eaten into the wood, remove the bolt and add one or two washers, then put the bolt back in its hole. If the nut inside the rail spins, so that the bolt cannot be tightened, drill or chisel out the wood plug that conceals the access hole. Remove the loose nut, clean the old glue from the hole, spread epoxy glue around the nut and replace it in the hole. Cut a new plug slightly longer than the access hole. Apply glue, and hammer the plug into place until its end hits the edge of the nut. Trim off any part of the plug that protrudes, and refinish the area.

Repairing a pin-and-hook fastener. To replace a worn wood block, chisel out the old block, and clean the hole in which it rested. Cut a new block to fit the hole, and mark positions for the pins by holding the block against the side of the metal hooks and tracing their outline on the block. Make a slot wide enough and deep enough for entry of the hooks, either by drilling a row of holes the length of the slot and clearing them with a slender mortising chisel or by sawing a channel the length of the block. Then drill holes for the pins, put the pins in the block, and glue and clamp the block into the hole in the bedpost. If the pins are damaged, cut new ones from bolts of the same diameter.

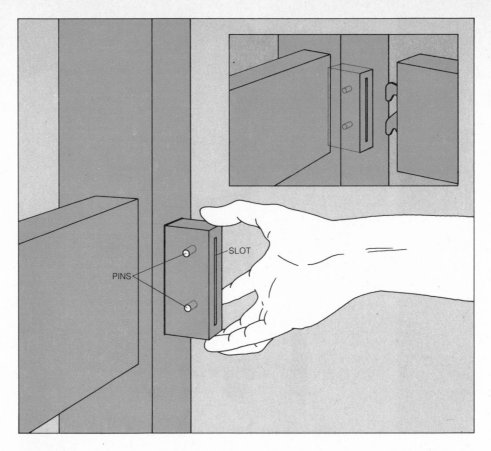

Strengthening a Loose or Sagging Slat Ledge

Adding reinforcement. Unscrew the ledge and gently pry it away from the rail with an old wood chisel, cleaning old glue from both ledge and rail. Fill in the existing screw holes in the ledge and rail with wood putty, then mark off and drill pilot holes for new screws along the ledge, using the distance between existing holes as a guide. Reattach the ledge to the rail, in the same position as before, with glue and screws. Glue and screw several wood blocks against the underside of the ledge for added support, placing the blocks about 18 inches apart.

If the ledge is badly warped or if it cracks while you are removing it, replace it with a strip of hardwood you have cut to the same length. Prepare the strip as described above, reinforcing it with wood blocks if desired.

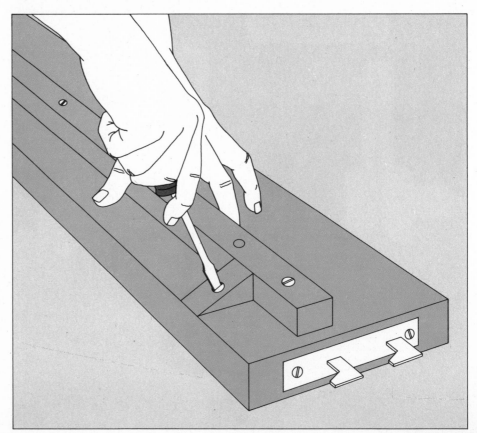

Reining In a Bulging Rail

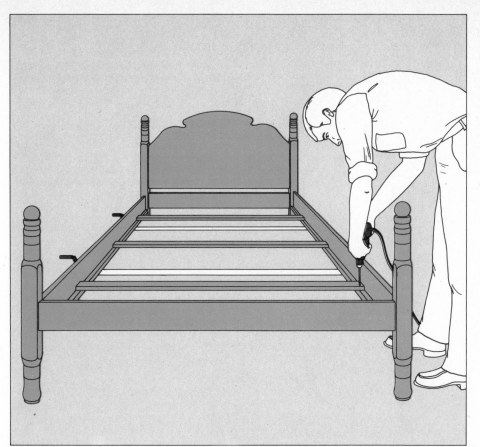

Correcting slight warps. Using two bar clamps, pull the side rail back into line. Position three slats spaced evenly along the length of the rails, making sure that each end of each slat forms a right angle with the rail. Drill a $3/16$-inch hole through both ends of each slat and into the ledge below, leaving a $1/16$-inch gap between the slat ends and the inside face of the rail. Countersink the holes, then insert flat-head, $3/16$-inch-diameter bolts in the holes, add nuts and tighten. Place the rest of the slats on the ledges but do not fasten them down.

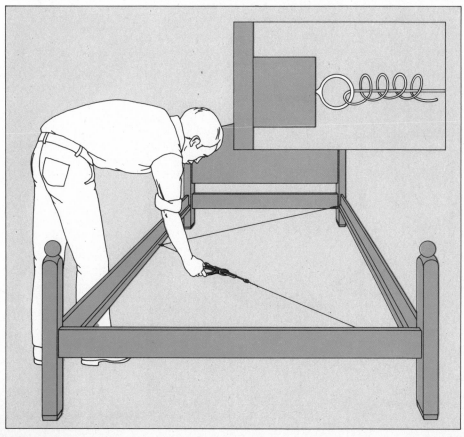

Using a turnbuckle for a bad bulge. Fasten eye screws to both bedposts on the side opposite the bowed rail, placing the eye screws at the height of the ledge. Attach a third eye screw to the ledge at the center of the bowed side rail; the eye screw should be long enough to penetrate the ledge and half the thickness of the side rail. Connect the three eye screws with two lengths of heavy picture wire, fastened at the bedposts by looping and twisting (*inset*), and joined with a turnbuckle that can be adjusted with pliers to pull the rail straight.

If the other side rail is also bowed, repeat the process on the opposite side.

Coming to the Rescue of Flawed Cabinets

Though cabinets come in many shapes and are constructed with a variety of joints, they do have some basic characteristics in common. Bureaus, vanities, armoires, desks and china cabinets all are of boxlike structures *(below)* that are fitted with doors, drawers or both. Since cabinets are not built to support weight, the stresses on them are different from those on chairs or beds. It usually is the moving parts that wear out or break.

When drawers stick or doors do not latch, look for simple remedies first. A loose nail may be catching on a drawer guide, and you will simply need to drive it back in. Door problems can often be traced to a loose hinge. Tighten the hinge screws. If the screw holes are enlarged, try a slightly larger wood screw, or plug the holes and redrill for the screws.

Some more serious problems, such as worn-out drawer guides, can be remedied without disassembling the frame. Most older cabinets have wood guides; frequently the bottoms of the drawer sides serve as runners. Even if these pieces have been kept waxed, the rubbing wood surfaces can wear down or become rutted. Professionals restore the drawer sides by reshoeing the drawer—replacing worn edges with new wood.

A rutted drawer guide can be replaced, but an alternative is to attach drawer-glide buttons. These are vinyl-coated or metal disks—like large thumbtacks—with points on the bottom that are driven into wood. Positioned atop guides, the buttons lift the drawer just enough to let it slide smoothly in the cabinet.

A drawer that is coming apart at the joints calls for some judgment in its repair. If all of the joints are loose, knock the drawer apart *(opposite)* and reglue. But if only one joint has worked free, it is easier to force glue in and clamp it together, leaving the rest intact. Open up sound joints only if you must; the force needed to separate a joint invites further damage to the drawer.

If the problems of an ill-fitting door cannot be traced to loose hinge screws, the solution may lie in repositioning the hinges—"throwing the hinges," in the parlance of professionals. A door warp can sometimes be straightened *(page 45)*, but many cabinetmakers prefer to disguise it by moving the hinges slightly. With this technique, you may be able to bring the protruding corners of a warped door back into line with the frame. With a similar technique *(page 29)*, you can tilt a sagging door so it does not bump the cabinet frame. Trim a door edge only as a last resort, when problems of fit arise from a distortion of the cabinet's frame.

If a cabinet caster is broken or bent, it should be replaced immediately; a cabinet that is not level is subject to stresses it was not built to withstand, and will be more susceptible to joint failure. Replacements are available in many sizes and designs. You may need to increase the size of caster mountings *(page 31)*, but select new casters of a style that complements the design of your cabinet.

Anatomy of a cabinet frame. Cabinets gain strength from a rigid boxlike construction. The carcass of a cabinet is composed of its top, sides and base. Most pieces are fitted together with rabbets and dadoes; others are mitered and the joints reinforced with splines *(bottom inset)*. Like the bottom and sides of the cabinet at right, rabbeted on each side, many cabinet sections are assembled just with glue. Other parts, like this solid-wood top, are screwed to frames. Here, two hardwood cleats attached to the sides with glued rabbet-and-dado joints *(top inset)* anchor screws driven up into the top.

Most cabinet backs are thin plywood or hardboard nailed into rabbets in the cabinet sides. The back adds rigidity—it keeps the frame from twisting out of square. When you need to make repairs, remove the back by tapping it from the inside with a wood block and a mallet.

From the front, most cabinets are enclosed by drawer fronts or doors. Drawers rest on dust panels—thin sheets of plywood set in a dado on the inside edges of a simple frame. If dust-panel frames are dadoed into the sides of the cabinet, they also help to hold the carcass square. Doors are hinged onto a face frame that is glued (and sometimes nailed) to the front edges of the cabinet frame. The leg assembly at right has an apron and mortise-and-tenon joints, much like those of a table *(page 19)*.

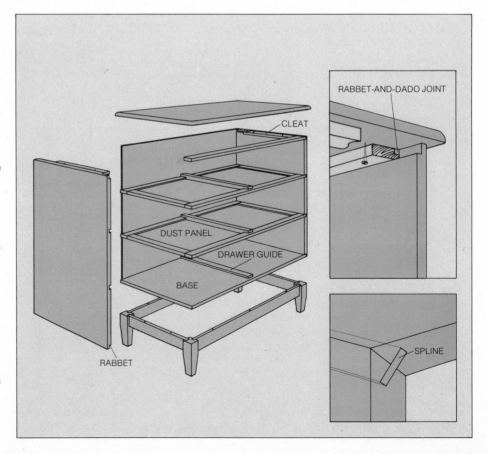

CLEAT

RABBET-AND-DADO JOINT

DUST PANEL

DRAWER GUIDE

BASE

RABBET

SPLINE

Gluing a Drawer Back Together

1 Knocking a drawer apart. To separate a loose dovetail joint, prop a block of wood inside the corner of the drawer and strike it sharply with a mallet or hammer. If the joint is very loose, a blow with your hand may be sufficient. Repeat at the other corners.

Two other common joints are shown in the insets; for each, an arrow indicates the correct direction of a mallet blow to separate the joint. The double-dado joint (*top*) is regularly found in older pieces. In dado-and-rabbet construction (*bottom*), the drawer front hides the end grain

of the sides. On both drawers, the bottom rests in a continuous dado in the front and side pieces.

Scrape the joint edges with a chisel, cleaning them of dirt and old glue. Remove the drawer handles to facilitate clamping.

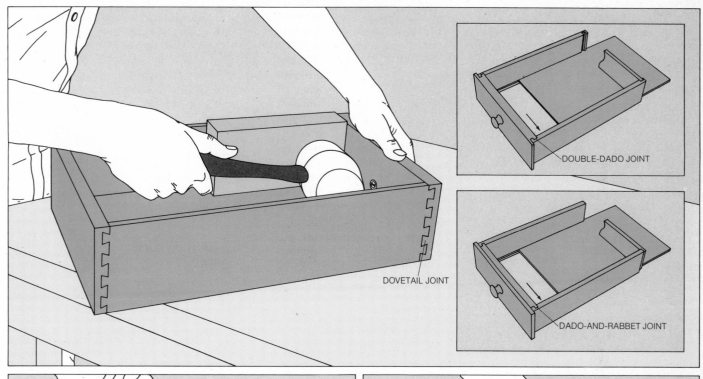

DOUBLE-DADO JOINT

DOVETAIL JOINT

DADO-AND-RABBET JOINT

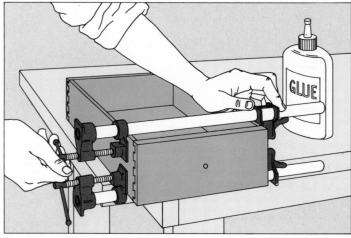

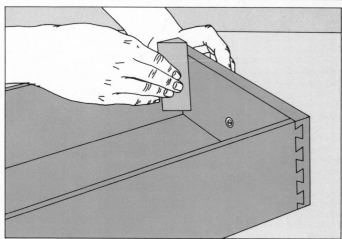

2 Regluing the joints. Apply white glue to all joining surfaces and reassemble the drawer. Attach pipe clamps on the top and the bottom, ½ inch behind the dovetails that join the sides and front of the drawer. Then rest the drawer on its front, and place a third pipe clamp across the back. Measure immediately to make sure the drawer is square: Diagonal measurements between opposite corners must be equal. Shift the clamps, if necessary, to square the drawer.

3 Adding glue blocks. To reinforce the joints of the drawer, cut four triangular blocks of wood as long as the drawer is deep , then glue one of them inside each corner. To set a glue block firmly without using a clamp, spread an even coat of white glue on two faces of the block and on the surfaces inside the corner. Press the block in place, and rub it up and down four or five times, until the glue begins to resist movement. The rubbing motion should cover only about ½ inch.

Easy Remedies for Drawers That Stick

Flipping a sagging drawer bottom. Using nippers to grasp the nailheads, pull the brads that fasten a warped bottom to the lower edge of the drawer back. Slide the bottom out of the dadoes in the drawer sides. You may have to use a chisel to pry off small glue blocks that join the bottom to the drawer front or sides. If the bottom also fits into a dado in the drawer back, the drawer will have to be disassembled.

Turn the bottom over and reassemble the drawer. If the bottom is split and cannot be mended (*page 55*), replace it with a new piece of thin plywood or hardboard.

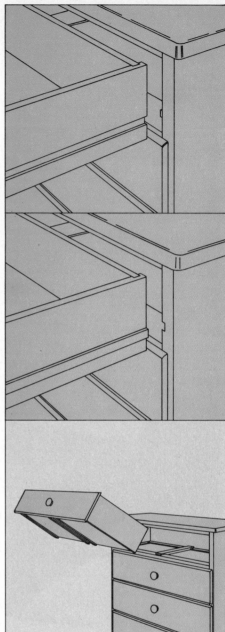

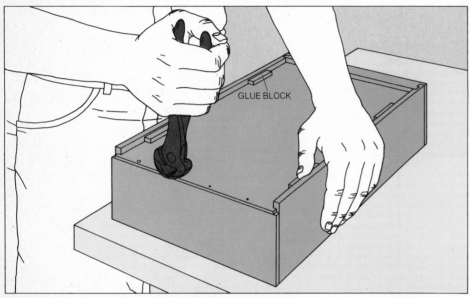

GLUE BLOCK

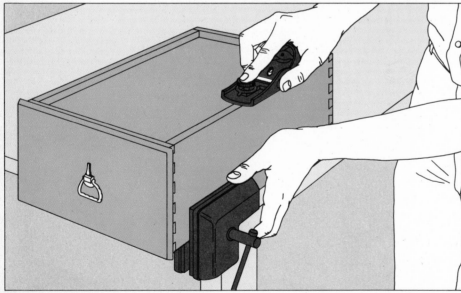

Reshoeing a drawer. If drawer sides that slide along wooden runners are so worn that the drawer does not move smoothly, plane the worn edges and rebuild them. Secure the drawer—or a side if the drawer is disassembled—upside down in a woodworking vise, then plane each worn edge to make it straight. Edges usually wear more at the front than at the back; to restore evenness, you rarely need to remove more than ⅛ inch of wood. If you are working on an assembled drawer and cannot plane to the ends of the edges, finish these areas with a chisel.

Cut strips of hardwood to the length and width of each side. Glue both strips in place, using straight-edged boards and large C clamps to secure them until the glue has dried. Then test-fit the drawer and, if necessary, plane or sand the new strips. Rub paraffin along the runners and the bottom edges of the drawer sides.

Replacing wooden drawer guides. Though there are several designs, most drawer guides made of wood consist of a cleat-and-groove assembly that can easily be replaced if the parts become worn. The drawer sides in the top drawing are dadoed to fit over cleats attached to the cabinet frame. At the center, the configuration is reversed: Cleats attached to drawer sides slide in dadoes in the frame. In the third design, directly above, two cleats on the bottom of the drawer form a groove that slides on a cleat in the center of the frame; the bottom edges of the drawer sides slide on cleats attached to the sides of the frame. To replace a cleat, trace its outline, remove it, then cut and install a duplicate. Use glue and screws to attach a cleat to a frame; use just glue to attach a cleat to a drawer.

PROTRUDING CORNER

FINGER LATCH

Effective Fixes for Balky Cabinet Doors

Throwing the hinges. If one corner on the un-hinged side of a cabinet door protrudes when the door is closed, the door is probably warped. On a flush cabinet door hung with butt hinges, you can remedy this displacement with a process known as throwing the hinges: Unscrew the hinge leaves from the cabinet, plug the screw holes with glue and dowels and, while a helper holds the door in position, mark new screw holes to re-position the loose hinge leaves laterally.

To determine how much and in which direction to reposition hinges, measure the displacement at the protruding corner. You can compensate somewhat by moving just one hinge a distance equal to the amount of the displacement, but it is more effective to divide this amount equally between both hinges. In doing this, move the hinge that is directly opposite the protruding corner inward on the cabinet frame, then move the other hinge outward an equal amount.

If there is one warped door in a set of double doors that meet at the center, divide the displace-ment equally among all four hinges (*inset, far left*). To determine which direction to move each hinge, follow the directions above for the door that is warped, but reverse the directions on the unwarped door. If both doors are warped, deal with each one individually.

On any double door, instead of moving hinges you can install a finger latch (*inset, near left*) in-side the cabinet to secure the warped corner.

Providing clearance for a sticking edge. If the unhinged edge of a cabinet door sticks as it closes—binding either just below the top cor-ner or along the bottom edge—first make sure the screws in the top hinge are tight. If they are, unscrew the hinge leaves attached to the cabinet, and remove the door. With a mallet and chisel, either deepen an existing mortise for the top hinge by 1/16 inch, or cut a 1/16-inch-deep mortise if there is none. Screw the hinge back in place, and check the swing of the door. On double doors whose edges rub together near the top, you can recess the top hinge on each door.

If this fails to clear a sticking edge, the prob-lem is probably due to a twisted cabinet frame. To remedy it, plane the door edges (*overleaf*).

Planing a door edge that sticks. After marking the spots that stick and removing the door from the cabinet, draw a line on the door's inside face ⅛ inch from the sticking point. Secure the door in a woodworking vise so the line is horizontal. On a lipped door, as shown, use a rabbet plane or a block plane to cut the inside lip down to the marked line. On a flush door, use a block plane to bevel the edge down to the line, being careful not to remove any more wood than is necessary where the edge meets the outside face of the door; if you shave away excess wood here, you will only increase the gap between the closed door and the cabinet's front frame.

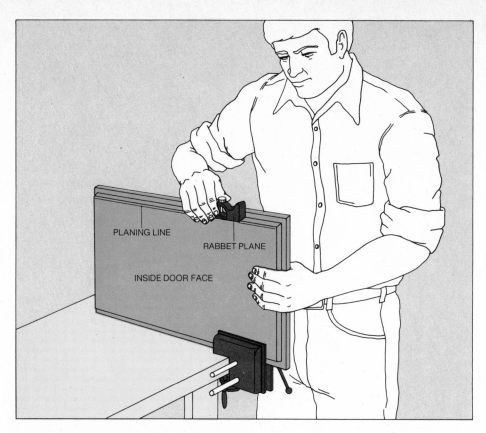

PLANING LINE

RABBET PLANE

INSIDE DOOR FACE

Analyzing Caster Troubles

Two basic designs. The commonly encountered types of caster differ primarily in the way they are attached to furniture. Plate-mounted casters are screwed directly onto the underside of the piece they support; they are quite strong and rarely require repair. They cannot, however, be mounted on small areas, such as the bottoms of narrow legs. Here stem casters are used. The roller of a stem caster is attached to a shaft that fits into a matching sleeve; the sleeve fits into a hole in the end of the leg. Though this design is more versatile, it is also more vulnerable to problems; the shaft may become loose in its sleeve, or the sleeve loose in its socket.

If the furniture design allows it, replace a faulty stem caster with a plate-mounted caster. Otherwise, repair it with the technique shown opposite. Both styles are available in various sizes, either with a wheel or with a ball-shaped roller.

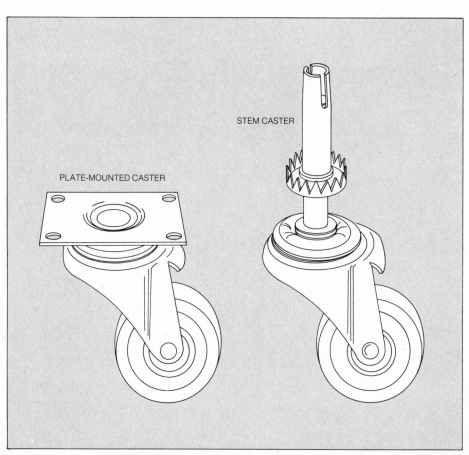

STEM CASTER

PLATE-MOUNTED CASTER

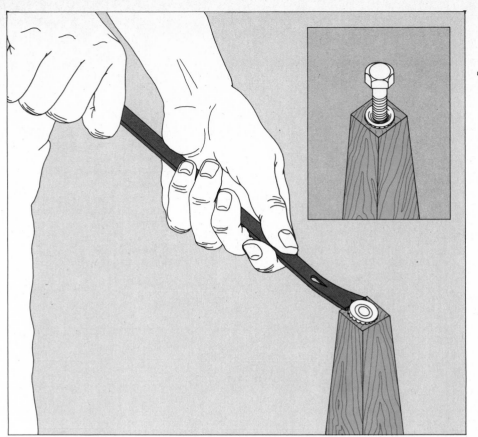

Replacing a Loose Stem Caster

1 **Removing the stem system.** After pulling out the roller and the shaft, try to work the clawed end of a small pry bar under the serrated flange of the sleeve so you can pry the sleeve out of its hole. If this fails, tap a threaded bolt of about the same diameter as the sleeve into the opening *(inset)*, just until it is wedged tight. Grip the bolt with pliers, and work the sleeve loose and out of its socket.

Use a drill to enlarge the old hole to fit the next larger size of stem caster. Wrap tape around the bit to mark the depth of the socket before drilling, and use a doweling jig *(page 20)* to center the drill bit. If the leg is too small for you to drill a larger hole, plug the old hole with a glued wood dowel, and drill a hole for a stem caster a size smaller than the old one.

2 **Installing a new stem caster.** Use a hammer and a wood block to tap the stem sleeve into its hole until the serrated flange bites into the wood *(far left)*. Push the stem shaft into its sleeve; if necessary, tap lightly on a wood block held against the stem collar just above the roller *(near left)* to force the stem into the sleeve. Repeat Steps 1 and 2 to put matching casters on the other legs of the cabinet.

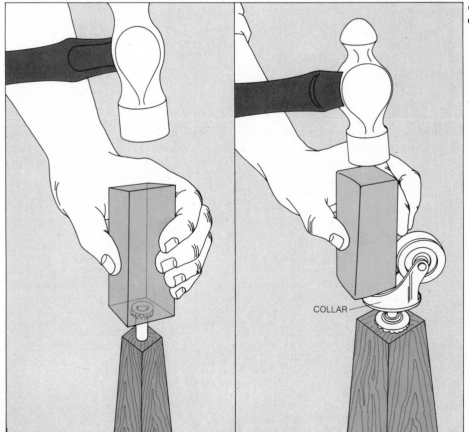

COLLAR

Technology's Look Comes Home

Weary of worrying about the fragility of conventional furniture and its inevitable need for eventual repairs, some people are adapting industrial materials for use in its stead. The new style of furnishing—usually called high tech—elevates steel storm drains to sofas *(page 34)*, shapes bars and sideboards out of wire food-storage shelving *(page 37)*, and supports tables on steel pipe *(page 35)*.

Behind this fashionable nuts-and-bolts look is more than just a search for durable furniture that will never need fixing. High tech is a spin-off of the trend toward functional design that began in the mid-1960s, when architects began exposing the structural and engineering elements of buildings, proclaiming steel trusses, heating ducts and plumbing pipes to be objects of esthetic value in their own right. Sometimes they even glorified these elements with bright primary colors. Typical of this concept, and perhaps its ultimate expression, is the Centre Georges Pompidou in Paris, a building whose exterior skin is actually its interior utility system turned inside out.

In seeking to apply this principle to the decor of a room, interior designers turned to industrial objects, since nothing could be more functional. The furniture they made from familiar and unfamiliar industrial objects and materials has in many cases proved to be not only more durable but also more imaginative than the furniture it replaced. The bold symmetrical shapes offer designers new possibilities for artistic expression.

On first sight, the high-tech furniture chosen for a setting may seem random and haphazard, but for designers this has never been so. The simple forms, sweeping curves and repetitive rectangular shapes of industrial objects are often used to emphasize the most subtle contours of surrounding traditional pieces—as the disk-harrow table, opposite, with its faintly Oriental lines, complements the Chinese side chairs it accompanies. The same conscious choice is exercised in terms of color: On page 36 the silvery finish of chrome-plated steel serves to highlight the metallic color of the canopy's painted-wood frame.

Sometimes high-tech furniture fits so well into a conventional setting that there is a certain whimsy in the juxtaposition. Surrounded by traditional furniture, a pseudoantique table made from the base of a Victorian water heater *(page 35)* blends so harmoniously that the anomaly is scarcely noticeable.

Like the furniture itself, the search for high-tech objects can be something of an adventure. For some people it is a game of chance—the tractor seat on page 39, for example, was discovered accidentally in a junkyard. Other people, with a specific object in mind, scavenge at demolition sites, on abandoned farms and through the trash of factories and stores that supply industrial equipment.

If you prefer to have something new, look for the catalogues of manufacturers of industrial equipment. The most comprehensive source for these is the Thomas Register, a multivolume compendium of thousands of American manufacturers, both great and small; it can be found at many public libraries.

A cultivated side table. Fitted with a glass top, a section of a well-worn disk harrow found on a New England farm serves as a side table between two Chinese chairs in an elegant New York City apartment. The cultivator's rusty-brown color complements the soft tones of the chairs, and its distinctive pagoda-like shape blends with the Oriental character of its setting. The harrow, originally more than 10 feet long, was sawed in two near a point on the shaft where the concave disks reverse direction, so that the bottom disk forms a stable downward-facing base. All but three of the top disks were removed to lower the 5-foot structure to table height.

Turning Sows' Ears into Silk Purses

In the design of industrial objects, form always follows function. But when devotees of high tech convert these objects to uses that were never intended, they stand the famous dictum on its head: Function follows form. Intended for one purpose but adapted to another, a drain culvert dictates by its shape how it will be used as a piece of furniture.

Simplest of the conversions is a table, since a great many objects can be made to serve that purpose. Even if an object does not itself have an appropriately flat surface, it will generally function as a sturdy base for a plain or fancy top. But furniture for sitting or sleeping is a different matter. In being adapted to sofas and beds, some ostensibly rugged industrial equipment must be shored up with framing. On the other hand, some industrial objects make the transition to domestic use easily, like the culvert-turned-closet below, which moved from one function to another with a minimum of change.

Galvanized living room. Sections of half-round drain culvert of corrugated steel assume the roles of a tall clothes closet and three low semicircular couches in this Swedish residence. Two pieces of the 3-foot-high culvert were stacked for the closet. The couches were fitted with steel-and-plywood frames and softened at the top edges with either cushions or rubber padding.

Utilitarian table base. Built to support the boiler of a gas-fired water heater in a turn-of-the-century kitchen, this graceful cast-iron base now cradles a thick slab of marble. Looking for all the world like a piece from a Victorian parlor, the table's only tip-off to its former role is the manufacturer's name, printed on the collar at the top of the pedestal.

Nontipping tables. Two former denizens of the underworld, a drainage-pipe joint and a section of 30-inch sewer main, decorate this New York City apartment. The weighty pipe-joint coffee table—approximately 75 pounds—is of rust-colored steel topped with a bronzed mirror. A similar mirror top serves to lighten the bulky base of the sewer-pipe end table.

Furniture from Erector-Set Parts

In the catalogue of high tech, the ultimate examples of functional furniture are those that are based on a system of metal grids. Among the favorites are industrial shelving systems originally meant for storing everything from auto parts on an assembly line to foodstuffs at wholesale markets. Other popular grid systems include wire panels intended for the display of retail merchandise; normally attached to walls and ceilings and fitted with hooks for hanging such items as pots and pans and clothing, these systems have been adapted to such free-standing constructions as the spidery bedstead below.

Construction scaffolding, with its pipes and its interlocking fittings and flanges, often is the inspiration for rugged utilitarian furniture like the table at far right; that piece was actually put together by a plumber. In fact, any object that must be assembled with wrench and screwdriver rather than with glue and clamps is a logical candidate for being put to use as high-tech furniture.

Metal-grid bed. Ringed by mirrors and soft lights, this gleaming chrome-plated canopy bed casts its airy shadows across the walls and ceiling of a New York apartment. The wire-mesh panels, designed for displaying merchandise, slide in and out of the grooved wooden bedposts, painted to look like metal. The platform bed is a separate element within the wood-and-wire frame.

See-through bar/sideboard. Sturdy steel-wire post-and-platform shelving, designed to let air circulate around perishable foodstuffs in commercial refrigerators, is at home in a residential setting, holding bottles, plants, baskets and artwork. Even in this guise the openwork design has a useful purpose: It makes any item, on any shelf, visible from any vantage point.

Roll-around table. Assembled from ordinary 1½-inch steel pipe with various couplings, this hardworking table has a top of rough-sawed marble that rests on plywood. The piece moves from room to room on casters welded to plates at the bottom of the legs and serves as either a desk or a table, depending on which room it happens to be in at the moment.

Born-again Storage Space and Seating

Not all high-tech furniture begins life as factory shelving or a storm drain. Some of it is furniture to start with. Cabinets, tables and seating originally designed for industrial use in schools, hospitals, offices and laboratories are prized for their clean styling and their sturdy construction. These no-nonsense pieces work every bit as hard in the home, serving related functions.

Though often intended for very specific purposes, as is the surgical-instruments cabinet below, many of these pieces become general-purpose home furniture with minor modifications. Since their specialized design overqualifies them for domestic chores, they will withstand any extra punishment they receive in their new environment. However, some of these recycled pieces need restoration before taking up a new life. The owner of the tractor seat opposite had to sand and refinish his junkyard find, to bring the castaway back to its former glory.

Antiseptic bookcase. A series of medical-supply cabinets designed to keep scalpels, scissors and gauze dry and dust-free does the same for valuable books in a Milanese living room. The cabinets come with clear or opaque glass doors: The owner mixed the two and otherwise adapted the cabinets to residential use by removing their tubular legs and stacking the units.

Filing-cabinet desk. Architect's filing cabinets support this spacious L-shaped desk top, made from two panels of veneered plywood mitered where they join. The owner, who could not find a standard desk with enough storage space, acquired the cabinets first, then designed a top to link them. The panels, edged with a 2-inch lip, are held in place by their own weight.

Tractor throne. Painted to resemble a cloud atop a rainbow, an antiquated tractor seat rides high in a living-room corner, cantilevered above a two-part base. The steel stem that gives the seat its comfortable bounce is angled as it was on the original tractor and, thanks to the stability of the plywood base, the seat can easily support a 200-pound person.

2

Surgery for Breaks and Gouges

A patch of veneer. In the delicate surgery required to patch a wounded veneer surface, a craft knife is used to cut out a diamond-shaped "grave," removing the damaged section and exposing the underlying wood. The edges of the grave are beveled inward to accept a similarly beveled patch of matching veneer. Both the beveled edges and the diamond shape serve to hide the lines of the cut. The patch is glued in place and pressed down with a roller; a light sanding brings it flush with the surrounding surface.

Unlike Humpty Dumpty, furniture with broken parts can often be put back together again almost as good as new, and indeed—given space-age glues and modern power tools—sometimes better than new. Solid-wood surfaces and veneers can be inconspicuously patched; broken chair legs can be spliced and pegged so the breaks do not show; rush seats can be rewrapped, cane seats rewoven and poolside chairs rewebbed.

Many of the techniques for doing these repairs have changed little over the ages. The ancient Egyptians knew how to salvage their valuable and elaborately cut veneered surfaces by regluing them, as is revealed by objects discovered in the tombs of the pharaohs. And the practice of turning new chair rungs on a lathe was common in American colonial times.

People have in fact been enormously resourceful and inventive in the ways they have patched furniture—not always, however, with esthetically pleasing results. In the 17th and 18th Centuries it was not uncommon to mend the split wood of a chair seat by nailing tin patches over the splintered areas. Cracks running along the grain were sometimes simply stitched together with leather laces woven through holes drilled on either side of the break. In one classic example of improvisational mending, the three legs of a delicate 1750 candlestand were refastened to the central column with baling wire.

But in many cases furniture repairs were made with amazing finesse and skill. Each year the Conservation Analytical Laboratory of the Smithsonian Institution examines up to 100 pieces of furniture acquired for its collections. Technicians use chemical analyses and infrared and ultraviolet light, among other things, to establish the date and origin of each piece. In addition, all repairs that have been made are carefully recorded. On a valuable early-19th Century side chair, for instance, there may be as many as half a dozen repairs, ranging from the simple regluing of a chip to the painstaking replacement of an elaborate finial. Some of these repairs are so finely done that only the trained eye of a conservator can spot them. It often takes an expert's knowledge of furniture design and wood-repair techniques to spot a skillfully duplicated leg that has been set among three original ones.

As a rule, museums and collectors disapprove of any repairs to fine furniture that remove or alter original elements of the piece. But on everyday home furnishings, you can employ any number of tried-and-true repair techniques. It is only good sense to patch, mend, or replace broken pieces as skillfully as possible, for it is by these measures that you restore furniture to usefulness and extend its value and service for many more years to come.

Home Remedies for Bent and Bruised Wood

Furniture made of solid wood, for all its sturdiness, sometimes seems as prone to damage as a new car in a busy parking lot. It gets dented, gouged, scratched and nicked and, in addition, it may even be assaulted by the atmosphere—moisture present in the air can penetrate the wood and cause it to warp.

If the piece is very old and the injuries are minor, they are often left alone—in an antique, slight nicks and bends can be desirable signs of character. But greater damage should generally be repaired, using a cure appropriate to the ailment.

Dents and warps can be steamed back into shape, and nicks and gouges treated according to the finish and the value of the furniture—the more precious the piece, the more painstaking the remedy should be. Whatever corrective measure is taken, the result should always be a piece at least as attractive and functional as before the damage occurred.

The simplest repair for slight scratches or nicks in solid wood is the wax-stick treatment, also used in repairing a damaged finish *(page 85)*. If the scratch or nick is wide but not deeper than ¼ inch, a quick and inexpensive repair can be made with wood putty. It dries rapidly, comes in tints to match many woods and

stains, and can be stained—although not always successfully. It should always be tested with the stain or finish that will be used over it.

A third, more elaborate, remedy for a scratch or gouge calls for enlarging the injured area and grafting in a new piece of wood. Shaping this graft has some steps in common with the shaping required for splicing a veneer patch in place *(pages 48, 49)*. When you select the wood, check its age and color—as well as the pattern, shading and texture of the grain, which should be a near match with the wood of the furniture. Also test the planned finish on a scrap of the patching wood before making a final decision.

Most patches will have to be cut to fit, but for damaged areas less than ½ inch across, you can save yourself time by purchasing wooden plugs, called bungs, cut to show the side grain rather than the end grain of dowels. Bungs come in various woods and, like any patch, should be matched to the original surface. If you have a drill press with a plug cutter, you can punch out the bung yourself.

For any of these spot repairs, begin by thoroughly cleaning the area of the damage, then sand it with very fine sandpaper to remove the existing finish. But to flat-

ten a warped surface, you may have to remove the finish from the entire surface to get at the base of the trouble; you may also have to take the afflicted part off its frame. Warping usually occurs when one side of a board is finished and the other side is not, or when the board is not securely fastened to its understructure. Moisture enters the board's unfinished side, and it causes the edges of the finished side to curl.

Warping can sometimes be corrected if you place the warped board, concave side up and finish removed, on a flat surface, and iron it with an ordinary laundry iron over a damp cloth until the warp relaxes. Or, on a sunny day, you can place the board, concave side down, on a freshly watered lawn. Within a day, or perhaps two—weights speed the process—the warp should be gone. In either case, the board should be refastened to its support immediately and refinished when the wood is dry.

For more severe warping you may have to resort to more involved techniques. If moisture and heat do not eliminate the warp, you will have to cut shallow slots in the underside of the board and attach hardwood battens across the slots to hold down the board's errant edges.

Removing a Dent with Water or Steam

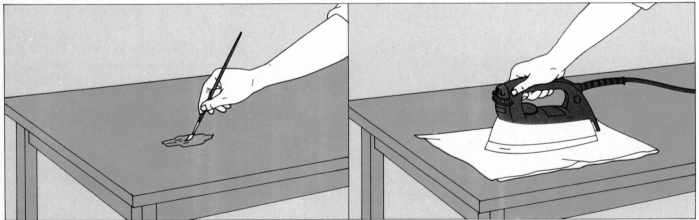

Raising wood fibers. Use an artist's brush or a finger tip to apply water to the crushed wood fibers *(above, left)*, taking care not to moisten the surrounding area. On softwoods, repeat the applications of water until the fibers rise; on hardwoods, apply water, then place a wet cloth over the dent and hold an iron set at low heat against it for 15 seconds. Check the dent and re-

peat the steaming process if necessary. If the dent does not respond, prick the surface with a pin, making holes to channel steam into the fibers. Try to raise the crushed fibers slightly above the level of the surrounding surface.

For tiny dents or dents close to glue joints that might be loosened by steam, isolate the steaming

process. Cover only the affected area with a folded wet cloth, then place a bottle cap upside down on the cloth over the dent and hold the iron against the rim of the cap.

Allow the raised fibers to dry thoroughly. Then sand the area and refinish it, using the techniques described in Chapter 3.

A Custom Patch for a Solid-Wood Surface

1 **Routing the grave.** Join four pieces of wood to form a jig for a router, outlining the area to be patched, called the grave; clamp the jig in place—directly, as shown here, or, if the jig is not near the furniture edges, by clamping two boards atop the jig. The jig must be oriented over the damaged area so that its sides will lie at an angle of about 45° to the grain of the wood. The jig should be just large enough to allow the router to take out the damaged wood, leaving the un-damaged wood alone. Rout out the grave to the depth of the damage, and square off the grave corners with a chisel. If you do not have a router, cut the grave with a hammer and a chisel. Make certain that the grave edges are vertical and that the bottom is flat.

2 **Applying the patch.** Tape paper over the grave, and trace the shape of the edges. Cut out this shape to make a pattern for the patch, and tape it to the patching wood, aligning the pattern so that the grain of the patch matches the grain surrounding the grave. Cut the patch slightly larger than the pattern.

With sandpaper or a plane, bevel the edges of the patch slightly inward (*inset*), testing the patch for fit frequently. When it fits snugly but lies slightly above the surrounding surface, apply white glue and fasten the patch into the grave. Cover it with brown wrapping paper or wax paper; weight it or clamp it overnight. Then sand it level with the surrounding surface, and refinish.

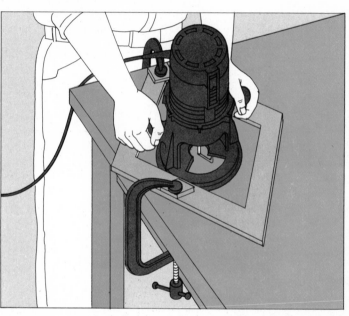

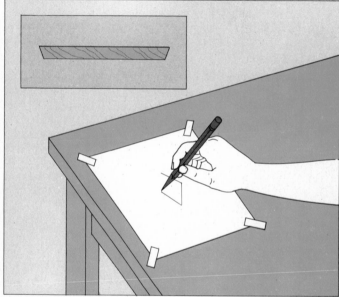

Wood Putty to Repair Edges

Filling in nicked edges. Rub paraffin or wax crayon on a scrap of wood that is long enough to span the area of edge damage, and clamp the waxed surface against the furniture edge, using edge clamps as shown, or C clamps with wood wedges to create the same effect. (The wax will keep putty from adhering to the scrap wood.)

With a spatula or a putty knife, force wood putty into the nick. If the nick is deeper or longer than ¼ inch, build up the putty in layers, giving each coat time to dry. Overfill the depression slightly, to compensate for shrinkage. When the putty has dried, remove the scrap wood, and sand the putty flush with the surface. Apply stain, if it is needed, then a sealer such as a coat of thinned varnish. Complete the repair with painted-on graining if necessary (*page 85*).

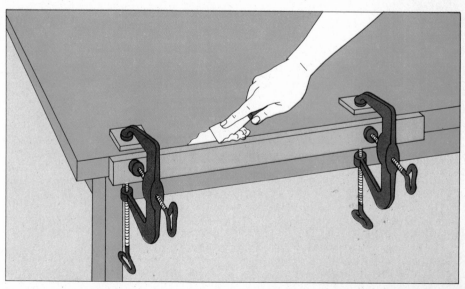

Molding a missing corner. Using wood putty and the same basic repair technique as for nicked edges (*page 43*), rebuild a missing corner by constructing a three-sided mold (*inset*). If a leg joins the piece of furniture near the corner, leave space for it. Wax all three sides of the mold that will touch the wood putty. Clamp the mold to the furniture, then fill in the damage.

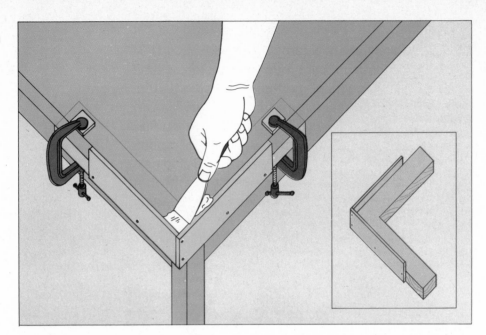

Reconstructing a Broken Corner with a Wood Block

1 **Preparing the corner piece.** Using a router or a mallet and chisel, prepare a smooth bed for the new corner by clearing away all the damaged wood on the existing corner. Then cut a wood patch to fit against the newly smoothed face of the corner, making this patch about ¾ inch longer and $1/32$ inch thicker than needed. Set the patch into place, and slide it back and forth until the grains of patch and of furniture are in the best alignment. Mark the patch in this position, then cut it down to size, leaving about $1/32$ inch of overhang at the sides.

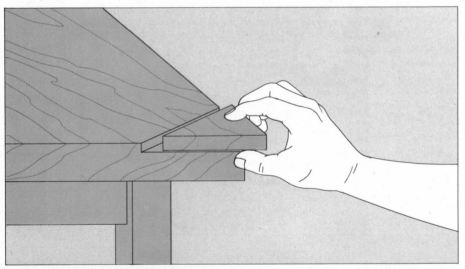

2 **Clamping the corner.** Apply glue to the horizontal and the vertical surfaces of the cleared corner, and set the corner patch in place. Slide a C clamp over the patch, and cock the clamp slightly off the vertical, until the swivel head atop the screw is ⅛ inch closer to the inner face of the patch than the top of the clamp is. In this position, pressure will be inward as well as downward against the patch. Tighten the clamp.

If the broken corner extends completely through the furniture, from top surface to bottom, construct a three-sided brace like the mold shown at top, coat it with wax or cover it with wax paper so glue will not adhere to it, then clamp it against the furniture. Wedge the new corner, coated with glue, into the brace. Or use two special edge clamps (*page 43, bottom*) to hold the new corner in place, but check periodically to make sure the corner has not slipped down.

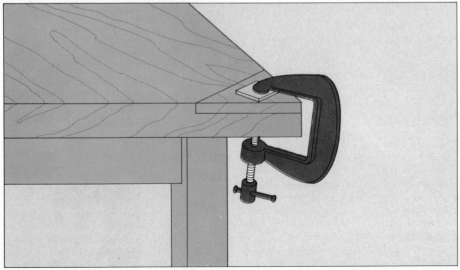

44

Saw Kerfs for a Severe Warp

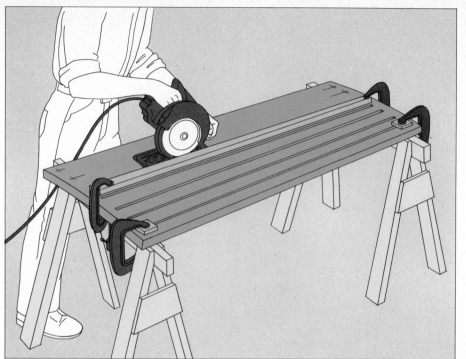

1 **Kerfing the underside.** When moisture alone does not straighten a warped surface, such as the table leaf shown here, clamp it bottom up against sawhorses or a worktable, and use a circular saw to make shallow, evenly spaced cuts, called kerfs, along its grain, stopping 1 inch short of the ends. To guide the saw, clamp a straight-edged 1-by-2 against the warped wood, and set the depth of the saw blade to half the thickness of the wood. Start with four kerfs, spaced at even intervals across the warped surface. If the warp persists, make additional kerfs, keeping them evenly spaced, but do not cut them any closer together than 2 inches.

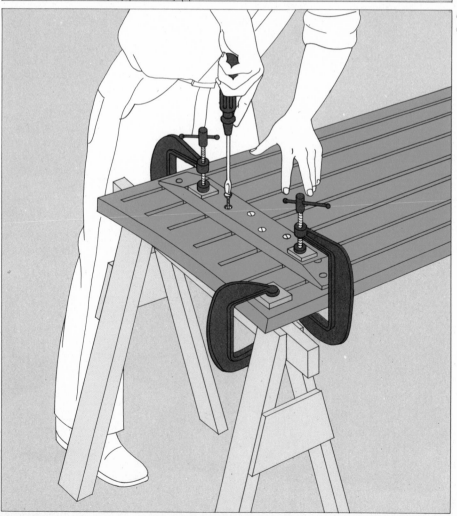

2 **Attaching battens.** If kerfing alone does not eliminate the warp, cut battens, preferably out of oak or other hardwood, ¾ inch thick, 1½ inches wide and as long as the warped board is wide. Bevel the batten ends to make them less conspicuous, and clamp the battens to the underside of the board, 8 to 10 inches in from the ends, or in locations where they will not interfere with the legs or frame of the furniture. Drill pilot holes about 6 inches apart for screws that will penetrate the board to within ¼ inch of its top surface; position the holes to fall between kerfs. Drive the first screws where the batten touches the high point of the warp. Then tighten the clamps on the batten slightly, and drive screws successively closer to the low edges of the warp. Continue in this fashion until all the screws are in place. Seal and finish the bottom of the board, and refasten it to the furniture.

Invisible Mending for Veneer

The richly colored, beautifully grained surface of a fine piece of furniture is likely to be a veneer—a thin layer of decorative wood glued over a core of less expensive wood or plywood. Sliced from selected logs, veneers are cut with the grain; varied patterns are achieved by cutting across the growth rings at different angles. In modern furniture manufacture, veneer is sometimes peeled from a spinning log in a continuous sheet, the wood unrolling much as paper towels roll off a kitchen roll.

The unique patterning of veneered surfaces makes them worth repairing, especially on older pieces that have veneers matched and finished with great care. Fortunately, even severe damage, if limited to small areas, can be repaired with scarcely a trace.

On old veneers the most common problem is blistering, or lifting, caused by the failure of the original hide glue (so called because it was derived from the hides of animals). Because this glue softens when heated, you may be able to repair the veneer by melting the glue with a warm iron and pressing the veneer back in place. Protect the surface from the iron with a dish towel. When the area has been flattened, weight it with heavy books for several hours, until the glue sets. Modern glues seldom fail, but surface chips, gouges and burns are suffered by new and old veneers. They are more complex to repair, requiring patching.

To cut the beveled edges of a veneer patch, you will need a craft knife that has a replaceable narrow slanted blade and pointed tip, of the type craftsmen and artists use (it is best known by one of its trade names, X-acto). Such a craft knife is also used for the delicate task of scraping away dried glue and paint in certain areas. Other special items that are useful are a tool with a thin, flexible blade, such as an artist's palette knife, for lifting veneer flaps; a wallpaper-seam roller or print roller for flattening a reglued blister or a new patch; and a glue injector, a sort of enlarged hypodermic needle for applying glue in constricted areas.

Craft stores usually have samples of available veneers, so you can select one to match your furniture. Veneer is sold by the square foot, in strips 6 to 12 inches wide or wider; buy a piece large enough to allow some leeway in selecting the area around the damage that must be cut away to accept the patch.

Although veneers come in many thicknesses, some paper-thin, those most commonly found on furniture are either $\frac{1}{28}$ or $\frac{1}{40}$ inch thick. On older furniture they frequently are thicker, $\frac{1}{20}$ inch or more; indeed, on a fine antique the veneer may be $\frac{1}{8}$ inch thick. It is best to use a patch of the thickest available veneer, then sand it down to the level of the surrounding surface. In some cases, the existing veneer may be so thick that you will have to glue more than one layer of new veneer to the underlying surface to bring the patch to the correct height. The underlayers need not match the surrounding grain.

Plastic laminates—used on less expensive furniture that is subject to heavy use—are usually attached to the underlying surface with fast-drying contact cement. Repair a lifted edge by scraping the old cement from both surfaces, spreading new contact cement according to the manufacturer's instructions, and pressing the laminate back in place; no clamping is required. Chipped laminate can be repaired the same way if the chip is saved. If the chip is lost, fill the damaged area with wood putty as shown on page 43.

Putting a Blister Back Down

1 **Cutting through the veneer.** If the veneer has risen to create a blister in the middle of the surface, cut diagonally across the grain of the veneer through the blister, with a craft knife, using a metal straightedge as a guide. Make a second diagonal cut, intersecting the first in the middle of the blister to form an X. Avoid cutting directly across the grain; this leaves an obvious line on the repaired surface.

If the veneer has risen at the edge of the surface, you may be able to scrape out the old glue (*Step 2*) without cutting through the veneer. If you cannot scrape the innermost part of the separated area, make a cut through the veneer, either parallel to the grain if the edge lies perpendicular to the grain, or diagonally across it if the edge parallels the grain (*inset*).

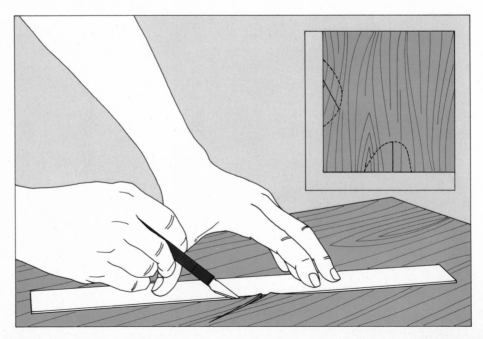

2 **Scraping out old glue, putting in new.** Using a tool with a thin, flexible blade, such as a small palette knife, gently raise one flap of a blister or a lifted edge and, with the tapered blade of a craft knife, scrape old glue from the bottom of the veneer and the top of the underlying surface. If the veneer is too stiff to bend easily, dampen it with a few drops of warm water. Scrape under other sections the same way, stopping occasionally to vacuum away particles of old glue.

When the inside of the blister or raised edge is clean and dry, apply a thin coat of white glue to the underlying surface, using a glue injector, a small putty knife or a fine artist's brush to reach inside. Then press the veneer back into place and wipe away excess glue.

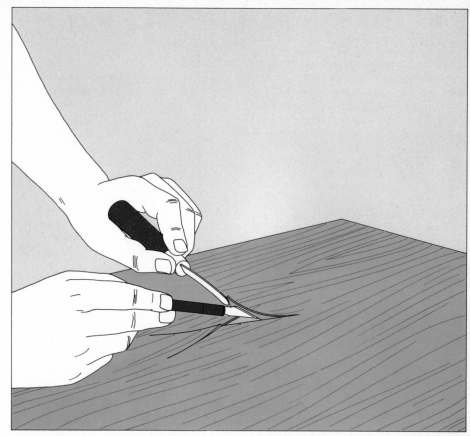

3 **Setting the glue.** With a wallpaper-seam roller, roll the repaired area, first lightly, then again with heavier pressure. Wipe away any additional glue forced out and cover the area with a piece of brown wrapping paper. Place a flat wood block, slightly larger than the repair, over the paper and weight it with several large books (inset), until the glue is dry.

Remove the weights and the paper. If scraps of paper stick, gently pare them away with a sharp chisel, beveled edge down. Refinish the repaired area, using the techniques in Chapter 3.

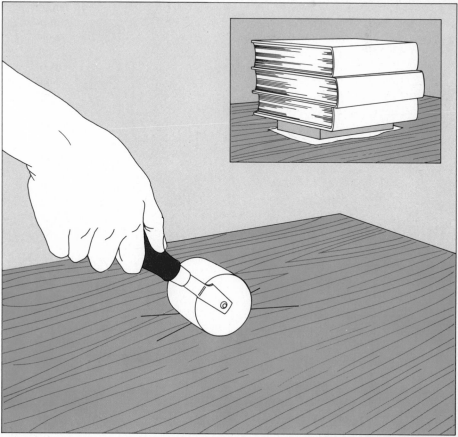

Grafting In a Veneer Patch

1 Cutting the patch. Using a craft knife and a metal straightedge, cut a patch of new veneer slightly larger than the damaged area. Plan the patch so that its grain will parallel the grain of the existing surface and match its striations as closely as possible. To avoid the obvious line of a blunt cut across the grain, make a diamond-shaped patch, as shown, to repair damage in the middle of a veneered surface, or a V-shaped patch for chipped edges or corners. In cutting the patch, use repeated light strokes of the knife and bevel the edges inward slightly by tilting the knife tip toward the patch at an angle of about 10°, to make the bottom of the patch somewhat smaller than the top (*inset*).

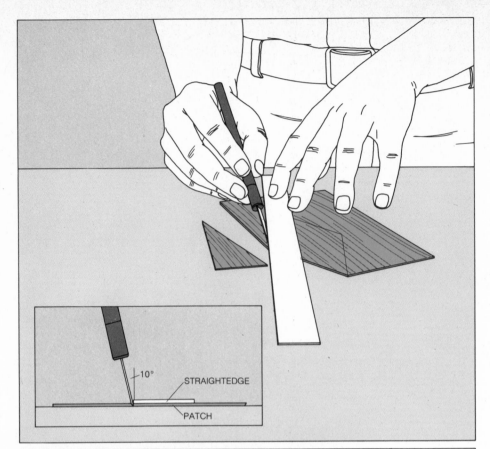

2 Marking the surface. Place the patch over the damaged area, aligning its grain with the surface grain, and outline its shape with a sharp pencil. Use a metal straightedge and a craft knife to cut just inside each pencil line to make a "grave"—a hollow for the patch. Bevel the cuts 10° toward the center, as in Step 1. Cut completely through the existing veneer with repeated light strokes, taking care not to cut beyond the corners of the diamond-shaped grave.

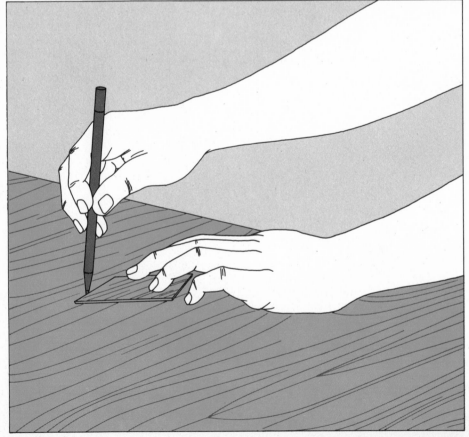

3 **Clearing the grave.** Starting at the center of the damaged area and working outward, remove the old veneer inside the diamond grave with a chisel held beveled side down. If the veneer is hard to loosen, tap the butt of the chisel lightly with a mallet. Use the chisel to scrape any remaining glue or dirt from the bottom of the grave, stopping occasionally to clean away debris with a vacuum cleaner.

If the surface under the veneer is damaged, level it with wood putty (*page 43*). Let the putty dry before you glue in the patch.

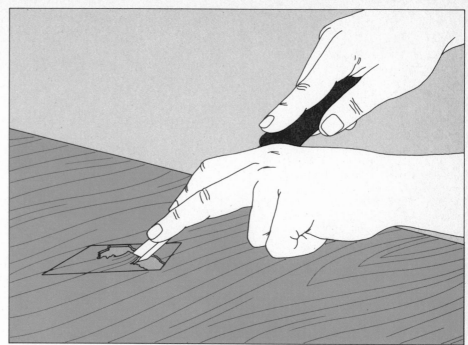

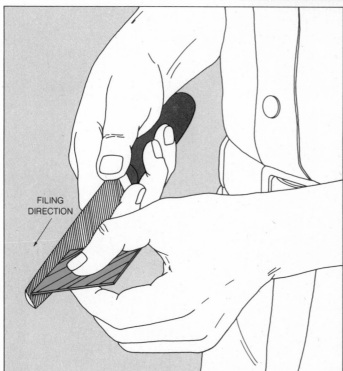

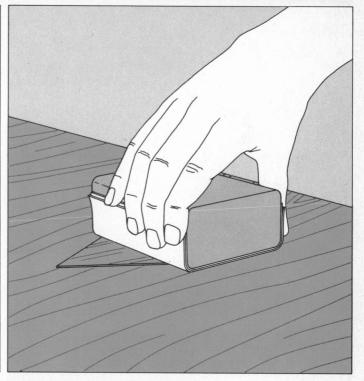

4 **Filing the patch to fit.** Lay the patch over the grave to check its size, then use a fine wood file to trim the edges of the patch for an exact fit. Be careful to maintain the edge bevel, and move the file only in the direction of the grain to avoid tearing the corners.

When the patch fits, brush a thin layer of white glue on the bottom of the grave, press the patch into place and wipe away excess glue. Roll and weight the patch as in Step 3, page 47.

5 **Sanding the patch flush.** When the glue has dried, sand the slightly protruding patch until it is flush with the surrounding surface, using 220-grit (very-fine) sandpaper wrapped over a flat, felt-covered sanding block with slightly rounded edges (*page 89*). Sand in the direction of the grain and use only light pressure to avoid chipping the corners of the patch or gouging the surrounding surface with the sanding block. When the patch is flush, refinish the area you have repaired, as shown in Chapter 3.

Pegs and Splints to Heal a Broken Part

A break in the supporting frame of a piece of furniture creates, in effect, a joint where none was intended, in an area originally designed to accept great stress. The repair of such a break must leave the broken part as strong as it was originally; at the same time it must be as unobtrusive as possible.

For certain breaks *(below, center)*, glue alone will do an admirable repair job. But since wood that breaks is in many cases dry and brittle, a quantity of glue must be worked into the pores, so that as it soaks in enough will be left on the surface for a good bond. Some breaks need support from added wood—either dowels or rectangular bracing blocks. When inserted in or attached to the area of the break, these braces stiffen the joint by providing more surface for the glue to grip.

Dowels can be hidden within a broken part or inserted into a hole drilled from the outside; in the latter case, the end of the dowel will show. If a part is broken cleanly in two and its centers can be drilled to receive a dowel, a hidden dowel is the better repair. But if a break is at an extreme angle, or is located at a curve in the part, it is easier to insert one or even two dowels from the outside—and the repair will be just as strong. The diameter of the dowel should usually be half the thickness of the part being mended and its length usually twice that thickness, though it can be longer if more strength is needed.

Braces are used to mend breaks in flat, thin parts, such as chair-back splats or sofa frames. In a visible part a bracing block should be recessed into a mortise cut to span the break, but in a hidden area, such as one beneath upholstery, a brace can be mounted across the break without a mortise. The thickness of a brace should be half the thickness of the broken part and its length about twice the width of the broken part. Both dowels and braces hold best if they fit the broken part snugly but not tightly—a piece too loose will leave glue gaps and one too tight will force the break apart or even split the wood around it.

These reinforcements should be made of hardwood, cut along the length of the grain for strength and flexibility. You can purchase short hardwood dowels ready-made, or you can cut them to any length from a dowel rod of the right diameter. Hardwood to be used for braces can be purchased at a lumberyard or scavenged from old, unusable hardwood furniture. It is sometimes possible to obtain a piece of matching hardwood from hidden parts of the broken furniture piece itself, perhaps the glue blocks or the drawer runners.

Adequate clamping is crucial whenever glue is used. A clamp must be placed so its force is applied perpendicular to the line of the break, to draw the ends together without pulling them out of alignment. Since most furniture is not constructed with perfect 90° angles, and since breaks do not occur that neatly, you may have to use some ingenuity in devising a special clamping technique for each repair.

C clamps, for example, can be used to sandwich an extremely angled break or to press a bracing block into a mortise. A C clamp can also be attached to a curved part to serve as an anchor point for a pipe clamp, which runs from the C clamp to the end of the broken part, perpendicular to the break *(page 53)*. A pipe clamp that cannot be placed so it applies force perpendicular to a break will tend to pull the broken pieces out of alignment, making the part bend at the break; by running a second pipe clamp from one end of the first clamp to another part of the furniture *(page 52)*, you can shift the force so the joint dries straight.

Three Common Ways That Wood May Break

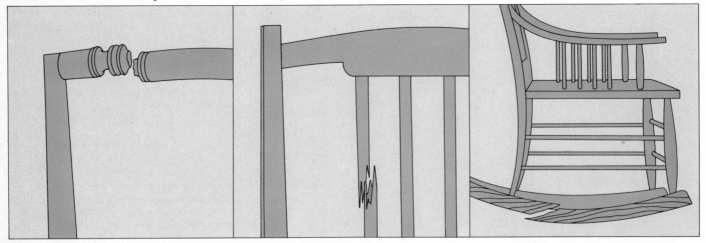

Three types of fracture. A wooden furniture part, held rigid by another part joining it or weakened by deep ornamental turnings, may snap cleanly *(left)*. Since there is little surface area for glue to bond, glue alone probably will not mend this kind of break permanently. The repair should be strengthened with a brace or a dowel. Wood that breaks jaggedly *(center)* is said to have a lot of tooth, and it provides a large, irregular surface for an effective glue bond. This kind of repair becomes the equivalent of a tongue-and-groove joint. Wood that breaks along the line of the grain *(right)* produces a long, angled break that has a large surface area but not much tooth for the glue to grip. Depending on how heavily the piece is used, the repair for an angled break may need to be strengthened by the addition of a dowel or brace.

A Clean Break Rejoined with a Hidden Dowel

1 **Drilling holes for a dowel.** Place the piece of furniture (in this case a chair with a broken leg) at a convenient height, broken end up. Clamp the furniture to a workbench or sawhorses if it is unsteady and clamp the piece that broke off in a vise, also broken end up. If the pieces are broken cleanly enough that you can use a doweling jig, drill into their exact centers as shown. If a doweling jig is unusable because of the shape of the break or the piece, you will need to estimate the centers visually (*page 15*). Use a small bit to drill a pilot hole in each piece, then drill the final holes with a bit the exact size of the dowel to be used. Clean drill debris out of the holes with a vacuum, or turn the pieces upside down and tap the debris out.

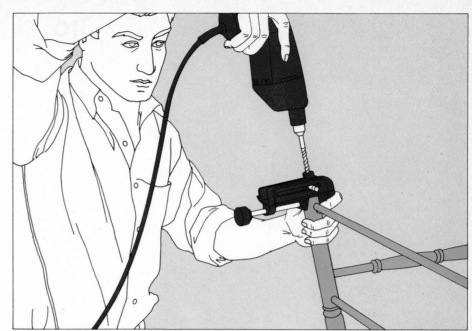

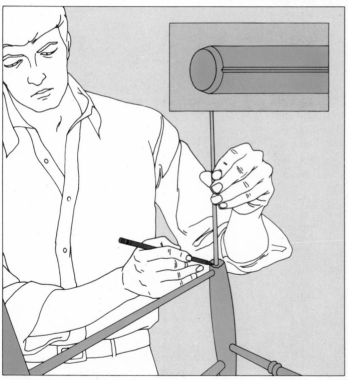

2 **Making the dowel peg.** Insert an undersized dowel or a pencil into each dowel hole and mark the depth on it. Cut a dowel of the right diameter for a snug fit to a length slightly shorter than the sum of the depths of the holes. Bevel the ends of the dowel slightly with a utility knife (*inset*) or sandpaper, and groove the sides of the dowel with the knife or with pliers to provide channels that will let the glue spread.

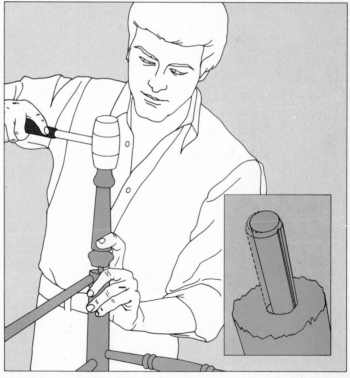

3 **Joining the pieces.** Put glue in one hole and on one end of the dowel and, with a mallet, tap the dowel into the hole as far as it will go. Then tap the other broken piece onto the protruding dowel, without glue, so you can check to see if the broken ends align precisely. If they do not, file down one side of the dowel or shave it a bit with a utility knife (*inset*) to allow the pieces to line up. When the pieces are aligned, put glue on the other end of the dowel, in the other hole and on the broken ends, then tap the pieces together securely. Wipe off excess glue.

4 **Clamping.** Apply a bar or pipe clamp extending from one end of the broken part to the other, running as nearly perpendicular to the break as possible *(near right)*. If the clamp cannot be placed exactly perpendicular and tends to pull the pieces out of alignment, apply a second bar clamp connecting the first clamp with some part of the furniture opposite it, in order to pull the pieces back into alignment *(far right)*.

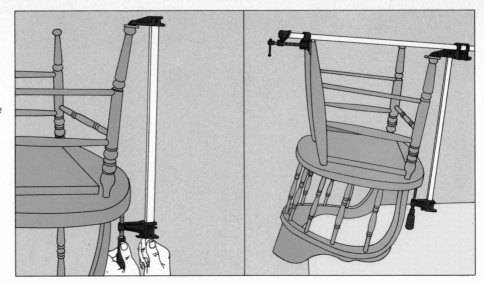

A Visible-Dowel Repair for an Angled Break

1 **Drilling the dowel hole.** Apply white glue to the broken edges and clamp the pieces together, using two strips of wood and two C clamps to hold them in place. At the least visible area, drill a pilot hole for the dowel hole through the first broken piece and partway into the second, at a right angle to the break. Using the pilot hole as a guide, drill a hole the same size as the dowel that is to be inserted. Clean the sawdust out.

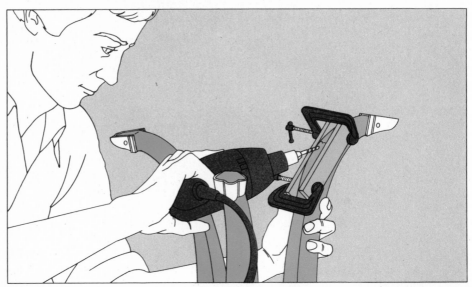

2 **Inserting the dowel.** Use a dowel grooved as in Step 2, page 51, but in this case cut the dowel slightly longer than the depth of the hole. Put glue in the hole and on the dowel; tap the dowel into the hole with a mallet. Remove the clamps and the wood supports, and wipe off excess glue.

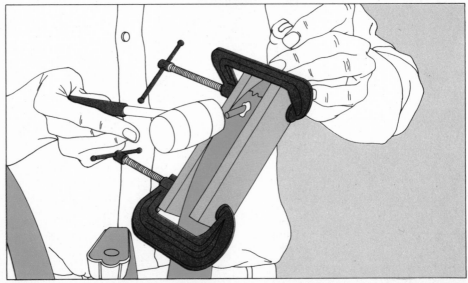

3 **Clamping a curve.** To apply force perpendicular to this break, you will have to attach a C clamp near the break to use as a bracket for applying force with a pipe clamp. Attach the pipe clamp in such a way that it runs from the C clamp to the end of the broken part, spanning the break and remaining perpendicular to it. When the glue has set, use a backsaw and sandpaper to trim the protruding end of the dowel flush with the surface of the broken part.

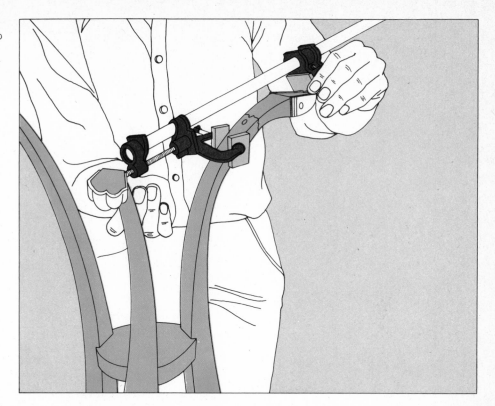

A Mortised Splint for a Flat Break

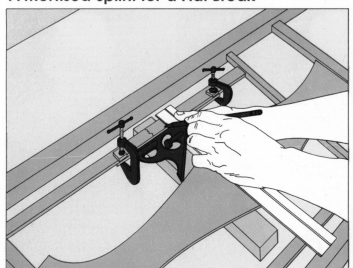

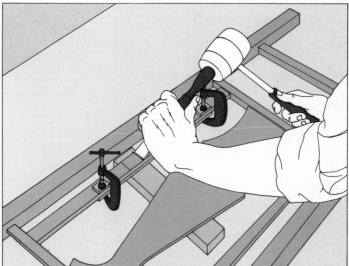

1 **Getting into position.** Clamp the furniture down on a bench or rest it on the floor with the back, or the least visible area, of the broken part horizontal and facing up. Apply glue to the broken edges and join them. Clamp the area of the break in position, using two C clamps, one on each side of the break, to secure a strip of wood spanning the underside of the break. Support the part from underneath with a second scrap of wood, if necessary, as shown. Guided by a combination square, mark where the ends of the mortise will fall on each side of the break, at right angles to the length of the part.

2 **Cutting the mortise.** Cut the mortise ends at the marks to the planned depth, using a backsaw. Or use a chisel, held vertically with its bevel facing the break as you tap it with a mallet. Then, keeping the chisel angled and the bevel side down, score the area between the cuts every ⅜ inch to a depth slightly less than that intended for the mortise. When you have scored the area, reverse direction in order to remove the chips, and then pare the bottom of the mortise smooth by shaving it with the chisel, still bevel side down. Smooth the bottom of the mortise with sandpaper or with a wood file.

3 Clamping the brace. Cut a hardwood brace to fit snugly into the mortise, then put glue in the mortise and on the back and ends of the brace. Insert the brace into the mortise, wipe away the excess glue and, without removing the original C clamps and strip of wood, clamp the brace into the mortise securely with additional C clamps. When the glue is dry, unclamp and sand the brace to match precisely the shape of the part.

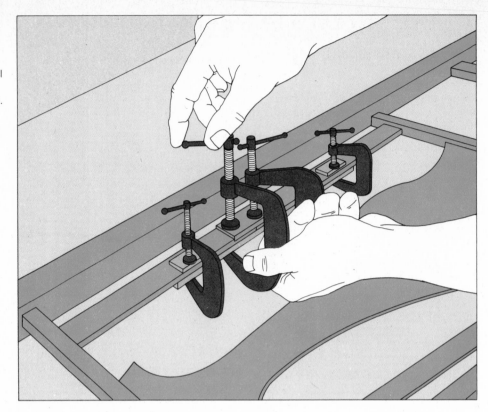

A Screwed-on Brace Concealed from View

A simple strengthener. Expose as much as possible of any concealed broken part; if the break is under upholstery, remove tacks or staples (*pages 102 and 103*) and fold back the fabric for several inches on each side of the break, without damaging the fabric. Apply glue to the broken edges and clamp them together with a pipe clamp running from one end of the framing member to the other. Drill pilot holes through the corners of a ½- to 1-inch-thick rectangle of wood that spans the break on the exposed side of the broken part. Spread glue on this brace and attach it with screws. When the glue is dry, unclamp the piece and retack the fabric.

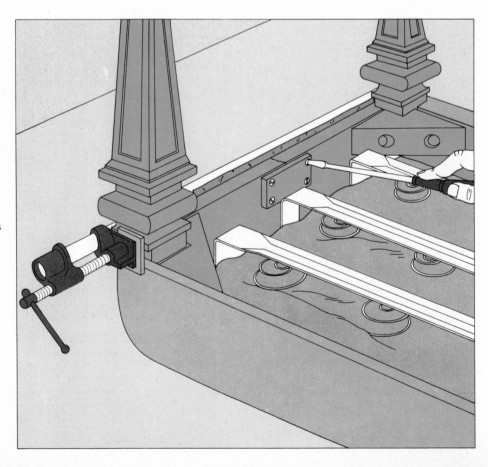

Fixing a Crack in a Tabletop

The boards that make up a tabletop may shrink and draw apart, producing cracks where they were glued together. If such a crack can be drawn closed by clamping, clean the crack with a thin blade and repair the break by forcing glue into the crack with a glue injector *(page 10)*, then clamping the crack shut.

A straight crack that cannot be drawn closed easily with a clamp can be sawed out. Remove the tabletop and draw a line along the crack from one edge of the tabletop to the other, then make a precise cut along the line with a table saw or a circular saw guided by a strip of wood clamped parallel to the crack. The saw blade cuts out the crack so that two pieces of the top can then be reglued at the new joint.

A wide crack can be filled with a narrow strip of wood called a spline. Cut the spline with the grain, from matching wood, and taper it with a file or sandpaper until it precisely fits the crack. Then glue it into position.

As with all glued repairs, apply clamps perpendicular to the break to draw the glued parts together. In the case of a round or oval tabletop, a caul clamp *(below, right)* facilitates this procedure.

Tracing a caul. To clamp a round or oval tabletop, you will need to cut bands to fit against the tabletop, providing straight edges for clamping. Remove the legs and place the top upside down on two 1-by-6 boards extending at least 2 inches beyond the tabletop at each end. Place the boards parallel to each other and to the crack in the tabletop, keeping the outer edges of the boards at least 2 inches beyond the edge of the top. Trace the outline of the top on the boards, and then cut along these lines with a saber saw.

Pad the edges of the tabletop with felt, or rubber cut from an old inner tube, and position the crescent-shaped boards—the caul—against it. Apply glue to the edges of the crack, then position pipe clamps so that they are perpendicular to the crack from one board to the other. If more than two clamps are used, alternate their positions *(inset)* to avoid warping the top.

A Spline to Fill a Wide Crack

Filling a tabletop crack. Cut a spline slightly longer and wider than the crack; sand or file the spline to fit the crack snugly. Apply glue to both sides of the spline and insert it into the crack, from the edge if it is a short spline, and from the top if it is a long one. Tap it in gently with a mallet, letting excess spline protrude. If the tabletop is rectangular, apply bar clamps perpendicular to the crack; for a round or oval top, make a caul clamp *(bottom)*. When the glue is dry, remove the clamps and trim any protruding parts of the spline; use a backsaw to cut the spline end flush with the edge of the tabletop, and a chisel, bevel side down, to pare away the part of the spline that protrudes from the top *(inset)*. Smooth the repair with sandpaper and refinish.

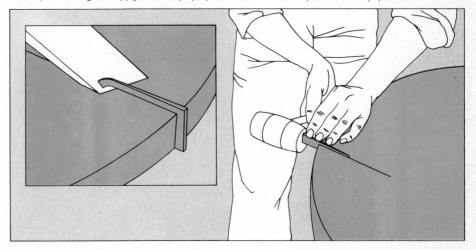

Clamping a Round or Oval Top with a Caul

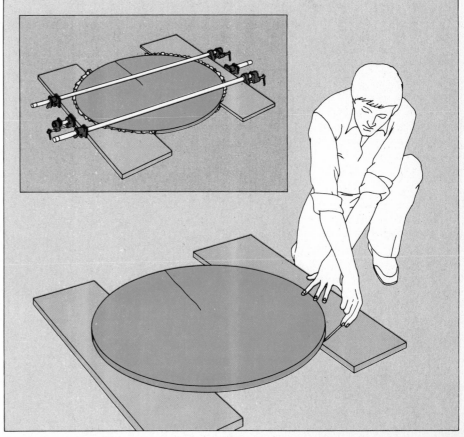

Restoring the Curves of Bentwood

Bentwood furniture is made of solid wood rods that have been softened by steam and bent into continuous curves that have great strength. The technique is ancient, but in 1842 a Viennese cabinet-maker, Michael Thonet, adapted it to mass production, eliminating much of the joinery of conventional furniture manufacturing. Bentwood chairs and tables are lightweight and sturdy—many of the millions of pieces built since Thonet's time are still in use, and 19th Century examples are valued antiques. But occasionally the severely stressed curves split, requiring special repair.

Most splits occur along the outside of a curve when wood fibers, stretched in the bending process, tear apart. You can repair these splits by steaming the wood to soften the tongue of the split, so that it can be glued back in position. To prevent a recurrence, the mended split may then be reinforced with dowels. Small splits, which can easily be pushed back together again, may need only gluing without either steaming or reinforcing. Repairs to the few joints used in bentwood pieces are made by the same techniques used for other furniture (pages 10-17).

Repairing Split Bentwood

1 **Cleaning the damaged area.** With the tip of a sharp, tapered tool such as a craft knife, scrape away dirt, old glue and paint from inside and around the split so that they do not interfere with sound bonding of the glue. Use a vacuum cleaner to remove debris.

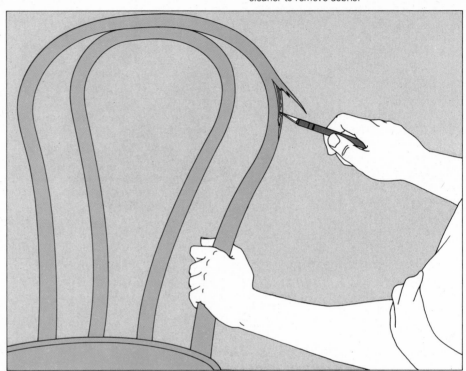

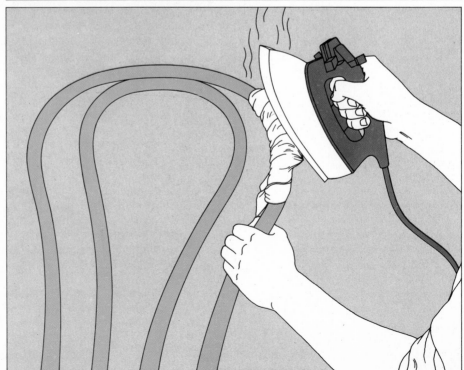

2 **Softening the wood.** Wrap the damaged section with several layers of cloth you have soaked in hot water, and steam the wood by rubbing a hot iron against the cloth from all sides. A steam iron is best to use, but you will still have to re-soak the cloth as it dries by dripping water onto it. Steam until the wood is pliable enough that you can press it back into its original shape—usually about 15 minutes. Then remove the cloth.

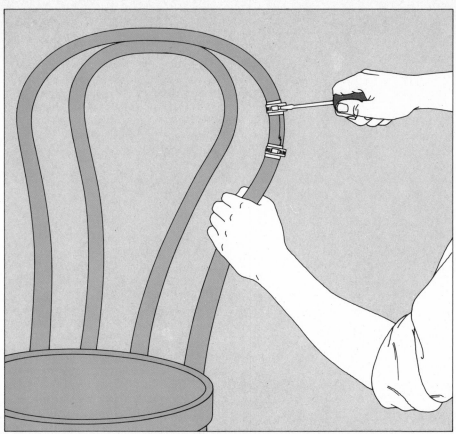

3 **Clamping the split.** Press the softened wood into its original position and clamp both ends of the split with automotive hose clamps, protecting the wood under the clamps with padding made of several layers of masking tape. Alternatively, use C clamps to hold the split closed, padding the clamp jaws with small pieces of plywood or cork. Let the wood dry for 24 hours in a warm place.

Remove the clamps and, as the split opens slightly, coat both inside surfaces with yellow glue. Use an artist's brush to apply glue to the throat of the split. Press the split closed and wipe away excess glue, then retape and reclamp the split until the glue has dried, about 18 hours.

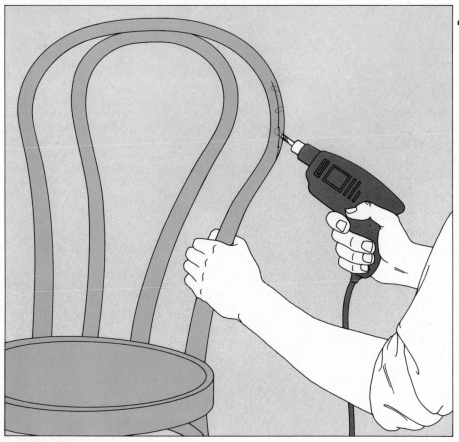

4 **Reinforcing the split.** If the split is deeper than one fourth the thickness of the wood, drill holes for ⅜-inch dowels at 2-inch intervals, beginning at the deepest point of the split. Drill about two thirds of the way through the wood, angling each hole differently to create an interlocking pattern.

Cut ⅜-inch dowels slightly longer than the depth of the holes and glue them in. Wipe away any excess glue, and sand or file the protruding dowel ends until they are flush.

Duplicating Parts by Copying the Originals

Parts of old furniture frequently wear out or get lost, or a part may be broken beyond repair. Fortunately, because most furniture is symmetrical it usually is possible to duplicate the part by using an existing part as a model—but keep in mind that the two parts probably were mirror images of each other, rather than exact copies, so the profile of the duplicate may have to be inverted.

Whatever the part or the furniture style, the process of duplication always begins in the same way: First you remove the existing part being used as a model. Though disassembling a piece of furniture to get at a single part may seem a bother, it is worth the effort. A copy is far easier to make if you can freely turn the part being copied to examine its profiles from different angles.

Sometimes, if the shape is relatively simple and the part has one flat surface, you can use the part itself as a pattern, tracing it directly onto the new wood. Professionals often sacrifice the model to get a flat surface, cutting the model in half lengthwise, although this means making two new parts instead of one.

More often, you will have to make a separate pattern, tracing all the profiles of the part—front, back and sides—onto a sheet of paper and using these silhouettes as patterns for transferring the profiles onto a block of wood. When you are duplicating a part on a lathe, the paper pattern will be a negative of the finished shape—that is, whatever is concave on the model will be convex on the pattern, and vice versa *(pages 64-65)*.

Accuracy is very important when these profiles are traced, especially when a joint is involved or when matching parts must function in unison—for instance, a pair of chair rockers. Use a mechanical pencil with its lead extended, so that you can hold the pencil absolutely vertical against the shape you are outlining. A profile tool *(page 65)*, pressed against the contours of a part, is helpful in making an exact tracing—although a profile tool usually is not long enough to capture more than one section of a part at a time.

Measuring tools such as a straight-rule caliper, a protractor and a T bevel are needed to transfer the dimensions of joinery parts such as dowels and sockets or mortises and tenons. But they are helpful also in copying profiles and in checking the shapes of new parts against old as the work progresses. In fact, only when you are using a tapering jig, or are tapering a square table leg, can the elaborate process of tracing and measuring be simplified.

In addition to tracing the outline of the part, you may also have to transfer a carving detail. Tape a sheet of paper over the carving, rub it with pencil or chalk, and then transfer the outlines of the carving to the new part with carbon paper and a sharp pencil or an awl.

The wood for a new part should match the old as nearly as possible, and its dimensions should be large enough to encompass the part with several inches to spare. In the initial cutting you will roughly shape the wood with a band saw, saber saw or coping saw *(pages 60-62)*, or carve it with a drawknife or a spokeshave *(page 63)*. For shaping the details, you will need gouges, chisels and a thumb plane; a router equipped with the appropriate bit is useful for reproducing missing parts such as sections of molding.

Transferring Dimensions of Diameters and Angles

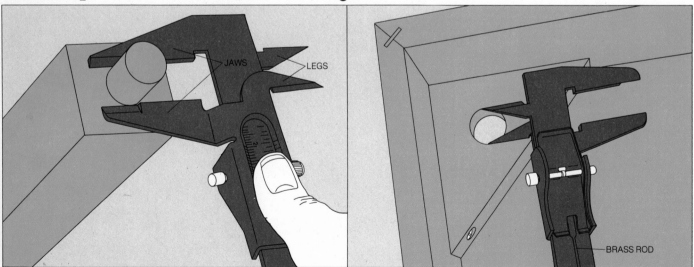

Using a straight-rule caliper. To measure and transfer the diameter of a dowel, loosen the caliper screw and open the caliper jaws until they rest against the widest part of the dowel *(left)*. Then lock the jaws by tightening the screw, and use the pointed tips of the caliper legs to mark the dowel diameter on a new piece of wood. At any setting, the caliper's jaw separation equals its leg separation.

To measure and transfer the diameter of a dowel hole, close the caliper legs and set them in the hole; then open them until they touch the walls of the hole *(right)*. Lock the caliper as above, and use the pointed tips of the legs to mark the diameter of the hole on a new piece of wood. To measure the depth of a dowel hole, rest the bottom of the caliper stem against the top of the hole, and extend the brass rod until it touches the bottom of the hole. Read the depth from the scale on the caliper stem.

Using a T bevel. Loosen the wing nut a bit, then position the handle and blade of the T bevel against the two sides of the angle that you want to copy *(top)*; tighten the wing nut. Move the T bevel to the new piece of wood, hold the handle against the edge of the wood, and mark along the blade to transfer the angle *(bottom)*.

To measure an angle in degrees, you can use either a protractor with the T bevel or a tool that is a combination protractor-bevel *(inset)*. Loosen the lock nut and align the bottom of the protractor plate with one side of the angle to be measured. Align the bevel arm with the other side of the angle, and read the angle in degrees on the plate of the protractor.

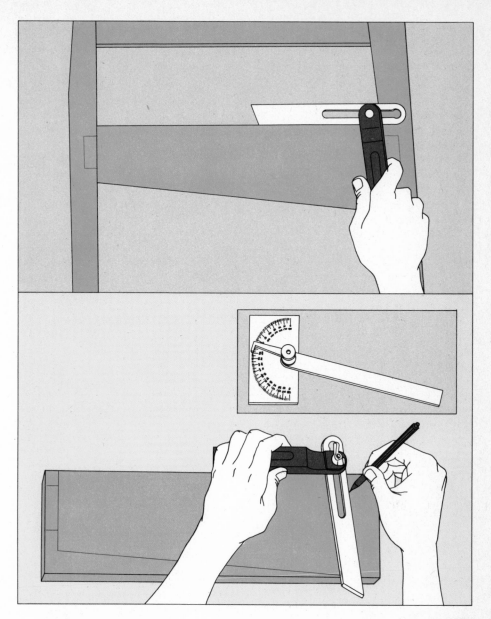

Laminating a New Rocking-Chair Runner

1 Tracing the lamination parts. On a board one third the thickness of the runner, trace three outlines, using the existing runner as a pattern. Arrange the outlines on the board so the wood grain runs a different direction in each one; insofar as possible, avoid short grains at the ends of the runners, as these are brittle.

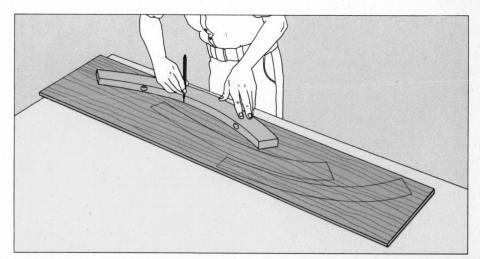

2 **Sawing the runner sections.** Clamp the board to a work surface or sawhorses and, starting at the board edge, cut out the runner parts. Support each runner as the saw nears the edge of the board, so that the piece does not fall and break.

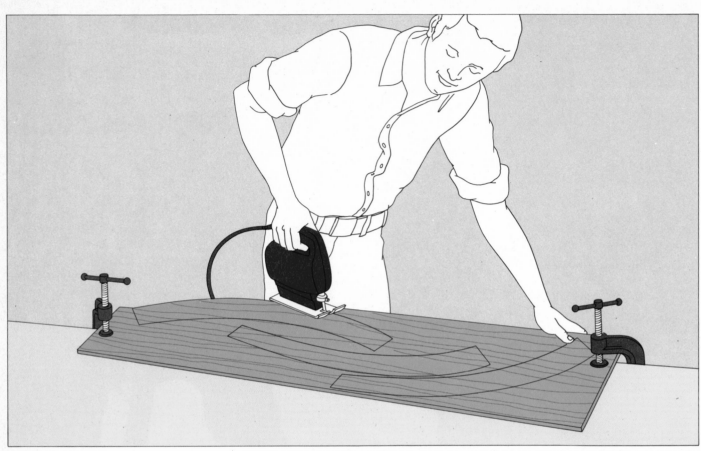

3 **Gluing the runner together.** Spread yellow glue on both faces of one runner section and on the interior faces of the other two sections. Assemble the sections, and clamp them between long blocks of wood to distribute the pressure evenly. Allow the glue to dry for 24 hours.

Remove the clamps, and smooth the curved surfaces of the new runner with a thumb plane, spokeshave or forming tool (*inset, page 63*). Then cut the holes for the dowels or tenons that will join the runner to the chair, taking care to position them the same distance from the ends as the holes of the original runner so that the chair will rock smoothly. Spread glue on the new runner and clamp it in place.

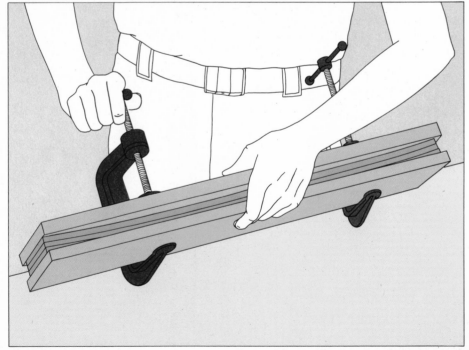

Shaping a Curved Rail
for a Ladder-back Chair

Cutting the compound curves. On a block of wood long enough to accommodate tenons at both ends, trace the curved front, back and top profiles of the new rail. Use a band saw to rough-cut the front and back curves, slicing off the back corners and hollowing out the front. Then refine both curves, working slowly and evenly along the profile to avoid gouging the wood or twisting and breaking the blade. Rough-cut and refine the top profile in the same fashion.

Smooth the front, back and top curves with a thumb plane or a forming tool. Measure the mortises on the chair stiles, and shape matching tenons on the rail with a dovetail saw and a chisel. If you cut the tenons as short as possible, you may be able to insert the new rail without pulling apart the rails already in place. Glue and clamp the new rail in place.

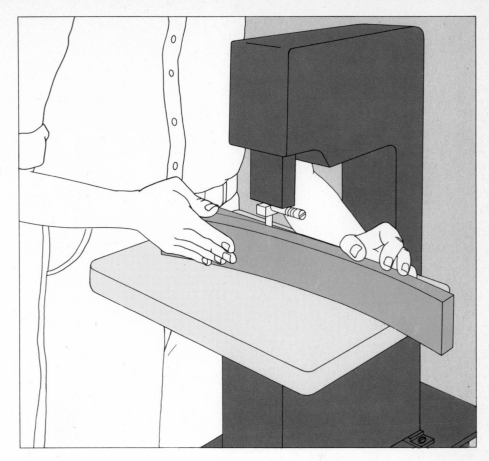

A Compound Rough Cut
for a Cabriole Leg

1 Tracing the profile of the original. Place the leg to be copied on its side on a sheet of paper, and trace its profile. With a caliper or a ruler, compare the measurements of the leg and the tracing; correct the tracing if necessary. Cut out the tracing with scissors and, using a block of wood large enough to encompass the whole leg plus a tenon, position this pattern so that the knee and foot are both touching the corner of the block where the two faces meet *(inset)*. Transfer the profile onto the wood, then turn the pattern over and move it to the adjoining face so that the knee and the foot touch the same points on the first tracing. Then transfer the profile onto this side of the block as well.

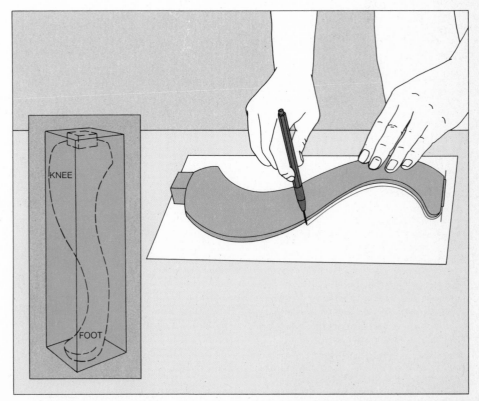

2 **Making the compound cut.** Place one profile, face up, on the table of a band saw and cut along both edges of the profile. Nail the cutout sections of waste wood back into place temporarily, taking care not to nail into the leg. Then flip the block of wood, placing the other profile face up, and again cut along both edges of the profile. Caution: Do not let the saw blade hit a nail, or the wood will kick and the blade may break.

After the last cut, use a forming tool or a thumb plane to shape the rough-cut leg to match the original. Carve decorative details with gouges and chisels, and sand the leg smooth.

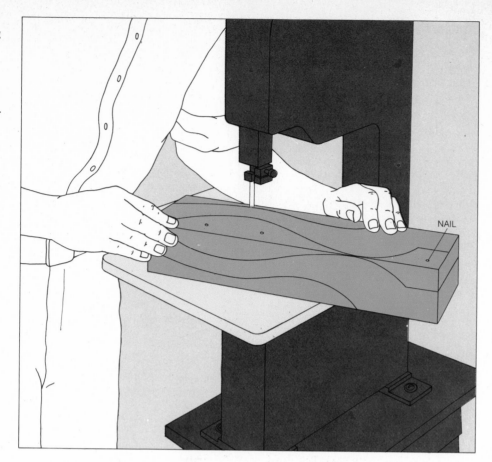

NAIL

Using a V-shaped Jig to Cut a Tapered Leg

An exploded view of a tapering jig. A tapering jig can be made from readily available materials: two 1-by-3s for the folding legs; a 2½-inch fixed-pin butt hinge screwed into one end of each leg; a sliding chest-lid support attached to the opposite end, to set and hold the angle of the legs; and a 1-by-3 stop on the outer face of the open end of one leg. Reference points, used in setting the angle, are marked on the inside edge of each leg, 12 inches from the hinge end.

To use a tapering jig, you must first determine the taper of the part as a ratio of inches per foot. On a leg, for example, measure the widths of the leg at top and bottom, in inches, and subtract to find the difference. Divide this figure by the length of the leg, in feet, using decimals if necessary. The result is the amount of taper in terms of inches per foot. Open the jig legs to this amount of taper at the reference points, and tighten down the wing nut.

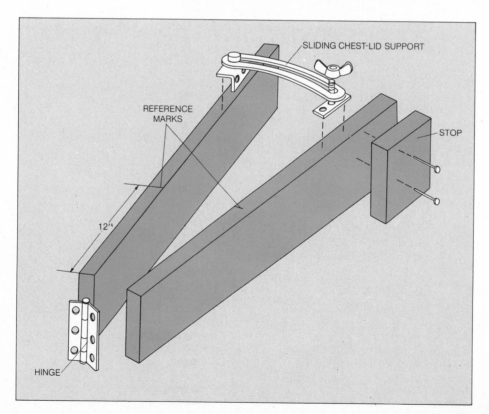

SLIDING CHEST-LID SUPPORT

REFERENCE MARKS

STOP

12″

HINGE

Using a jig for a tapered cut. Start with a block of wood as long as the original leg and as wide as the top width of the leg. Resting the block against the jig, push jig and block through the saw. Turn and cut the other three faces of the block, but double the angle of the taper whenever a tapered face rests against the jig: Cut the third side at the same angle as the first, and the second and fourth at double that angle.

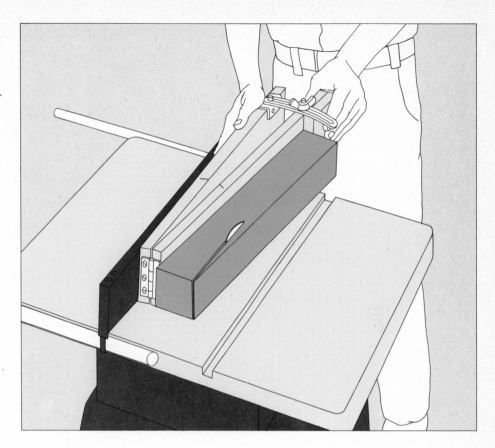

Sculpting a Free-Form Shape with Hand Tools

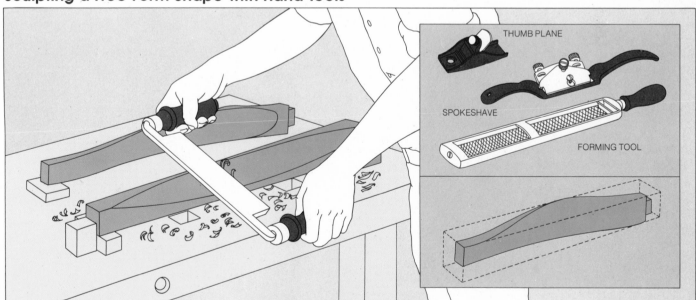

Using a drawknife to cut a chair arm. Trace the outer limits of the arm's curved surfaces on a block of wood large enough to encompass the overall dimensions of the arm. Secure the block of wood to a worktable and, with the beveled edge of the blade down, pull a drawknife across the top face of the wood. To take off thin shavings, keep the handles of the knife nearly parallel with the face of the wood; tilt the handles down for thicker slices. Work slowly, and check frequently against the original, using a caliper and a ruler. Turn the wood as needed, sculpting all four faces as you go.

To finish the shaping, use a thumb plane, a spokeshave and a forming tool (*inset, top*) that is fitted with interchangeable coarse, medium and fine plates. Use the thumb plane—3 inches long and held in one hand—to maneuver into tight corners and over subtle changes in contour. Use the spokeshave, which is held as a drawknife is, to smooth the surfaces already rough-cut; for curved surfaces, spokeshave blades come with special convex and concave faces.

Fashioning a Template for Lathe Work

A spindle or leg that is a straight cylinder can be replaced with a dowel of the same size. But for a shaped spindle or leg—or a drawer knob with a convoluted design—using a lathe is the only feasible way to make a duplicate. To do the job by hand takes hours of laborious shaping, first with a drawknife, then with a gouge and chisel, and the results usually are crude.

If you do not own a lathe, you can farm out the work to a professional, but you can save both time and money by providing a two-part template. One part is a guide for marking the break points—the highest and lowest cutting points—on the smooth cylinder *(right)*. The other guide is a negative profile of the part, to hold against the work in progress for comparison. If you plan to do your own work, you will need to make the template for yourself.

2 **Cutting out the template.** Using scissors, cut along the center line and the template line. Glue the tracing to ⅛-inch-thick plywood or hardboard, using rubber cement. Clamp the wood or hardboard to a worktable, and saw along the profile line. If the saw blade will not turn sharply enough to follow the outline, saw as close to the detail as possible, staying outside the line when you depart from it, and finish shaping the profile with a file.

If your original has a squared section, as some table legs and chair spindles do, make the template for the curved portions only. The squared section will not be shaped on the lathe.

Making a Pattern from an Existing Part

1 **Tracing the original part.** Place the part to be copied on heavy wrapping paper spread over a hard smooth surface, and, using a mechanical pencil with the lead extended, trace the front and back profiles. Then, using calipers, compare the cross-section measurements of the original and those of the tracing at each break point, and correct the tracing, if necessary, to correspond exactly to the original.

Draw a center line down the length of the profile. Then draw a second line—this is called the template line—parallel to the center line and 3 inches outside the widest point on the profile edge *(bottom)*. Draw perpendicular lines, known as break lines, from the break points to the template line. Mark on each break-point line the diameter of the original part at that point; measure with the calipers.

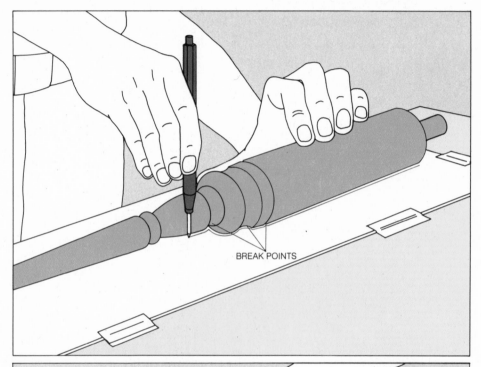

BREAK POINTS

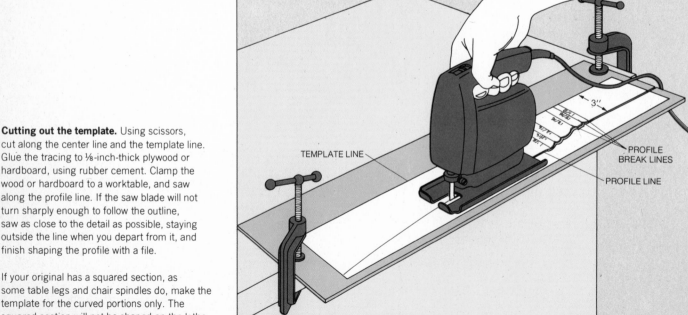

TEMPLATE LINE

3″

PROFILE BREAK LINES

PROFILE LINE

3 **Using the template.** Before starting to shape the part on the lathe, hold the straight edge of the template on the slowly spinning cylinder of wood so you can rest a pencil point at each of the break-point lines to mark these lines on the cylinder. Begin to cut and shape the part, stopping the lathe as you near the end to compare the profile of the wood with the profile edge of the template. When the differences between the two are slight, fold sandpaper over the profile edge and, with the lathe running at very slow speed, hold sandpaper and profile edge against the wood. Use calipers often to check the diameter at the break points; but stop the lathe while you are using the calipers, to avoid gouging the wood.

When cutting a part such as a knob or finial, on which the design is cut into the face of the wood as well as into the lengthwise grain, check the side profile with a template as described in Steps 1 through 3. But check the face profile with a profile tool (inset). Set the profile tool by holding it against the original part and pushing the teeth into the design.

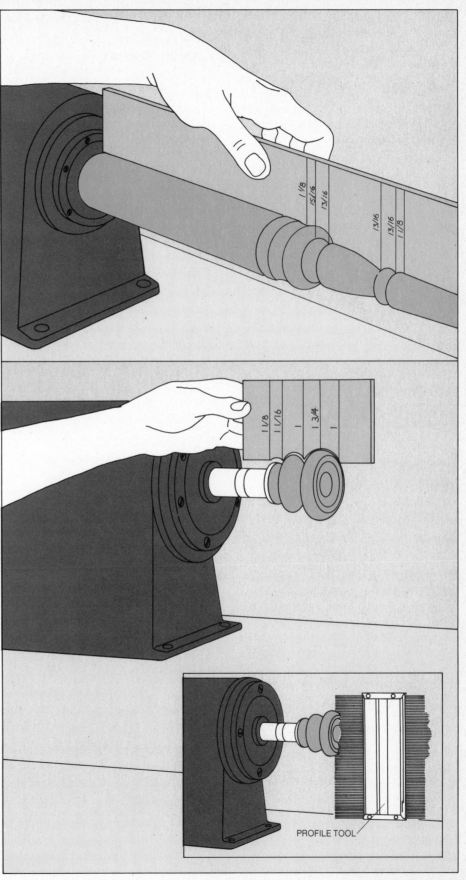

PROFILE TOOL

Reweaving Chair Seats of Splint, Rush or Cane

The techniques for weaving chair seats have been known and used for a very long time. Egyptians were using bulrushes to make seats for chairs and stools some 3,000 years ago. The rustic splint-bottomed chairs associated with rural America had their precursors in splint seats made of hickory or ash by European peasants in the 16th and 17th Centuries, when chairs first came into general use. In the same period, European gentlewomen added caning to their accomplishments, copying the intricate patterns of caned furniture brought from India by Portuguese traders.

Rush, splint and cane seats are still popular, and the techniques and materials for weaving them have changed little. Fiber rush made of twisted paper has largely replaced expensive natural rush except on antiques. And most splints are now cut from the core of the rattan plant, a climbing palm, instead of from the inner bark of trees. Perhaps the greatest change has been the introduction, in the late 19th Century, of prewoven caning and the spline-and-groove method of attaching it to the seat. The groove runs around the perimeter of the seat, and edges of the caning panel are forced into it, to be held in place by a flexible spline made of reed.

Cane furniture fitted with prewoven caning is much simpler to repair than a cane seat woven from scratch. But not even the complex caning patterns are difficult to reproduce. The process is handwork, requiring few tools but much patience—hand caning a typical 12-by-14-inch seat can take as long as 14 hours. The rush, splint or cane needed for the job is available from handicraft shops or from mail-order suppliers who specialize in materials for basketry and caning. Most such sources also carry prewoven caning for spline-and-groove seating.

In choosing a material, be guided by what was there before, since rush, splint and cane cannot usually be used interchangeably. If you are starting with a seatless chair, the frame may well provide a clue to the original seating material. As a general rule, the slat-backed chairs known as ladder-backs are woven with splints or rush; for a splint seat the front and back seat rails must be flush with the side rails, but for a rush seat the front and back rails can be lower than the side rails.

For hand caning, the seat frame must have holes drilled around its perimeter. Prewoven caning can of course be applied only to a chair with a groove. It is sometimes possible to add a groove to a chair that has none, but you should consult a professional furniture maker about the feasibility of such a step.

A splint seat is the simplest to replace. For this job you will need, in addition to splint, only three other supplies: ⅜-inch carpet tacks for fastening the splint to the frame; a stapler for splicing; and a spring-loaded clamp (which looks like an oversized clothespin) for holding the splint temporarily in place on the frame.

Just before weaving, soak the splint for 15 minutes in a bucket of lukewarm water, then round it at both ends with scissors, to make the weaving easier. In soaking the splint, coil it with its smooth side outward, facing the bucket walls, so that the curve of the splint will be in the right direction. (The smooth side is the side that does not splinter when the splint is bent between your fingers.) It is best to soak only five to six strands at a time, replacing them as you work, and to do the weaving in stages over the course of several days, to compensate for changes in the pattern as the splints dry.

Rush seats also are relatively easy to wrap; they require the same ⅜-inch carpet tacks and spring clamp used in weaving splint. In addition, you will need a mallet and a drafting triangle of clear plastic, the latter for checking pattern rows to make sure they lie at right angles to each other—the sign of a well-made rush-bottom seat. Before beginning the wrapping, dip the fiber rush (made of twisted paper) in water for about 30 seconds; if left longer, the paper will begin to untwist and the rush will be damaged. And plan to do the job in easy stages, stopping occasionally to check that the pattern is right.

Hand caning is by far the most difficult of the three techniques, typically done in a six-step pattern with a seventh step to lock the cane to the chair. You will need, in addition to the weaving cane, a supply of wooden pegs—golf tees will do—to hold the strands of cane in the holes, and a small amount of binding cane (cane one size larger than the weaving cane you are using).

With prewoven caning, installation is a much simpler process. You will need a hardwood wedge 4 inches long to drive the caning into the groove and several hardwood wedges 1 inch long to hold it there. To secure the caning permanently, use a flexible reed spline with a tapered edge; the taper of the spline as well as that of the wedges should conform to the width of the groove.

Like splints, both cane strands and prewoven caning need to be soaked in lukewarm water for 15 minutes before using. Cane strands should be coiled in the bucket, with the shiny sides out. To soak prewoven cane, which must be kept flat, you may have to use a bathtub.

Before beginning any weaving project, repair broken chair parts, remove traces of the previous woven material and refinish the chair frame, if necessary. To remove an old hand-caned seat, cut as close to the frame as possible with shears, then use a mallet and chisel to cut through the loops on the underside, so they can be pulled from the holes. On a prewoven cane seat, clean the groove completely before recaning; you can use a mallet and chisel to remove the old caning and spline, and vinegar will often soften old glue.

Also set up a comfortable place to work. Because weaving takes time, put the chair on a stool or table—padded with a blanket to protect the finish—so that you will be working at a level that will be easy on your back.

Once woven, each type of seat may need special finishing and care. Dampening splint and cane may raise stray hairs, which should be removed with tweezers or scissors before finishing the seat. You can stain a splint-woven seat if desired, although splint will darken naturally with age. Dampen the seat at least once a month to help retain the shape. For a fiber-rush seat, brush on one or two coats of shellac, and repeat this application once a year to prolong the life of the fiber rush. Cane also darkens naturally with age, but it too can be stained. For a high-gloss finish, apply a lacquer sealer, followed by clear lacquer.

A Variety of Weaving Materials

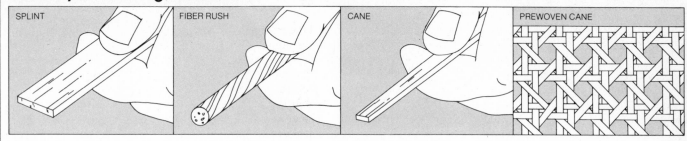

SPLINT · FIBER RUSH · CANE · PREWOVEN CANE

Splint

Splint was originally cut from the inner bark of hickory and ash trees, but most modern splint is the so-called flat-reed splint, cut from the core of the rattan plant. It is available in various widths— ⅝ and ½ inch are most common for chair seats—and is sold by the bundle. One bundle will generally cover the average 12-by-14-inch seat. Though more expensive and harder to use, tra- ditional ash splint is still available when precise restoration is important. A fiber splint of kraft paper is also available, but it can be used only on chairs that will never be exposed to moisture.

Fiber Rush

A counterpart of natural rush, this cord-like material is also made from kraft paper, twisted by machine into strands ranging in width from $3/32$ to $7/32$ inch. It is considered the most durable seating material, and comes in an array of earthy colors. Fiber rush is sold by weight; about 2½ pounds will cover an average 12-by-14-inch chair seat.

Cane

Cut from the outer bark of the rattan plant, cane strands are sold in widths and thicknesses suited to the size and spacing of the chair's holes. The commonest sizes are fine, narrow-medium and medium. Fine cane is for holes $3/16$ inch in diameter, spaced ½ to $9/16$ inch from center to center; narrow-medium is for holes ¼ inch in diameter, $9/16$ to ⅝ inch apart; and medium is for holes ¼ inch in diameter, ⅝ to ¾ inch apart. Cane comes in 250-, 500- and 1,000-foot hanks. A 250-foot hank covers a seat 12 inches square, unless there are more than 72 holes around the frame.

Prewoven Cane

Also called cane webbing, this material consists of strands of natural cane that have been loom-woven into various patterns. The traditional six-way pattern shown is sized according to the width of the holes in the mesh; sizes range from ⅜ to 1 inch. It is available in rolls 12 to 36 inches wide, from which suppliers will cut pieces to size, based on the dimensions of the chair seat. Buy such caning to bridge the widest part of the seat, measured from the outside edges of the groove, adding an inch for the material to be driven into the groove. The reed spline, driven into the groove to hold the cane in place, is sold by the linear foot in widths based on the width of the groove.

The Overs and Unders of a Woven Splint Seat

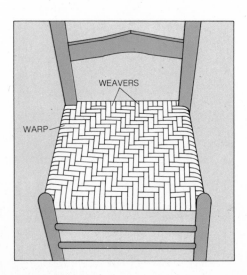

WEAVERS

WARP

The basic herringbone pattern. On any seat woven with splint, strands of splint are wrapped over the side rails to create the first layer of weaving, called the warp. Additional strands, called the weavers, are then woven through the warp and wrapped over the front and back rails to complete the seat.

In the standard herringbone pattern illustrated at left, the weaver passes over and under alternating groups of three strands of warp. On the first row, the first weaver passes over the first strand of warp, then alternately under three and over three, all the way to the back of the seat.

On the second and third rows, the weavers pass over the first two and three strands of warp respectively, then continue with the under-three, over-three pattern.

With the fourth, fifth and sixth rows, the pattern reverses; these weavers start by passing under one, two and three strands of warp respectively, then continue with an over-three, under-three pattern. The starting pattern for the weavers continues to reverse in this fashion with every three rows going first over one, two and three strands of warp and then under one, two and three strands of warp, until the seat is complete.

How to Weave with Splint

1 **Wrapping the warp.** Beginning at the back of the chair and using splints that have been soaked in water for 15 minutes, tack one end of a strand of splint to the underside of one of the chair's side rails, placing the rough side of the splint against the rail and allowing 4 or 5 inches to extend beyond the tack. Pull the splint over the rail from the outside, across to and around the opposite side rail, and then back to the original rail. Keep the smooth side of the splint exposed on both the upper and lower passes around the rails. Do not pull the splint completely tight as you wrap because it will shrink as it dries.

Continue wrapping the first strand of splint until you have made the last complete pass you can make across the top of the seat. Then trim the splint, leaving an end of 6 to 8 inches, along the lower pass; spring-clamp the loose end to the nearest side rail while you splice a new strand to the first strand with staples *(inset)*. Overlap the strands at the splice by about 3 inches and use about three staples per splice.

Continue wrapping, splicing as necessary, until the side rails are covered. Clamp the final strand to a side rail; tack its loose end to the inside of the front rail, with 4 or 5 inches extending beyond the tack. Dampen the warp with a wet cloth just before proceeding to Steps 2 and 3.

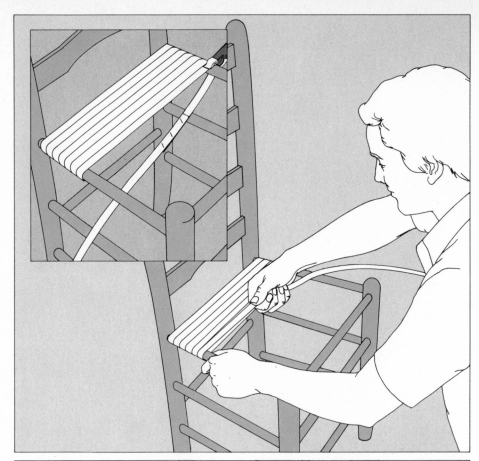

2 **Squaring off an angled seat.** If the front rail of a chair is longer than the back is, fill in the small triangular area on each side of the front with short rows of weaving. To locate the inner leg of the triangle, find the difference in length between the front rail and the back rail, divide in half, then make a pencil mark indicating the resulting measurement at each end of the front rail. Starting at the left front corner, weave the first splint through the top layer of warp, following the pattern shown on page 67 and keeping the splint parallel with an imaginary line running from the end of the back rail to the pencil mark on the left side of the front rail. Stop when the splint butts into the side rail, and leave an end long enough to weave back through the bottom layer of warp hanging over the front rail.

Continue weaving lengths of splint through the triangular corner area, following the pattern sequence, until the triangle is filled. Then turn the chair upside down and, starting with the row closest to the side rail, weave the splint back through the bottom layer of warp, maintaining the same pattern as on top. Tuck the loose ends of splint at the back into the space between the top and bottom warp, and tack each row of splint to the bottom of the front rail *(inset)*.

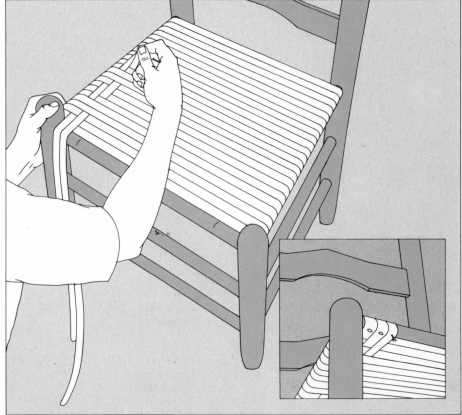

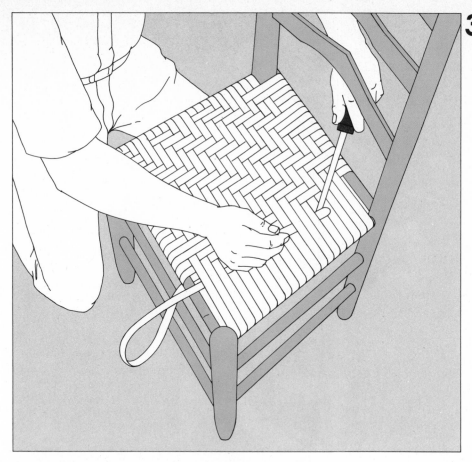

3 Completing the pattern. On the main body of the seat, weave a long strand from the front rail to the back, on the top layer of warp, continuing the pattern sequence. Pull the excess through, and tack the front end to the underside of the front rail. Carry the splint over the back rail, weave back through the bottom layer of warp and then start a new row on top. Snug each new row of splint against the one just completed, and whenever you need to splice on new splint, make the splice on the underside of the seat, following the directions in Step 1.

When you completed a third of the seat, allow the splint to dry for 24 hours and adjust the position of the rows if necessary. Stop again when you have reached the two-thirds point in the weaving. As you near the end of the weaving process, use a blunt screwdriver to lift the warp so that you can slide the weaver beneath it.

When you complete the last row before the pencil mark on the right, cut off the splint, leaving a loose end long enough to tuck up into the seat, and tack the end to the underside of the front rail. Then weave in strips to fill the triangular corner area, as in Step 2, trimming the width of the last strip if necessary.

Remove any splint hairs that remain on the finished seat, using either a razor blade or tweezers. Rub the surface with fine sandpaper, then allow it to dry for 24 hours.

Wrapping a Fiber-Rush Chair Seat

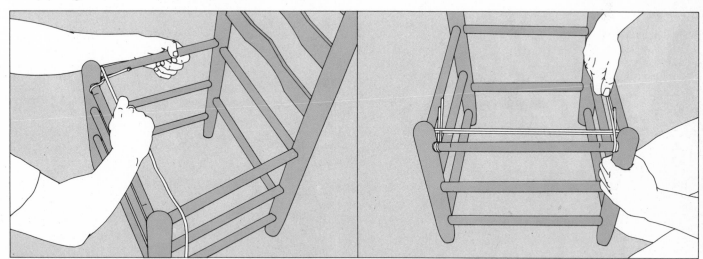

1 Establishing square corners. After marking the front rail for squaring off as in Step 2 *(opposite)*, tack one end of a length of rush cording to the inside face of the left rail, 3 inches back from the front corner. Bring the cord under, then over the front rail; loop it back under itself, then under and over the left rail *(above, left)*. Pull the cord across to the opposite side of the seat, and loop it under and over the right rail; then carry it back under itself, and under and over

the front rail. Tack it to the inside of the right rail, directly across from the point where it is tacked to the left rail.

Tack a second length of cord to the inside of the left rail, behind the first *(above, right)*, and wrap it in the same pattern until you have filled the triangular areas between the front corner posts and the pencil marks on the front rails. To keep the intersecting runs of cord at right an-

gles, pull the cord taut across the seat but relax pressure while wrapping the corners.

When the chair corners are squared off, hold a drafting triangle against the intersecting cords to make sure they are at right angles to each other. If the cords cross the rails too far out, gently tap them back with a small block of wood and a rubber mallet; if they cross the rails too close in, flatten them with a mallet to widen the weave.

2 **Completing a circuit.** After the chair has been squared off, lightly dampen about 20 feet of cord, roll it into a manageable coil and tack one end to the left side rail, just beyond the last squaring-off cord. Wrap it around the two front corners in the same way as you wrapped the corner cords (*Step 1*), but instead of tacking it to the right rail, continue the pattern to the right back corner, then to the left back corner, and finally to the left front corner, to complete an entire circuit—called a bout (*inset*). Continue wrapping bouts until the cord runs out. Then attach a new length of dampened cord with a square knot, positioning it so that the knot falls on the underside of the chair and at a rail.

After about six bouts, secure the cord to a rail with a spring clamp, and check to make sure the cords are forming right-angle intersections. Adjust the cords as in Step 1, if necessary. Then continue wrapping bouts, stopping periodically to check for right angles.

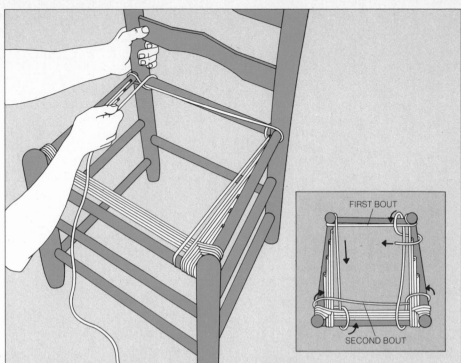

FIRST BOUT

SECOND BOUT

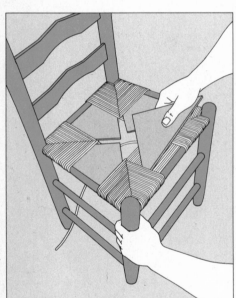

3 **Stuffing the seat.** When the side rails are covered by cord except for about 4 inches, slide a triangle of cardboard into the pocket between the upper and lower layers of rush along each side rail. Continue to weave bouts over the cardboard until about 4 inches of space remains on the front and back rails. Then insert cardboard triangles in the pockets along the front and back rails. If these rails are lower than the side rails, as is the case with many chairs, they will probably need additional layers of cardboard to fill the pocket. When all of the cardboard is in place, cut off the points of all four cardboard triangles to allow more room for weaving. Continue weaving until the side rails are filled.

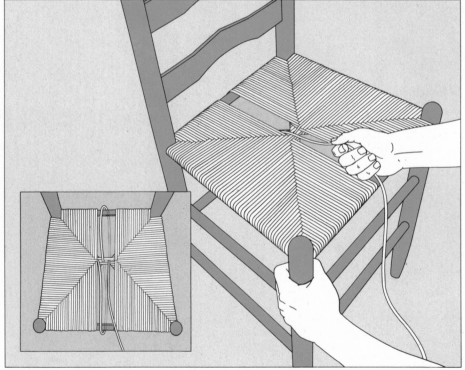

4 **Completing the chair.** To fill the remaining space on the front and back rails, bring the cord up through the center opening, over the front rail, up through the center opening again and over the back rail, then up through the center opening once more to form, in effect, a figure 8 (*inset*). Continue weaving figure 8s until the front and back rails are filled, then use a hammer and a block of wood to flatten the

layers of cord where they cross in the center. Tack the end of the fiber rush to the back rail, and cut off the excess.

To make sure that all rows of cord lie in the same plane, rub the seat with a block of wood or, if necessary, use a stiff wooden ruler to poke additional cardboard stuffing between cords on the underside of the seat.

Restoring a Chair Seat with Prewoven Cane

1 **Cutting the pattern.** After removing all the old cane, spline and glue from the groove and sanding it clean, tape a piece of paper over the seat. Mark the paper by running a pencil along the inside edge of the groove, then cut along the marked line to make a pattern for the prewoven cane. Tape the pattern onto a section of prewoven cane, positioning it so that one set of double strands runs straight down the center from front to back, and one set of double strands runs parallel with the front rail (on a square seat) or with a line between the front legs (on a round seat). Cut the caning 1 inch larger than the dimensions of the pattern.

Soak the prewoven cane for 15 minutes where it can lie flat, then place it across the seat in the correct position. Remove any strands that run along, rather than across, the groove.

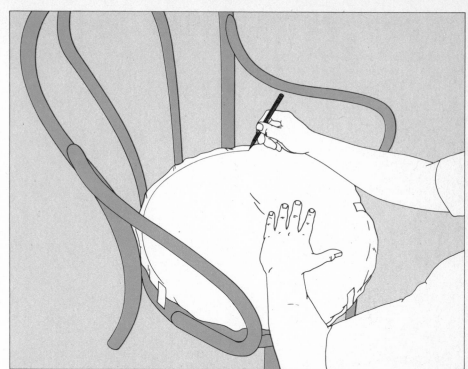

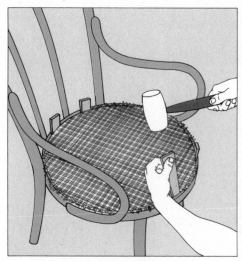

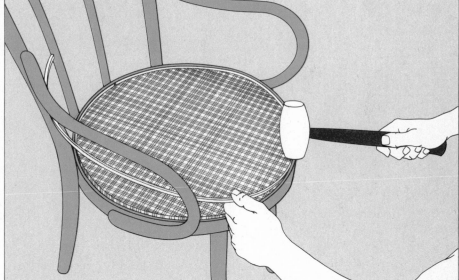

2 **Inserting the cane in the groove.** Using a rubber mallet and a 4-inch-long wedge of hardwood, drive the prewoven cane into a 2-inch section of the groove at the center back of the chair. Lock this section in place with a 1-inch-long hardwood wedge. Then pull the cane tightly across to the front, and drive it into a 2-inch section of the groove at the center front, again inserting a locking wedge. Continue working along the groove, first on one side and then on the other, inserting cane in 2-inch-wide sections and locking them with wedges, until you have driven cane into the groove all the way around. Sponge the cane periodically to keep it pliable.

Use a razor knife or a mallet and sharp chisel to trim off any cane ends that stick out of the groove, removing the locking wedges as you go.

3 **Inserting the spline.** Square the ends of a length of reed spline at least 1 inch longer than the circumference of the groove, and soak it in water for 20 minutes. Run a uniform bead of white glue into the groove on top of the cane. If the groove outlines a rounded seat, as here, start the spline at the back, tapping it lightly with a rubber mallet just enough to position it in the groove. When you have completed almost the entire circuit, lap the spline over itself, mark the overlap point, and cut the spline with a razor knife. Then use a wooden wedge and a rubber mallet to seat the spline firmly in the groove, so that it is flush with the surface of the frame and so the ends form a

butt joint. Sponge off any excess glue and allow the chair seat to dry for at least a day.

If the groove goes around a square-cornered seat, use the same basic techniques to fit spline into the groove; but use a length of spline for each rail, and miter the ends to fit together at the corners. Take care to cut the miters so they make neat joints.

Use tweezers or fine sandpaper to remove any whiskers that were raised by the soaking process, and cut off larger filaments with scissors. Prewoven cane darkens naturally with age, but it can be stained if you choose to do so.

Hand Caning a Chair Seat

1 **Lacing the first vertical row.** On a square seat, insert 3 or 4 inches of soaked cane in the center hole along the back rail—or in the center hole nearest the left rail if the number of holes is even—and peg it in place with a golf tee. Find the corresponding center hole in the front rail, and pull the strand of cane through it, top to bottom, keeping the glossy side up. Carry the strand along the underside of the front rail, and bring it up through the first hole to the right of the hole just passed through. Then pull the strand of cane across the seat, and thread it through the corresponding hole in the back rail. Continue lacing in this manner, working from the center to the right, but do not lace through the corner holes. Pull the cane smooth but not completely taut, for it shrinks as it dries.

When a strand is used up, leave 3 or 4 inches hanging below the rail, and peg the end in place; peg a new strand into the nearest hole, again leaving 3 or 4 inches hanging below the rail. If empty holes remain on the front rail after the holes on the back rail are filled, weave an individual strand from each empty front hole to a selected hole on the side rail so that the strands will be parallel and equally spaced (*inset*); leave ends of 3 or 4 inches at both front and side. Lace the left side of the seat in the same way, again leaving the corner holes empty.

On a round chair, use these same basic techniques but take special care to start on corresponding holes in the center front and back of the seat. In lacing to fill the curved sides, choose holes that will keep the lines of cane parallel and evenly spaced. Do not worry about leaving empty "corner" holes on a round seat.

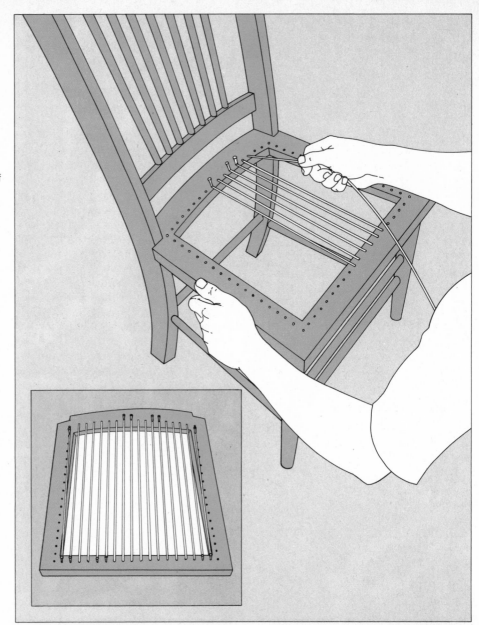

2 **Tying off ends.** Before continuing the cane weaving, turn the chair bottom up, and tie off any pegged cane ends by knotting them around the loops on the underside of the chair. Thoroughly sponge each end of cane and its adjacent loop, then lift the loop gently with an awl, and slip the end underneath. Keep the rough side of the cane up, and carry the cane under the loop from the inside to the outside edge of the chair rail. Then pass the cane through the new loop it has formed (from the outside of the rail to the inside) and, placing your thumb over the knot, pull the cane tight. Position the knot in the center of the loop to allow for more than one knot per loop if needed. Trim cane ends to ½ inch.

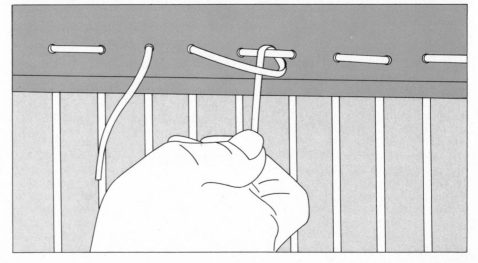

3 Lacing the first horizontal rows. On a square seat, begin the horizontal lacing at the back, working between side holes but skipping the holes at the back corners. Peg the end of the cane as in Step 1, and lace it from side to side, over the top of the vertical strands, glossy side up. Stop after you pass through the last set of holes short of the front corners *(inset)*. Tie off the pegged ends as in Step 2.

On a round chair seat, lace the cane using the same sequence described in Step 1. Begin by lacing from center side to center side, then lace from there toward the back. Then return to the center and lace toward the front.

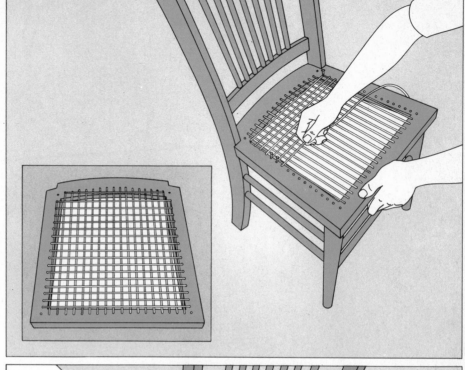

4 Lacing the first diagonal rows. On a square seat, start lacing diagonal rows at the right front corner; peg the end of the cane in the first hole at the left of the right front corner hole. Thread the free cane down through the first hole on the right side rail next to this corner, and up through the next hole on the same rail. Then carry the cane back to the front rail, going under each vertical strand and over each horizontal strand. Lace the free cane back to the side rail in the same manner. Continue weaving diagonals until you pass through a corner hole. You may have to weave two diagonals into the same hole on one side, and skip over a hole on the other side, to keep the rows of cane even.

During this step and all subsequent steps that require intricate weaving, frequently dampen the free end of cane, as well as the top and the bottom of the woven seat. To make longer passes across the seat go more smoothly, trim the free cane end to a point, and pull all the excess cane through after every four or five stitches to avoid bending the cane into too many S curves.

Weave diagonals through the second half of the seat in the same manner, starting on the back rail in the hole next to the left back corner hole and running the cane between the back and left rails. When the first diagonals are completed *(inset)*, there should be two strands of cane passing through the holes at the left front and right back corners. Tie off pegged ends *(Step 2, opposite)*. On a round seat, weave the first diagonals following the same basic techniques used for a square seat, using your eyes to judge the appropriate holes for each row.

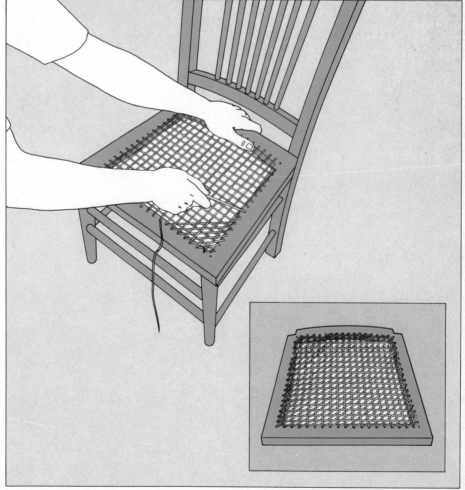

5 **Lacing the second vertical rows.** Using the same methods as in Step 1, page 72, lay a second set of vertical strands between the front and back rails, placing them slightly to the right of the first vertical canes and stringing them over the top of all work done thus far. As before, tie off the pegged ends (*Step 2, page 72*).

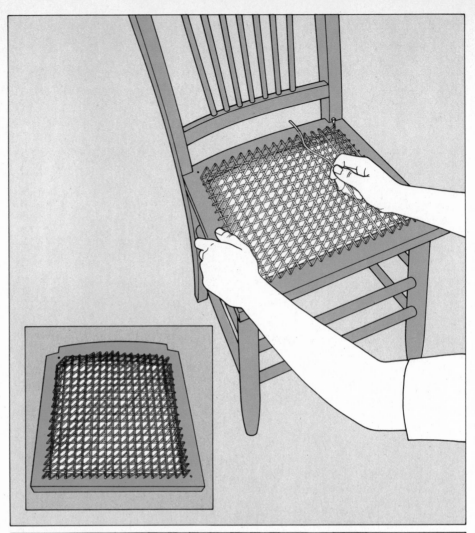

6 **Lacing the second horizontal rows.** To make this step easier, use two pegs as tools to separate each pair of vertical strands. Beginning in the hole on the right rail next to the right back corner hole, weave a second set of horizontal strands, just behind the first horizontal strands. Follow the same sequence of rows as in Step 3, page 73, but as you weave, go under all the first diagonal rows and over the first vertical rows, but under the second vertical rows. Straighten the rows as you work, and check carefully for mistakes. When you have finished weaving a second set of horizontal rows across the entire seat, tie off any pegged ends (*Step 2, page 72*).

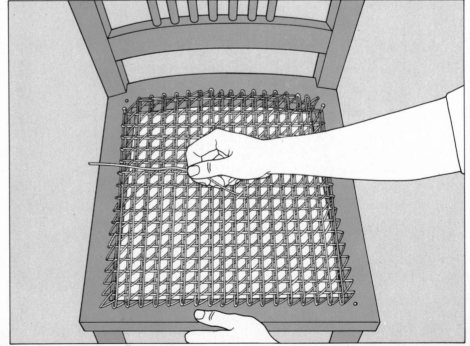

7 **Lacing the second diagonal rows.** With an awl, carefully compact the strands already woven into each hole to make room for additional strands of cane, then weave diagonal rows at right angles to those already laid (*Step 4, page 73*). Start in the hole in the front rail next to the left front corner hole, and weave under the first diagonal and over the second diagonal that go to this corner hole. Then thread the strand of cane down through the hole on the left rail next to this corner hole, and up through the next hole on the same rail. Continue to weave between the front and left rails, carrying the strands over the vertical rows, under the horizontal rows and alternately over and under the diagonal rows. To avoid confusion at the edges, remember that you should never go under or over two consecutive diagonal strands.

To maintain symmetry in the pattern, skip holes or double the rows in a single hole where necessary, as in Step 4, page 73. Stop when you reach a corner hole, then weave diagonals across the second half of the seat in the same way, starting on the back rail in the hole that is next to the right back corner hole and weaving between the back and right rails (*inset*). Tie off the pegged ends (*Step 2, page 72*).

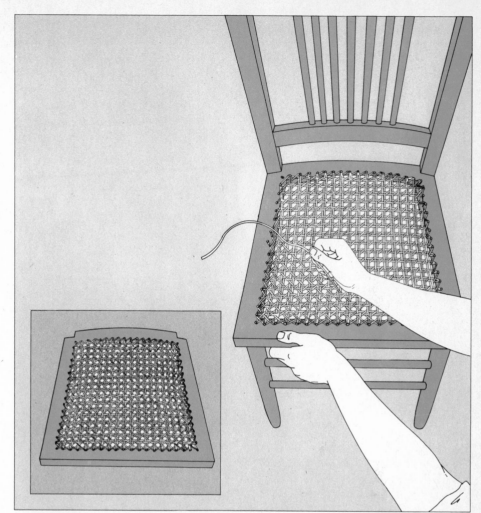

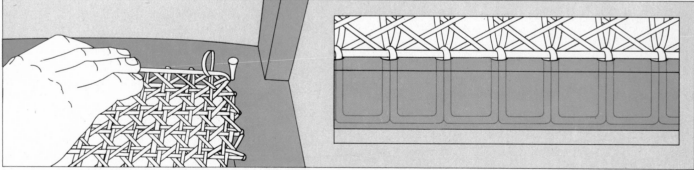

8 **Binding the edge of the seat.** For a square seat, cut a length of binder cane—cane one size larger than the weaving cane—for each rail, making it 2 inches longer than the rail length. Soak the four binder canes and four strands of weaving cane, then peg one end of the binder cane for the back rail in the hole at the right back corner, allowing about an inch of cane to hang beneath the seat. In the next hole along the back rail, thread a weaving strand from under the rail; loop it over the binder, from back to front, then push it down through the same hole, anchoring the binder against the rail. On the underside of the rail, tie off one end of the weaver

(*Step 2, page 72*) and pull the free end tight, making sure the weaver is at right angles to the binder and that the binder cane lies flat (*inset*). Loop in this manner at every hole along the back rail. Insert the binder and the weaver in the left back corner hole and peg them in place.

To start the binder cane for the left side rail, slip one end under the back rail binder, insert it in the left back corner hole, and peg it in place; then fasten the binder along the left rail as you did along the back rail. Complete the front and right rails in the same way, and insert the last end of binder cane down into the right rear corner,

where you started. To hold the binder ends in place, whittle a softwood plug to fit each corner hole, and hammer the plugs in place from the top with a rubber mallet, making sure they are flush with the chair frame. Finally, rub the binding stitches with the wooden handle of an awl to flatten them, and remove any stray hairs from the cane with tweezers or a razor blade.

On curved chair seats, use a single piece of binder cane for the entire seat perimeter. On chairs that have angular back corners and a curved front, use two pieces of binder cane—one for the back and one for the sides and front.

New Webbing for Outdoor Furniture

Aluminum lawn chairs with plastic webbing can take an occasional drenching in summer storms, but constant exposure to the elements will eventually cause their webbing to stretch, fray or tear. A half hour's labor is all you need to install new woven polypropylene straps or to rewrap a chair in tubular cushion vinyl.

As for expensive, designer-label furniture, though it is commonly sent back to the factory for rewebbing, new vinyl lace put on at home can save you as much as half the retail price of the chair.

Polypropylene webbing and tubular cushion vinyl are commonly sold in kits that contain sufficient webbing for a standard lawn chair; they are available at hardware stores. However, if you are rewebbing a number of identical chairs, it is cheaper to buy the material in bulk.

For polypropylene webbing, estimate your needs by measuring the lengthwise and crosswise dimensions of one chair, from screw hole to screw hole. Add 3 inches to each measurement; multiply each of the two totals by the number of the old straps that run in that direction. It takes 120 feet of tubular cushion vinyl to wrap an average lawn chair.

The flat vinyl lace on more expensive chairs is sold in fixed lengths—a 75-foot roll is enough for a typical chair with seat and back of open basket weave. But vinyl lace is not commonly available at retail stores and must be purchased from the manufacturer's local distributor.

Before rewebbing any chair, clean the aluminum frame. Scrub unpainted frames with soap-filled kitchen scouring pads; wash enameled frames with nonabrasive household cleaners. Then coat the frames with car wax. To reweb a vinyl-lace chair, you will also have to recruit some help: Because the lace is attached in one long strand, you will need an extra pair of hands to hold the webbing taut while you knot it. You will also need a pair of padded, spring-loaded clamps to hold the knots temporarily. To make vinyl lace more pliable for stretching, soak it in hot water for 20 minutes before you start working on the job.

Wrapping a Chair Frame with Polypropylene Straps

1 Securing strap ends. Starting with the first crosswise strap at the top of the chair back, fold in both corners at one end of the strap, to form a point at its center (*inset*). Use an awl to pierce a screw hole ½ inch from the tip of this point, going through all four thicknesses of the fold. (A punch designed for leather or paper will greatly speed this job.) Fasten the strap end to the frame with a washer-head screw in the hole nearest the top of the chair back; repeat for the other end of the strap. Fasten other crosswise straps in the same way.

To fasten the straps without using screws, eliminate the fold and substitute C-shaped clips (*inset*). Lap ¾ inch of webbing over the clip at one end of the strap, and snap the clip over the frame. Repeat at the opposite end. The clip is covered when both ends are fastened.

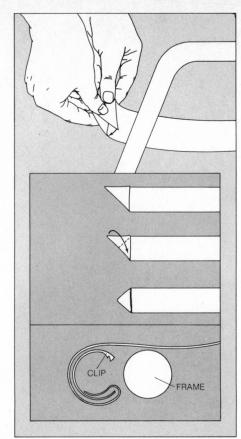

2 Weaving the straps. Passing the lengthwise straps alternately over and under the crosswise straps, stretch and fasten them between the front of the seat and the top of the back. Carry each strap behind the bar at the seat back.

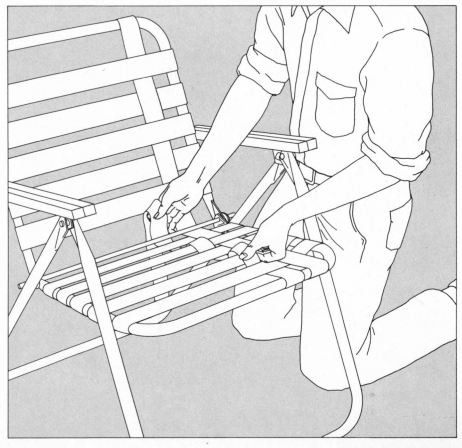

Stretching Tubular Vinyl Webbing

Wrapping the chair frame. Fold over 1 inch at the end of the roll of tubing and pierce a hole for a screw through both thicknesses of the fold. Fasten the tubing against the frame with a sheet-metal screw in the hole just below the bend at the top of the frame. Pull the tubing across the back of the frame, then stretch it across the front of the chair back. Continue wrapping down the chair back, keeping the tubing taut and making each successive turn support the bottom edge of the tubing just above it. At the bottom of the chair back, cut off the tubing, fold the end under and secure it with another screw.

Repeat this procedure for the seat of the chair, wrapping the frame from back to front. Fasten the end of the tubing at the hole on the inside bottom edge of the frame.

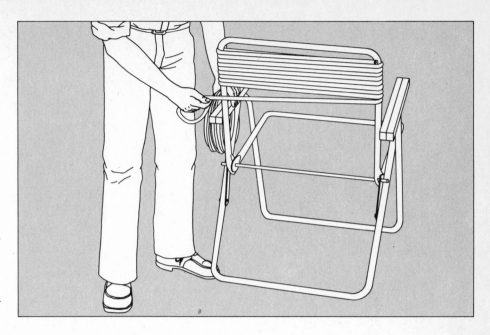

Weaving with Vinyl Lace

1 **Tying the starting knot.** Have a helper hold the roll of lace while you knot the loose end to the front seat bar, 3½ inches in from the right corner of the seat. Wrap the lace over the bar from back to front, then carry the loose end over the lace and through the loop, following the direction of the arrows as shown below. Pull the knot tight, holding the loose end against the inside edge of the bar (where it will later be held in place by another knot). Hold the knot in place temporarily with a spring-loaded clamp.

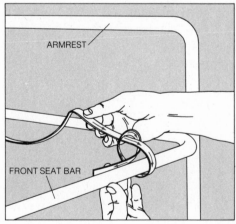

ARMREST

FRONT SEAT BAR

2 **Passing the back seat bar.** In carrying the webbing from the front seat bar to the back seat bar, pass the lace over and under the back seat bar, and back over itself, following the arrows shown below, left. Have a helper hold the roll taut as you tighten the knot; take up any slack and align the knot with the opposite knot on the front seat bar. Clamp the knot.

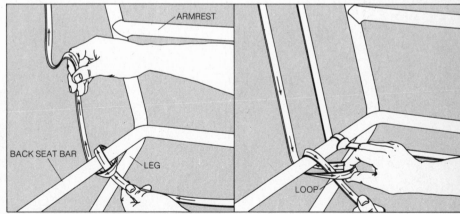

ARMREST

BACK SEAT BAR

LEG

LOOP

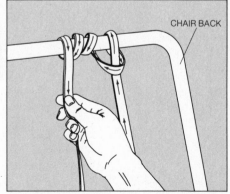

CHAIR BACK

When you are carrying the webbing in the opposite direction, from the chair top down to the back seat bar, reverse the direction of the knot that you tie against the back seat bar (*below, right*), and leave a loop about 2 feet long. While you hold the loop, have a helper pass the roll of lace under and over the bar, then down through the loop. Clamp the knot.

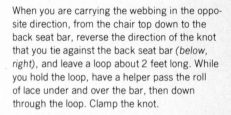

3 **Knotting the lace on the outer frame.** To knot the lace anywhere along the chair's outer frame—at the top, seat front or sides—carry the lace over the bar, across the webbing, then under and over the bar again, as shown by the arrows at left. Wrap the lace over the bar two more times to space the rows evenly. Pull out any slack as you tighten the knot.

Press the edges of the wrapped lace close together except at the corners. There, spread the wrapped lace apart and add an extra wrap, if necessary, to keep the rows of webbing even.

4 **A route for the webbing.** Using the knots described in Steps 2 and 3, follow the route plotted with arrows on the chair at right to fill in the frame with a continuous strip of lace. Space the parallel runs of lace 1½ inches apart, clamping each knot until the following knot is tied.

Tuck the loose end of the starting knot inside the first knot to its left on the front seat rail. To make right-angle turns in the lace at the two top corners on the chair back, give the lace one extra wrap around the bar, and space these wraps ⅜ inch apart. To pass the obstructing bars of the right arm and rear left leg, make one wrap fewer in the turnaround knot.

After a right-angle turn, weave the lace alternately under and over the stretched runs of lace already in place. Have a helper turn the roll parallel to the existing webbing and do the actual weaving while you keep the new run in line. For the last three crosswise runs at the back of the seat, weave and knot the lace very loosely so there is room for the roll to fit beneath the back bar; when these three runs are in place, go back and pull out all the slack before moving up to weave the back of the chair.

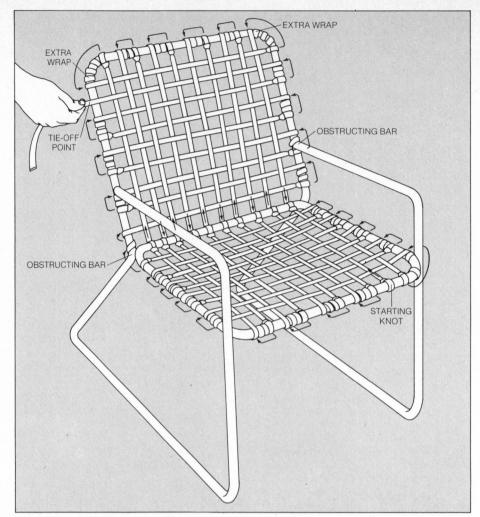

EXTRA WRAP

EXTRA WRAP

TIE-OFF POINT

OBSTRUCTING BAR

OBSTRUCTING BAR

STARTING KNOT

5 **Tying off the lace.** After weaving the final run on the back of the chair, pass the end of the lace over and under the side bar, wrap it from bottom to top over the run of lace, then draw it through the loop you have created (*near right*), passing behind the run of lace. Pull out any slack and tighten the knot, drawing the lace end downward to the rear of the chair.

Move to the rear of the chair and secure the loose end by drawing it from right to left through the loop on the back of the knot just tied (*far right*). Again pull the lace tight, and then tuck the end once more down through the loop you have created. Trim off any excess lace.

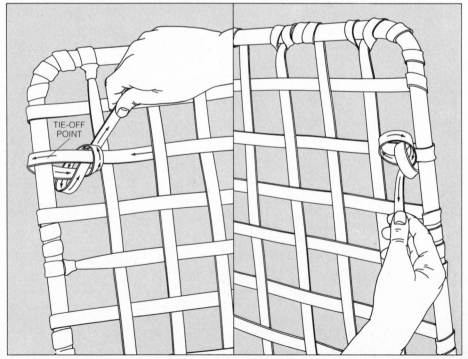

TIE-OFF POINT

Webbing a Rounded Frame

Turning right angles on a curved bar. To turn the lace from a vertical run up the back of the chair to a horizontal run across the top, tie a knot as shown at near right. Leave a sufficiently large loop in front of the last run of lace to allow the roll to be doubled back through the knot. To turn the lace from the horizontal run back to a vertical run, pass the roll through the knot shown at far right. Tie each of these knots a second time on the next two courses of the weaving pattern. Make the second knots identical to the first but, since the lace will be going in the opposite direction, reverse the path of the arrows.

Tying off around joining bars. On the last run of lace use the knot at right to tie off the lace end at the point where the armrest and back post intersect. After looping the lace around the two bars in the sequence shown, pull it snug (the knot is shown loose here for the sake of clarity). Complete the knot with a downward motion to the rear of the chair, so that the knot is hidden neatly behind the two bars.

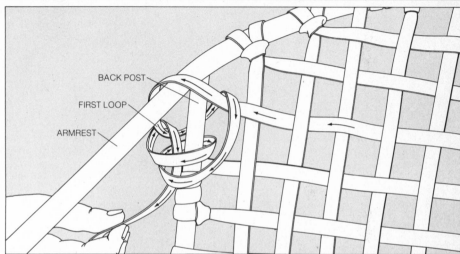

A route for a rounded-back chair. Follow the webbing route marked by the arrows to fill in the frame of this chair; space parallel runs of lace 1½ inches apart and use the knots shown on page 77, Steps 1-3. The starting knot should be 5½ inches from the right corner on the front seat bar.

Use the two knots shown at the top of this page to make the right-angle turns in the weave as you go around the curve of the top rail. At the left front corner of the seat frame, space the three wraps of the turnaround knot (*Step 3, page 77*) evenly around the leg bar. At the left back corner of the seat, skip one wrap in this same knot as the lace moves from the side bar of the seat to the side bar of the chair back. In reversing direction at the start of the last run, make a standard turnaround knot against the side bar of the chair back, but loop the final wrap of this knot over the top of the armrest. Tie off the lace at the opposite end of this run, using the knot shown tied at the back post in the center drawing above.

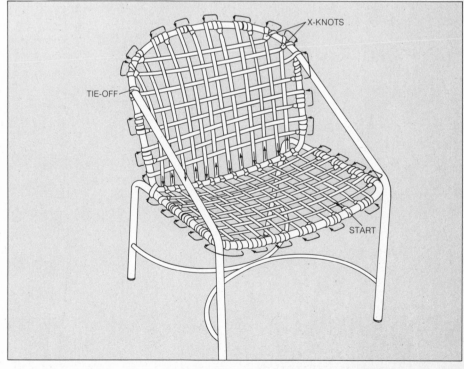

3

From Touch-ups to Refinishing

The finishing touch. A clear oil finish, brushed liberally onto the bare surface of an oak chair, sinks into the wood and highlights the beauty of the grain. In preparation for this step, the chair was treated with chemical strippers that removed old paint, layer by layer; then the wood was smoothed with increasingly finer sandpapers. An oil finish is one of the easiest to apply; it can be spread on the surface with a cloth or even a bare hand as well as with a brush.

For some 5,000 years of furniture building, wood has been the most popular material—and no wonder. It has been abundantly available and, though strong, it is flexible and light enough to be easily worked. Yet wood has disadvantages: It is susceptible to damage from insects, moisture and misuse. Because it is so vulnerable, most wood furniture has through the ages been covered with a protective coating. In earlier times, this coating was often so extravagantly ornate that it completely hid the wood. King Tut's wood throne was armored with gold, and many medieval wood pieces were encased in gesso, a plaster-like substance. Nowadays nearly all furniture that is made of fine wood is covered with clear finishes that allow the grain to shine through while protecting the wood itself.

Modern finishes guard the wood against moisture, dirt and damage such as scratches or bruises. The most familiar finishes are divided into two groups: those that soak into the wood and those that rest on it like skin. Within these groups, each finish performs certain functions better than others. So if you plan to refinish a piece of furniture, choosing a finish will depend on the use the furniture will get, your preference for looks and ease of application.

Commonest among penetrating finishes are boiled linseed oil, tung oil and rubbing oils, such as Danish oil or penetrating-resin sealer sold under various brand names. All are usually applied with a bare hand or with a rag, and they seal the pores of the wood without piling up any surface bulk; they emphasize the grain and the color of the wood rather than obscuring them. They dry quite hard and some, like tung oil, resist moisture very well, but oil finishes are so thin that they offer little protection from surface abrasion. Though they remain in the pores of the wood, in time oil finishes wear off the surface—so they require periodic reapplication.

Surface-coating finishes include shellac, lacquer and a multitude of varnishes. These are usually brushed or sprayed on, often over a sealer that prevents them from penetrating the wood; they dry into a hard film that lies on top of the wood. The surface-coating finishes form an effective barrier against dirt and damage, but their reaction to moisture varies tremendously: Polyurethane varnish is virtually impervious to water, while lacquer can cloud and soften simply from high humidity. Most surface-coating finishes obscure the natural texture of the wood slightly and impart a coated appearance.

Maintaining the beauty and protective powers of any finish can involve a wide range of procedures, from simple spot repairs to an elaborate process of stripping and refinishing. But you have the satisfaction of knowing that in renewing the finish, you are maintaining a part of the furniture that is as essential as its very structure.

Saving a Damaged Finish with Minor Repairs

The original finish on a piece of furniture can sometimes be its greatest asset. It seals the wood against loss of moisture, prevents spills and stains from penetrating the wood pores and, with age, may take on a mellow patina that enhances the furniture's value. Therefore it may be preferable to correct a flawed finish instead of stripping it.

The corrective measures to be used will depend on the type of finish and the cause of the damage, and often the two are closely related. The white haze that clouds a tabletop, for example, is likely to be the result of a chemical interaction between the shellac or lacquer finish and moisture in the environment, which softens both finishes. (The white rings that form when wet glasses sit too long on a shellac or lacquer surface are localized versions of this same phenomenon.)

Both shellac and lacquer belong to a class of finishes called solvent-release coatings. They are solutions of resin in a solvent that evaporates, leaving behind a thin resin film. Solvent-release coatings have the special property of redissolving readily when the proper solvent is brushed over them. With care, it is sometimes possible to respread such a coating to a smooth new finish in a process that is called amalgamation.

A second major class of finishes, the chemically reactive coatings, harden through a much more complex process: They absorb oxygen from the air to change from liquid to solid. Two familiar examples of these coatings are varnish and enamel, which harden into a thin film; unlike shellac and lacquer, they cannot be amalgamated. Two other reactive coatings are boiled linseed oil and tung oil, both of which sink into the pores of the wood.

Distinguishing between these finishes requires no particular expertise. Application of the proper solvent (chart, opposite) in a hidden spot will cause shellac or lacquer to dissolve and quickly redry. If the finish does not respond this way it is probably varnish, enamel or paint, which will crinkle and soften when paint remover is applied. Indeed, the finish can in some cases be identified by its response to the materials used in the preliminary cleaning process. The simplest

of these cleaners consists of mild white soap and warm water, which are used to float away surface dirt. Water should be tested first on a small area, for it may tend to cloud a shellac or lacquer finish.

Alternatively, you can clean the surface with turpentine or mineral spirits, both especially useful for deep grime or built-up layers of wax. Mineral spirits may also remedy the flawed finish. If the finish is clouded by a smoky blue haze that disappears when cleaned with mineral spirits, the problem is one of incompatibility—the furniture has been oiled or waxed over a silicone polish, which repels the other coatings. The silicone, as well as oil or wax, is dissolved by mineral spirits.

In the normal course of repair, you will need two kinds of refinishing aids—abrasives and chemicals. The abrasives commonly used are extra-fine steel wool, grades 3/0 and 4/0, and silicon-carbide paper in grit sizes of 220 to 400, very-fine to superfine. Abrasive papers should be used with a sanding block (page 89).

Two other abrasives used in refinishing are rottenstone and pumice, both of which are mixed with mineral oil into a paste. Rottenstone is a very mild abrasive made of powdered limestone; pumice, which is much stronger, is powdered volcanic glass. It should be used only in fine grade, 3/F, or very-fine grade, 4/F, and be applied with a well-padded sanding block or a blackboard eraser so it will not mar the finish. In lieu of either of these two substances, a gentle but slightly abrasive car polish also makes an excellent abrasive for furniture finishes.

Chemicals useful in repair work include solvents, dyes, stains, oils and polishes. Solvents combine with the existing finish—as denatured alcohol amalgamates shellac, and lacquer thinner amalgamates lacquer—to remove hazing and to restore a crazed or crackled finish to its original smoothness. Dyes, stains, oils and polishes can improve the entire finish or be used for more localized repairs—they disguise scratches, scuffed areas and similar blemishes.

The simplest remedies for spot repairs are ordinary furniture oils and polishes, which have a wetting effect that may be sufficient to darken minor scratches to match the surrounding finish. When

these do not work, colored furniture polish or an oil-base stain may do the job. Two of the handiest products for disguising blemishes are dye-impregnated felt-tipped pens and small vials of dye with brushes attached to their lids, both available at furniture-refinishing shops.

Sometimes makeshift home remedies work almost as well as these professional products. A nutmeat rubbed over a scratch may darken it enough to hide it, and iodine will disguise a scratch in red-stained mahogany. Shoe polish in the right color will do for a scuffed table precisely what it does for scuffed shoes. With any of these coloring agents, begin with a lighter color and move to a darker one as necessary, since a scratch dyed too dark can seldom be lightened to match its surroundings.

For deeper scratches as well as other deeper blemishes, such as burns and chips, some sort of filler is needed. Sometimes it is possible to fill in a scratch by rubbing a child's crayon over it. On painted or varnished surfaces, a slight depression can be built up with successive coats of the same finish, layered on with a fine-tipped artist's brush. But the professional way to patch burned, chipped or gouged areas is with wax sticks or shellac sticks, both available at furniture-refinishing shops.

Whether you use a wax stick or a shellac stick, patching is done in essentially the same way: The stick is held against a hot knife and the wax or shellac is guided into the depression as it melts. But of the two, shellac-stick patching is much more difficult to do, and takes practice. The shellac hardens into a patch that is practically impossible to remove, so you may have to live with a mistake, whereas a patch made with a wax stick can easily be taken out and redone.

After any of these spot repairs, the area of the repair should be buffed with a fine abrasive to blend it into the surrounding finish, and then waxed or polished. A hard paste wax, the kind used on cars, provides the best protection and needs renewing only three or four times a year. An oil-base polish such as lemon oil imparts a lovely glowing shine, but the polish is not very durable and must be renewed about once a week.

Repairs at a Glance: Local Defects

Material \ Problem	White rings or spots	Minor scratch	Deep scratch	Small burn	Small chip in finish
Furniture polish		Apply to entire furniture surface with clean cloth; rub well into scratch; buff.			
Colored furniture polish		Rub into scratch with cotton swab, and then, if desired, apply to entire surface with clean cloth.			
Furniture dye		Apply to scratch with brush or felt-tipped applicator; wipe away excess with a clean cloth.			
3/0 steel wool	Dip in mineral oil or linseed oil, rub over spot with grain in short strokes, wipe away excess with clean cloth.				
Rottenstone	Mix to creamy consistency with mineral oil, rub into spot with finger wrapped in clean cloth. Wipe off excess mixture with damp rag; dry with soft cloth.				
3/F pumice	Mix to creamy consistency with mineral oil, rub gently over spot with grain, using well-padded sanding block. Wipe off excess with damp rag; dry with soft cloth.				
Furniture-wax stick		Rub into depression to fill it, wipe away excess with a clean cloth.	Choose color that matches light grain of finish; melt wax into depression with a hot knife. Cool, scrape smooth. Paint in darker grain with artist's oil or watercolors; seal with spray varnish.	Scrape out all charred material with utility knife. Choose color that matches light grain of finish; melt wax into depression with hot knife. Cool, scrape smooth. Paint in darker grain with artist's oil or watercolors; seal with spray varnish.	
Polyurethane varnish or enamel			Using artist's brush, fill with successive coats of finish color. Build up higher than surrounding area, then smooth down with very fine abrasive paper on a sanding block.		Using artist's brush, fill with successive coats of finish color. Build up higher than surrounding area, then smooth with very fine abrasive paper on a sanding block.
Denatured alcohol (for shellac finish) / Lacquer thinner (for lacquer finish)	Wet a small, lintless pad with solvent, wring out. Stroke damaged area, remoistening pad, until spot disappears.				

Remedies for local damage. Listed across the top of this chart are local damage or spot defects that commonly afflict furniture finishes. Corrective measures for them use the materials in the far left column of the chart. The technique for using a specific material is described in the column beneath the problem. In most cases there are several alternatives, ranging here from mild at the top to more extreme at the bottom. Try the more conservative measures first; for example, to hide a minor scratch, try furniture polish before furniture dye.

Repairs at a Glance: General Damage

Material / Problem	Stubborn wax or grease, silicone haze	Scuffed, dull surface, multiple light scratches	White haze	Cracking, alligatoring
Furniture polish		Apply with a clean cloth; buff.		
Colored furniture polish		Apply with a clean cloth, working into marred surface to color it; buff.		
Turpentine or mineral spirits	Rub in with clean cloth, changing cloth as needed until all traces of coating are removed.			
Mixture of 3 parts boiled linseed oil to 1 part turpentine		Rub in along grain with lintless cloth, wipe away excess with dry cloth.		
3/0 steel wool		Dip in mineral oil or linseed oil, rub with grain over entire surface, giving special attention to scratched areas. Remove excess oil with clean cloth.	Dip in mineral oil or linseed oil, rub with grain in long strokes over entire surface. Remove excess oil with clean cloth.	
Rottenstone		Mix to creamy consistency with mineral oil. Apply with clean cloth, rubbing with grain, giving special attention to damaged areas. Wipe off excess mixture with damp rag; dry with soft cloth.	Mix to creamy consistency with mineral oil. Apply with clean cloth, rubbing with grain. Wipe off excess mixture with damp rag; dry with soft cloth.	
3/F pumice		Mix to creamy consistency with mineral oil and apply with padded sanding block. Rub along wood grain with an even touch. Wipe with damp rag; dry with soft cloth.	Mix to creamy consistency with mineral oil and apply with padded sanding block. Rub along wood grain with an even touch. Wipe off excess mixture with damp rag; dry with soft cloth.	
Denatured alcohol (for shellac finish) Lacquer thinner (for lacquer finish)		Amalgamate, using varnish brush to apply in light strokes with the grain until scratches have melted away. Work horizontally.	Amalgamate, using varnish brush to apply in light strokes with the grain until haze disappears. Work horizontally.	Amalgamate, using varnish brush to apply in light strokes with the grain until cracks are smoothed out. Work horizontally.

Restoring a generally damaged surface. Across the top of the chart above are listed problems that typically affect the entire furniture finish. The materials that can be used to correct the damage are in the column at the left. The technique for using a specific material is shown in the column beneath the problem. The solutions range from mild at the top to more extreme at the bottom. You can save time and effort by trying the more conservative solutions first. For example, to remove a white haze, try fine steel wool before switching to quicker-cutting pumice.

Patching with a Hot Wax Stick

For this repair to be almost invisible, you need a furniture-wax stick the exact color of the lightest grain in the wood, and a tube of artist's color—either oil paint or watercolor—in the same color as the darkest grain. If you cannot find a matching wax stick, you can mix your own by melting and blending shavings of several colors in a spoon or a metal jar lid, then allowing the mixture to cool and harden.

Caution: Do not melt a wax stick directly over a flame or electric burner; it is a combination of paraffin, beeswax, oil and dye, and is dangerously flammable. Instead, heat the spoon or lid, take it off the fire, then drop the shavings into it; they melt quickly and can be blended before the spoon or lid cools.

Other supplies needed for the hot-wax patch are a curved knife, a sootless heat source, a fine-tipped artist's brush, spray varnish and 4/0 steel wool. Professionals use a curved knife called a burn-in knife, but you can substitute a grapefruit knife—or any knife with a slender blade.

Making an Invisible Plug

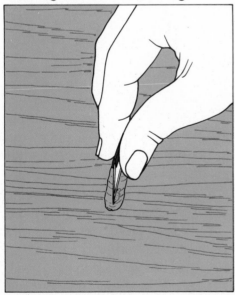

1 Preparing the surface. To repair a burned area, as shown here, first scrape away all charred material with a single-edged razor blade or a utility knife, then clean the depression with mineral spirits. To prepare gouges or deep scratches for filling, simply clean the blemish thoroughly.

2 Forming the patch. Warm the knife over an alcohol lamp or electric hot plate and, holding the end of the wax stick against the heated blade, guide the melting wax into the depression. Reheat the blade as necessary, adding wax to the patch until it is slightly higher than the surrounding surface; the wax will contract as it cools. When the patch is cool, pull a single-edged razor blade across it to level it, and give it a final smoothing with your fingertip.

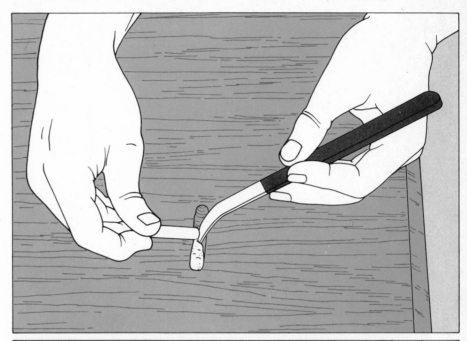

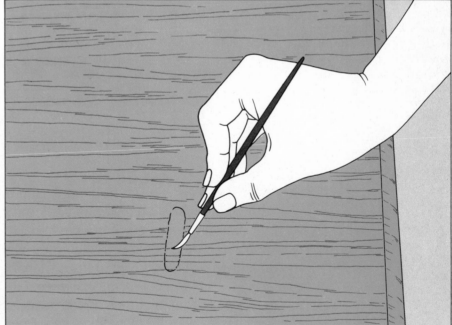

3 Painting the grain. Dip a fine-tipped artist's brush into artist's colors used undiluted, straight from the tube. Wipe the brush over paper, leaving the brush almost dry. Then paint feathery strokes over the wax patch with the nearly dry brush, blending them into the pattern of the surrounding wood grain. If the lines look too crisp, smudge the color lightly with a finger or a cloth for a more natural effect.

To fix the patch permanently, spray a light coat of clear polyurethane or acrylic varnish over the repair area and the surrounding surface.

Caution: Spray in a well-ventilated room, away from any open flame, and do not smoke. When the sprayed area is dry, buff with 4/0 steel wool to blend it with the texture of the finish. Wax or polish the entire surface.

Stripping a Finish Down to Bare Wood

Some old finishes, clear or opaque, are worth preserving; after years of polishing, they lend character to a piece of furniture. But many others—bubbled and brittle, or so thick they obscure carving or hide grain—are better removed.

There are three ways to remove a finish: dissolve it with chemicals, heat it so it bubbles away from the wood, or scrape or sand it away. Speed and potential damage to the wood are the main considerations in choosing a method.

By far the easiest—but not the best—way to strip furniture is to send it to a professional who will dunk it in a chemical dip tank. This process gets the finish off, but it can also bleach the wood and soften glue to loosen joints and veneer; it is not generally recommended for valuable pieces. However, it may be the only practical way to strip furniture that otherwise would require long hours of tedious handwork—wicker, for example.

Several heating devices are excellent for rapidly stripping away many layers of paint. One is a heat lamp with a 600-watt bulb. Another resembles a hair dryer and blows air heated to 700° onto the paint surface. A third, a heating iron with a pivoting handle, is held just above the paint to soften it. But none of these devices are effective on such solvent-release finishes as lacquer and shellac, and may scorch the wood. Propane torches, sometimes used for stripping house paint, increase the risk of scorching and should not be used on furniture.

Power sanders used with coarse sandpaper, or sanding attachments for electric drills, speed the job of clearing finished surfaces. But neither is recommended for fine furniture or veneers, and both should be used with caution, as they may gouge the surface and leave scratches that must be removed before the furniture is refinished. Hand-applied chemicals, though slower, allow more control and usually leave the surface ready for refinishing. Sometimes you will have to use more than one of these techniques.

The best all-purpose chemical strippers are solutions containing methylene chloride; other all-purpose chemicals, such as lye and oxalic acid, are more dangerous and difficult to control. Trisodium phosphate, methyl alcohol and lacquer thinner work only on specific finishes. Methylene chloride strippers come as liquids and pastes; the paste type is much easier to use because it clings to vertical surfaces and evaporates more slowly.

Some paste and liquid strippers are labeled "no wash"; others are thickened with wax, which must be removed after use with a wash of denatured alcohol. A third type calls for a water wash; but these are less satisfactory, as the water is likely to raise the grain of the wood and may separate veneer from its base, requiring sanding or regluing.

Although some makers of chemical strippers recommend removing the entire finish with one application, the best technique is to proceed layer by layer. One-step removal requires prolonged soaking with stripper, which may saturate and soften the wood so that the scraper gouges the surface easily and the stripped wood looks bleached and rough.

Because chemical strippers can irritate your lungs and skin, protect yourself by working in a well-ventilated space and wearing goggles and rubber gloves. Cover the workroom floor with newspapers and put foil piepans under furniture legs to catch drips; stripper can dissolve some types of plastic and linoleum flooring as well as rubber soles on shoes. Work carefully, and allow plenty of time for each job and the subsequent cleanup.

Both heat and mechanical removal require precautions to limit surface damage. Always turn a heat lamp or coil away from the surface as soon as the paint softens, to avoid scorching the wood surface or igniting the finish. When using a power sander, apply only light pressure, to avoid digging into the surface with the edge of the sanding pad. Wear goggles and a dust mask when using any sander.

Removing a Finish with Chemicals

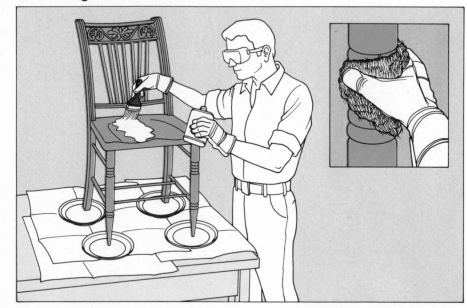

1 Applying the stripper. Beginning with a large horizontal surface, pat the stripper evenly over the surface with an old paint brush; let it work for five minutes. When the finish begins to bubble, use a wide putty knife to scrape the stripper and the dissolved finish into a can at the edge of the surface, or wipe it onto an old newspaper with the putty knife. Scrub the surface with 2/0 steel wool, working parallel to the grain, to expose the next layer of hard finish. Repeat until you reach the bare wood.

Brush on a final thin coat of stripper to soften any residue of finish in the pores of the wood. Scrape gently with the putty knife and then scrub the surface smooth with 3/0 or 4/0 steel wool, following the wood's grain.

Turn the piece so another large surface is horizontal and repeat the stripping process. Then strip smaller elements, such as chair legs and rungs, by patting on stripper and rubbing with 2/0 steel wool.

2 Stripping cracks and crevices. To remove the softened finish from cracks or crevices in a carved surface, position the furniture so the carved surface is horizontal and pat on stripper, then use a pointed dowel or an orange stick to lift out the finish. Work gently, since the wood may be softened by the stripper and easily gouged. Use 3/0 steel wool wadded into a small, tight ball to scrub gently inside the crevices.

If you are doing extensive stripping of heavily carved surfaces, you may need to have special tools. Old toothbrushes, an awl, a small soft wire brush, toothpicks, and a pen knife *(inset)* are all useful for this purpose.

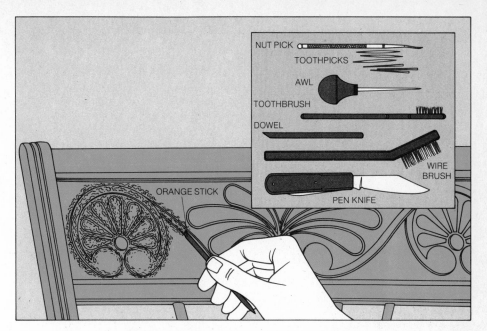

Softening Paint with Heat

Heating and scraping paint. Hold a heat gun or heating iron designed for paint removal 2 to 4 inches above the paint surface. When the paint bubbles, remove the heat source and gently scrape away the paint, using a wide-bladed putty knife. Repeat layer by layer until you reach bare wood; finally, smooth with fine steel wool.

Mechanical Paint Removal

Electric-drill stripping accessories. To remove paint from a contoured surface, you can use a flap-drum stripping attachment. Hold the core of the drum 1 inch above the surface, so that the sandpaper flaps will bite into the paint without leaving gouges. Keep the drum constantly in motion to avoid changing the contours.

To remove paint from the insides of concave curves, use a small sanding drum *(inset, right)* with replaceable belts. For gently contoured surfaces, use either a foam-padded disk with adhesive-backed paper *(inset, left)* or sandpaper backed with a rubber disk *(inset, center)*. Work with the disk held at a 30° angle to the surface, sweeping it from side to side.

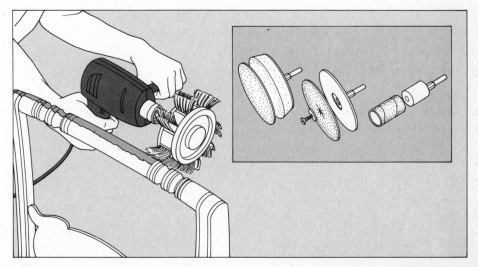

Preparing a Smooth Foundation

A good foundation is absolutely essential to any furniture finish, since the tiniest nick or scratch will be worsened by whatever is put on top of it. The key to a smooth base is a series of sanding steps, using progressively finer abrasives *(chart, bottom right)*. For the initial sanding, power sanders are useful, provided the surface is large and flat. But hand sanding is needed for the final stages, and for curved or detailed surfaces, followed at the end by a buffing with fine steel wool to remove the last hairlike roughness. (Steel wool for wood finishing ranges in grade from 2/0 to 4/0, roughly corresponding to the grades of very-fine to superfine sandpaper.)

The best power sanders for furniture work are in-line and orbital sanders, which allow precise control and reduce the possibility of gouging—a problem with belt and disk sanders. An in-line sander has a rectangular pad that vibrates in line with the grain of the wood and does very fine work, but it is slower than an orbital sander. The latter has a similar rectangular or square plate that rotates in a ⅛-inch circle, 9,000 to 12,000 times a minute, but leaves tiny circular scratches that must be removed with hand sanding. Some sanders can be operated in either an orbital or an in-line mode.

Hand sanding to remove the last scratches left by power sanding, as well as to smooth curved or detailed surfaces, uses various sanding blocks to ensure equal pressure over the surface of the wood. For flat areas, the block is usually a rubber-faced rectangle, available at most hardware stores, or a homemade wood block padded with felt. You can make blocks in different shapes for sanding convex surfaces and inside corners.

For the final smoothing, use 4/0 steel wool, and wet the wood with a damp cloth so any loose wood fibers swell and rise. Let the surface dry overnight, then whisk off the fibers with the steel wool. To find remaining rough spots, put your hand inside an old nylon stocking and run it over the surface; if there are fibers that catch, go over the area again with the same steel wool.

After the final smoothing, some open-pored woods—such as oak, walnut, mahogany and rosewood—will need to have the pores filled with a wood filler if you plan to use a glossy clear finish. Fillers usually are thick pastes, made of silica powder mixed with oil, and they come in colors to match most woods. But for an exact match, you can buy a neutral filler and add penetrating stain or oil paint to get the right color. Test the color wet; although it will lighten as the filler dries, a clear finish will darken the color again. When wood is to be stained, apply the stain *(pages 90-91)* before the filler.

To use filler, thin the paste with turpentine to the consistency of house paint, then scrub it on with an old paintbrush, pushing it into the pores. Let the filler dry until the surface is dull, then wipe it off across the grain with burlap or an old bath towel until it is no longer visible on the surface. Let the filler dry for 24 hours, then sand lightly to remove surface granules before applying a finish.

A Range of Sandpapers for Varied Uses

Descriptive term	Grade	Grit size	Use
Medium	1/0	80	Paint removal and rough shaping
Fine	2/0 3/0	100 120	Preparatory sanding, softwoods
	4/0 5/0	150 180	Preparatory sanding, hardwoods
Very fine	6/0	220	Finish sanding, softwoods
Extra fine	7/0 8/0	240 280	Finish sanding, hardwoods
Super fine	9/0 10/0	320–360 400	Polishing between finish coats; often used wet

Choosing the right sandpaper. The grade is usually printed on the back of sandpaper according to one of the three systems shown here. One uses words to designate fineness and coarseness; a second uses zeros; the third and most modern system indicates a grit number.

The best papers for woodworking are covered with minerals such as garnet, silicon carbide (also called emery) or aluminum oxide. These papers retain their abrasive qualities much longer than ordinary flint-covered sandpaper.

There are two types of abrasive coating: closed, with a dense covering of grit; and open, with more widely spaced grit. Closed-coat papers cut faster but clog quickly on softwoods or old finishes; they are best for the final sanding stages. Open-coat papers clog less easily and are best for rough sanding and power sanders.

Padded Blocks for Sanding

Making a felt-faced block. Cut a 4½-inch block of 2-by-4 and a 5-inch square of 1/16-inch-thick felt, obtainable at a variety store or craft shop. Spread rubber cement on one face of the block; then tack an edge of the felt to one side of the block, stretch it across the cemented face, and tack it to the other side. When the cement is dry (about five minutes), use a utility knife to trim overlapping felt. To use the block, cut standard 9-by-10-inch sheets of sandpaper into quarters and hold the sandpaper over the felt with your fingers as you sand.

Make sanding blocks for curves and grooves by cementing felt to dowels or triangular blocks of wood *(inset);* hold the felt in place until the cement sets. Do not use tacks; they might scratch the surface that is being sanded. Wrap these blocks with small pieces of sandpaper, also held in place with your fingers.

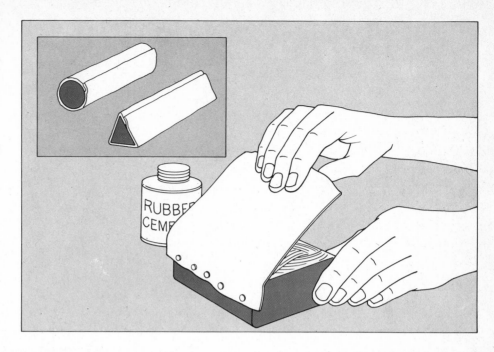

A Sequence of Sanding for Exceptional Smoothness

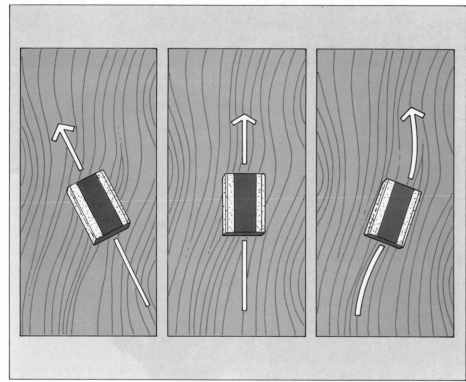

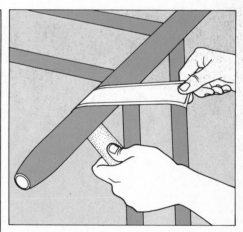

Sanding round parts. To sand parts such as chair legs or spindles, place a length of 1-inch cloth tape against the back of a 1½-inch-wide strip of sandpaper, to reinforce it. Holding the sanding strip at each end, draw it back and forth around the part as you do when shining a shoe. Begin with 100-grit paper and progress to 220-grit paper. Finally, sand along the length of the leg or spindle with 280-grit paper or 4/0 steel wool until surface scratches are smoothed away and raised fibers are removed.

Smoothing flat surfaces. To remove ridges, superficial stains, or damage resulting from stripping, make sanding strokes at a slight angle to the wood grain *(left).* Start with 180-grit paper; if the sanding progresses too slowly, switch to 100-grit paper until most of the roughness is reduced, then switch back to 180-grit and continue sanding until the only remaining roughness is from the diagonal sanding scratches.

Remove the diagonal scratches by sanding with strokes parallel to the grain *(center).* Use 220-grit paper, and sand until the diagonal scratches are entirely removed.

Finally, sand the surface with short back-and-forth strokes following the grain *(right).* Use 240- to 280-grit paper, and sand until the wood is smooth enough to reflect oblique lights.

Changing the Color of Wood

For most of the thousands of years that furniture makers have worked with wood, they have used only the innate colors of the materials, sometimes altered slightly with vegetable dyes or the coloring properties of the oil, varnish or shellac finish. But developments in organic chemistry since the mid-19th Century have made it possible to achieve a vast array of wood shades and tones easily and safely. Concentrated bleaches can freshen stripped or raw wood darkened by age or even eliminate the natural color entirely. Stains and dyes can make one wood resemble another or can call attention to the pattern of the grain by tinting it with a purely decorative color.

Bleached wood—with the natural color chemically removed from its fibers—became popular in the 1930s when blond furniture was in fashion. In the simplest method, ordinary chlorine laundry bleach is used; diluted with water, this will lighten wood, accentuating the pattern of its grain. Oxalic acid, dissolved in hot water, can be used similarly; it is somewhat stronger than chlorine bleach. (Used at full strength, chlorine bleach will also remove dye, ink or water stains from wood. Oxalic acid is especially effective for removing water stains from oak.)

Either of these bleaches should be applied with a synthetic-bristled brush or a plastic-mesh scrubber (natural fibers deteriorate in bleach) and allowed to stand for 15 minutes. Repeat the process until the wood is sufficiently lightened. Then neutralize the bleach to prevent it from attacking whatever finish you apply later. For chlorine bleach use white vinegar at full strength or a soap-and-water wash; for oxalic acid use vinegar or a wash made of one part ammonia in 10 parts water. Allow the bleached wood to dry thoroughly, then sand off the fibers that have risen on the surface *(page 88)*.

The strongest bleaches are sold as a two-part package, a combination of hydrogen peroxide and lye. With enough applications, these products can totally eliminate the natural color of the wood, turning a dark wood white. Because they are so powerful, they must be used with great care, following the manufacturer's instructions. All bleaches are caustic. Wear rubber gloves, and use a dust mask when sanding, since the sanding dust will be impregnated with irritating chemicals from the bleach and neutralizer.

Stains are used to change the color of natural wood or to recolor bleached wood. There are two chief types. The penetrating stains are made of aniline dye dissolved in water, alcohol or oil; they soak into the wood and color the wood fibers. The other stains, made of pigments suspended in oil or in a finish such as varnish, cover the wood with a colored film and fill the wood pores; a stain in which the pigments are suspended in oil is called a wiping stain. Because they are absorbed differently by the hard and soft parts of the wood, penetrating stains accentuate the grain, while pigment stains are often used to obscure the grain and disguise cheaper woods.

Stains are available in a wide range of standard colors, and to create other colors you can mix stains that have the same solvent base. You can also make your own stains: Artist's oil paints and pigments mixed with linseed oil and turpentine make good oil-base wiping stains, and cold-water-based fabric dyes can be used as penetrating stains, providing a variety of colors from natural wood tones to vivid, if unconventional, rainbow hues. For both of these homemade stains, the proportion of pigment to water or oil depends on the depth of color desired. Always test the mixture on a hidden or inconspicuous area before you use it, and keep a record of proportions so you can duplicate the stain later if you need to.

Before applying stains, carefully clean and sand the surface, whether unfinished or stripped. Residual wax or rough spots will absorb stain unevenly, making light and dark patches. Begin working on the least conspicuous part of the piece to determine how the wood takes the stain. When applying a penetrating stain, avoid runs, drips and overlaps, which can result in dark spots. For maximum control, thin the stain by adding solvent and apply two or more coats until the desired depth of tone is achieved. If a coat is darker than you would like it to be, you can lighten it by wiping the surface with a solvent-soaked cloth. To avoid staining your hands as well as the wood, be sure to wear rubber gloves.

Applying the Two Types of Wood Stain

Wiping on the stain. Using a sponge or a folded square of cheesecloth as an applicator, wipe on penetrating or wiping stain in broad strokes with the grain, pressing lightly to force the stain into the pores of the wood. Do a small area at a time, working with the surface horizontal whenever possible. On vertical surfaces, work from the bottom, stroking upward, to prevent runs that may penetrate unevenly. Keep a clean cloth handy to wipe off excess stain or to rub the surface with solvent if an area is too dark. Wipe the high spots on carved areas to lighten them, which will emphasize their contours and give them an aged appearance.

When using a penetrating stain, allow each coat to soak into the wood before applying the next. With a wiping stain, wait until the surface is dull (indicating the solvent has evaporated), then wipe away excess pigment with a dry cloth. Usually, wiping stains are applied in one coat.

How to Get Precisely the Color You Want

Standard Color / Color Sought	Antique Pine*	Brown Mahogany	Red Mahogany	Cherry	Honey Maple*	Antique Maple*	Fruitwood	Dark Oak	Swedish Walnut**
Mahogany	1 part	1 part	1 part	1 part					
Light Oak		1 part		1 part	3 parts	1 part	4 parts	1 part	2 parts
Walnut	4 parts	5 parts	1 part	1 part	1 part	1 part	1 part	1 part	4 parts
Maple					2 parts	2 parts	1 part		

*Thin with enough solvent to lighten the tint. **Add a drop of lampblack.

Mixing stains. To obtain wiping stains in the custom colors listed on the top row of the chart, mix the standard stains listed at the left, using the proportions indicated. For more color variations, add artists' pigments or oil paints in such colors as raw sienna, burnt sienna, raw umber and yellow ochre. Black or white pigments shade the stain or make it paler; additional solvent lightens it. Penetrating stains can be custom-mixed in different colors as long as they have the same solvent base, but proportions vary according to the type of solvent used and the kind of wood being stained. Test any penetrating-stain mixture carefully before using it; wait until the sample is dry to judge the result.

Selecting the Stain Best Suited to the Wood

Stain Type	Solvent	Use	Advantages	Disadvantages	Application
Penetrating	Water	All woods; in warm reddish tones is especially good for mahogany, walnut, cherry	Inexpensive and easy to mix; easy to handle; broad range of colors; will not fade or bleed	Raises wood grain; needs 24-hour drying time; not ready-mixed; not widely available	Dampen the surface with clean water first. Apply with brush or sponge; wipe off excess. Sand when dry
	Alcohol	All woods, but best on close-grained woods such as maple, beech, birch. In greenish tints especially suitable for oak	Does not raise grain; extremely fast-drying (10 to 15 minutes); available ready-mixed	Fades in direct sunlight; application with spray gun takes practice and experience	Spray over small areas so that overlapping areas are wet
	Oil	Coarse-grained woods: mahogany, oak, rosewood, walnut	Does not raise grain; easy to use; rich tones; long-lasting	Saturates soft woods quickly, producing zebra effect. Hard to remove. Will bleed through varnish unless coated with a sealer	Brush or wipe evenly with no overlaps. Wipe off before it sets, let dry for 24 hours
Nonpenetrating	Oil	Close-grained woods such as birch, cherry, maple	Disguises cheaper woods and makes different woods look the same. Lightens coarse-grained woods and tones down grain with uneven color distribution	Darkens soft, porous woods; does not take well on hardwoods; accentuates dents and scratches	Stir well before and during use. Premix if using more than one can to get even color. Wipe on, wait until surface dulls, wipe off
	Varnish Shellac Lacquer	Cheap woods	Fills, colors and adds gloss in one step. Dries in 3 to 12 hours	Almost completely obscures grain; not a high-quality finish	Apply like varnish

An assortment of stains. Wood stains are classified according to the coloring medium they contain: dye in penetrating stains, pigment in nonpenetrating stains. Dye, which is dissolved in water, alcohol or oil, saturates the pores of the wood; pigment, mixed with oil or clear finish, just rests on the wood's surface. Some of the commercial stains are a mixture of both and in addition may contain a sealer that prevents the stain from bleeding into any subsequent finish. Stains vary in their usefulness, as the chart above indicates, and some of them are easier to work with than others. For the amateur, oil-base stains usually are the easiest to work with and give the most uniform results.

The Pros and Cons of Five Clear Finishes

If furniture is made of fine, beautifully grained wood, the most desirable finish is generally a transparent one. The clear versions of five finishes *(box, opposite)*— shellac, varnish, oil, wax and lacquer—are commonly used, either alone or in combination. Shellac, for example, can be used as a base coat for varnish or as a complete finish by itself. On some fine antiques the finish consists of six or more thin coats of shellac, each rubbed down before the next coat was applied.

The relative merits of the five finishes are partly a matter of esthetics. Shellac and varnish highlight the grain of the wood, for example; an oil finish mellows its appearance. But practical considerations—such as the need to protect the wood against wear and spills, and the relative ease of application of various finishes—also enter into the choice. Shellac, for example, is vulnerable to moisture damage, and varnish is not. On the other hand, varnish is more difficult to apply; it tends to bubble if it is not brushed on carefully with a special brushing technique *(page 94, Step 1)*.

Similarly, though oil finishes are the simplest of all to apply—you can stroke them on with the palm of your hand if you like—they take as long as two weeks to dry thoroughly. Lacquer dries in minutes—so fast that it is difficult to apply with a brush without leaving telltale stroke marks. Lacquer is best applied by spraying, but the spray is so volatile that you must take elaborate precautions against fire or explosion.

There also are choices to be made within each category of finish: tung oil versus linseed oil, white shellac versus orange shellac. Most dizzying of all are the choices among varnishes. These are formulated for floor, outdoor, marine and furniture use, and are labeled as such on the cans. Furniture varnishes normally are less glossy than those made for other uses. They are, nonetheless, available in a range of glossiness from dull to mildly glossy. Furniture varnishes are also somewhat less durable than varnish products made for other uses.

If you want a particularly tough finish, use a high-gloss floor or outdoor varnish, and tone down the shine by buffing. Some special-purpose outdoor varnishes, however, do not produce the hard surface desirable on indoor furniture.

With any of these finishes, work where there is no dust, little humidity, even light and good ventilation. If you cover the work surface with newspapers to catch drips, as most people do, dispose of the papers as soon as the job is done, for all these finishes are flammable and their solvents are dangerously so. Be equally careful with oil-soaked rags.

If you plan to do extensive work with spray lacquers, you will have to construct a refinishing booth. An effective spray booth partitions off a corner of the workshop, isolating the potentially explosive spray from any spark or flame. It may be built of either sheet metal or fire-resistant wallboard. All motors and electrical switches are located outside the booth. In addition, one end of the booth must be equipped with a special kind of exhaust fan, one that traps the drifting lacquer spray with filters and expels the lacquer fumes outside the house. The other end of the booth must be open to allow the free flow of air.

To apply shellac or varnish, you will need a good brush, such as a varnish brush, with tapered bristles. Pour the finish a little at a time into a clean metal container, such as a coffee can, and reclose the original container. To thin varnish (and to clean brushes), use turpentine or mineral spirits; avoid thinning and stirring varnish if you can, since stirring introduces bubbles that will mar the finish. To thin shellac, use denatured alcohol. To make a linseed-oil finish, you will need to add turpentine.

For the important task of removing sanding dust between coats of finish, one of the most useful pieces of equipment is a tack rag. It can be bought at a hardware store, but you can easily make your own from a 24-inch square of cheesecloth. Dampen the square with water and wring it out well. Then sprinkle the cloth with a few teaspoons of turpentine, and again squeeze out the excess moisture. Sprinkle the cloth, a final time, with a small amount of varnish. Fold the four edges to the center, and wring the cloth tightly to remove any remaining water; the tack rag should be just damp enough to pick up dust without leaving a mark. When not in use, the tack rag should be stored in an airtight screw-top jar.

A Guide to Finishes That Let the Grain Shine Through

The five types of clear finishes described below encompass hundreds of commercial products, which vary in their suitability for particular needs. Varnish and oil finishes are the most versatile—they include products formulated for both indoor and outdoor use. Shellac, lacquer and wax finishes are intended only for indoor furniture. But the five also differ in durability, ease of application and the qualities they bring to the natural beauty of wood grain.

Lacquer

Modern lacquer finishes are synthetic compounds made from a cellulose derivative (usually nitrocellulose), a solvent and a plasticizing ingredient (to prevent brittleness). Lacquer hardens on a surface when its solvent content evaporates—a process that happens in a very few minutes. This short drying time has made lacquer the finish of choice in production-line furniture factories.

Lacquers for brushing are available but, because of their rapid drying time, they have a tendency to retain the shape of the brush that is used for applying them. Consequently, lacquer is usually applied as a spray.

For small jobs, lacquer is available in aerosol cans. More extensive work may require a compressed-air gun. When lacquer is to be used with a gun, it must be thinned to spraying consistency with the solvent recommended by the manufacturer. The usual proportions of lacquer to thinner are 2 to 1, but it is best to start out with a slightly thicker mixture and test it on a piece of scrap wood. If lacquer is too thin, it will run; if it is too thick, it produces a bumpy texture that professionals refer to as orange peel.

Sprayed lacquer dries mirror smooth, but you can tone down the surface shine to a gloss or sheen, if you wish, by rubbing it with very fine steel wool. Several coats of sprayed lacquer can be built up within a few hours. A lacquer finish has fair resistance to wear but little resistance to moisture.

Oil

Oil finishes are the easiest of all to apply and are prized for their soft sheen and subtle beauty. Tung oil and linseed oil, both derived from crushed seeds, are the most commonly used in furniture finishing. They penetrate the pores of the wood, and with repeated applications they gradually form a clear, hard film on the wood by reacting with the oxygen that is in the air.

Linseed oil can be used undiluted, but more often it is combined with an equal portion of turpentine. Only boiled linseed oil is suitable for finishing wood; raw linseed oil does not dry.

A linseed-oil finish can easily be touched up or recoated, but it is not particularly durable and has virtually no resistance to moisture. Tung oil has greater durability and offers good resistance to moisture. In addition to being a finish in itself, tung oil is also used as an ingredient in some specialized finishing mixtures based on varnish.

Shellac

Shellac, made from secretions of a tropical insect, is sold ready to use or as flakes or buttons that must be dissolved in denatured alcohol. White shellac is clear and colorless; orange shellac imparts a slight tint to wood, but is somewhat more resistant to moisture and keeps longer in the can. All shellac solutions, however, have a limited shelf life—after approximately six months they lose their ability to harden.

Shellac is easily applied with a brush and leaves no marks. It can be built up in successive coats that bond strongly to each other, forming a good base coat for finishes such as varnish, which are more difficult to apply. But between coats and before varnishing, shellac should be roughened by sanding.

A shellac finish can be rubbed with fine steel wool or polished to modify its gloss or sheen. Though shellac will protect wood from moisture, it discolors in contact with dampness and dissolves in contact with alcohol.

Varnish

The term "varnish" encompasses a diverse group of clear, tough, extremely durable finishes for wood, most of which are based on synthetic materials. The types best suited to use on furniture are alkyd-resin, phenolic-resin and polyurethane varnishes. In a heavily diluted form, varnish is also an ingredient in furniture finishes that are labeled "rubbing oil" or "antiquing oil."

Both alkyd- and phenolic-resin varnishes give a warm, glowing tone to wood and are sufficiently durable for most furniture needs, though less rugged than polyurethane varnish. Alkyd-resin varnish is the type most easily recoated to build up a deep-looking finish; phenolic-resin varnish, commonly labeled "spar varnish" or "marine varnish," has a tendency to darken or yellow. It is especially formulated for outdoor use and, even when dry, remains slightly soft to accommodate the shrinking and swelling of the wood beneath it. This softness makes it less suitable for interior use.

Polyurethane varnish is prized particularly for its extreme durability and moisture resistance. It produces an extremely glossy finish and is somewhat difficult to recoat. Many polyurethane varnishes are modified with oils or alkyd resins to make them easier to use.

Wax

Simple paste wax is used as a polish over other clear finishes; the wax serves as a buffer against grime and wear. Since wax will yellow if allowed to get old, it must be removed once or twice a year and renewed.

Either paste wax or beeswax, melted and then thinned with turpentine, can be used alone as a finish on hardwoods such as maple or oak. If wax is applied to raw, unfinished softwoods, however, it precludes later refinishing because it cannot be removed from the pores. But even a softwood can be given a clear wax finish if the wood is stripped of an old finish that sealed the grain.

Building Up a Varnish or Shellac Surface

1 **Brushing on successive coats.** Starting from the center of a surface and working outward, brush on a thin, even coat of the finish, lifting the brush slightly at the edge of the wood to avoid run-overs on the adjacent surface. Whenever possible, work horizontally, especially when doing large surfaces. When working on surfaces that rest on the floor or workbench, prop up the piece to keep the finish from puddling around it at the bottom. Props strong enough to support a chair can be improvised from scraps of wood held together with glue and nails.

When working with varnish, which is trickier to apply than shellac, load the brush quite heavily; dip it to half the length of the bristles and apply each brushload in a single smooth stroke. Spread the varnish across the grain in a limited area first, then go back over the area, this time stroking with the grain. Finally, smooth the finish by running the tip of an almost dry brush lightly over the entire area, with the grain; during this operation hold the brush almost vertical.

To avoid contaminating your finish supply with particles of dust or dirt, pour a working batch into a clean coffee can. Twist a section of heavy wire through holes that you have drilled or punched near the top of the can, and strike the brush gently on this wire to control the load.

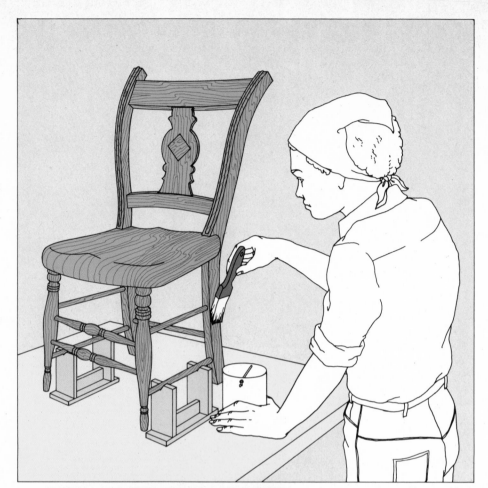

2 **Sanding between coats.** After each coat of finish dries, rub the surface lightly with 3/0 steel wool or 320-grit sandpaper (*page 88*). Sand lightly and evenly, always with the grain; take special care at the edges, where abrasives tend to cut through the finish entirely.

When the surface is smooth and free of imperfections, remove sanding dust with a tack rag. Then apply the next finish coat. Give each coat adequate drying time. To test for dryness, press your thumb against the surface, then wipe the area with a soft cloth; if the thumbprint remains, more drying time is needed. For a very deep finish, you may want to apply as many as six coats. When the last coat has dried, polish the finish to a soft sheen with 4/0 steel wool or, for a glossier look, with 6/0 steel wool.

3 **Waxing for protection.** Cover the final coat of shellac or varnish with paste wax, and buff by hand or with an electric drill fitted with a padded buffing wheel. Apply the wax with a soft damp cloth and allow the wax to stand 30 minutes before buffing. Use two coats.

Finishing Furniture with Tung or Linseed Oil

Applying oil finishes. Pour undiluted tung oil, or boiled linseed oil mixed in equal portions with turpentine, onto the furniture and rub it over the surface with a soft cloth or the palm of your hand. Allow tung oil to stand for a few minutes, then wipe away any excess that beads on the surface, and let the wood dry overnight. Apply as many additional coats as desired, depending on the depth and tone you want the finish to have. To add sheen to the final coat, rub the surface with 4/0 steel wool.

When finishing with linseed oil, continue to apply oil until the surface is saturated and will not absorb any more. Then wipe away the excess and allow the wood to dry for two weeks. Finally, buff the surface with a dry cloth.

Sanding a Paneled Surface

STILE   MOLDINGS

RAIL

PANEL

Sanding complex panels. When you sand furniture panels in which the wood grain runs in different directions, hold a cardboard shield at the point where opposite grain patterns meet, to prevent the sandpaper or steel wool from cutting across the grain of the adjacent panel. If the paneling is contoured, sand the moldings first, then sand the inset panels, and finally go on to do the rails and stiles of the frame.

4 Reupholstering for a New Look

The inner support structure of a seat. Pulled taut with a sharp-toothed stretcher and tacked to the underside of the wood frame, interwoven jute webbing supports the coiled seat springs above. Twine anchors the spring tops to one another and depresses all the coils slightly to give the seat both firmness and bounce.

Few improvements change the countenance of a room more quickly or yield bigger dividends in comfort than newly upholstered furniture. If you do the work yourself, refurbishing old furniture will also introduce you to the fascinating techniques of a centuries-old craft.

The first upholsterers were tentmakers, purveyors of shelter to nomadic peoples of the Middle East and, as such, elite among craftsmen. Famous among them were the Persian poet Omar Khayyam and the disciple Saint Paul. Although the tentmaking tradition continued through the Middle Ages—the coat of arms granted to London's Worshipful Company of Upholders in 1465 bore a picture of three tents—the focus of the craft shifted from shelter to seating as men found more time for sitting still and wanted softer furniture.

The upholders softened their first seats with leather, but by the middle of the 16th Century various hair and fiber stuffings had been introduced; upholstered side chairs, structured much in the same way as they are today, soon became standard household accouterments. The focus of the upholders then shifted again, this time to the task of embellishing the common side chair with an abundance of jeweled, fringed finery.

Upholsterers of the 16th Century received such instructions as these, which came from an inhabitant of Kenilworth Castle in England: "A chaier of wallnuttree...the seate all lozenged with silver twiste, trimed with fringe of crimson silck and silver; the back of the chaier lyned with crimson sattin." In 1581 Queen Elizabeth I, not to be outdone by lesser nobles, ordered more than 65 pounds of gold and silver fringes to decorate an assortment of 60 chairs and stools; the price of the precious metals alone accounted for more than one third the total cost of the job.

The following centuries saw such decorative furniture covering carried to extremes and, some felt, to the point of bad taste. The leg of a Victorian chair, much like the ankle of a Victorian lady, was considered indecent if allowed to be uncovered, so pieces of this period were draped from top to bottom in heavy silks, satins, velvets and damasks. Victorian furniture, in the words of one critic, "shrieks its own agony to all observers."

Today, styles in upholstery range from sumptuous to stark. But the craft has changed very little because no way has been found to make a more satisfactory seat than the one the first upholders perfected. Seat springs were introduced around the middle of the 19th Century, and more recent innovations have taken the form of synthetic stuffings, paddings and fabrics, but the basic tools and procedures illustrated on the following pages are those that fine craftsmen have used to upholster and reupholster furniture for thousands of years.

The Basic Upholstery Tools and Supplies

In addition to patience and methodical labor, reupholstering requires a few unique tools and some special supplies. The tools are specifically designed for ripping away old fabric and attaching new. Both tools and supplies are available from hardware stores, upholstery-supply outlets and mail-order houses.

You will also need a sewing machine equipped with a zipper foot. If you do not own a machine, or if you are working with fabric that is too heavy for home models, you may be able to get a professional upholsterer to sew your cut fabric for you. Similarly, farming out button-making chores will save you the need for a button press, and ready-made welt will save time if you can find a color suitable for your fabric.

Some tools and materials long used by professionals have begun to give way to innovations. The traditional snout-nosed, magnetized upholsterer's hammer, for example, has been replaced in many commercial shops by the pneumatic staple gun, which is powerful enough to drive a long staple through heavy materials into a wood frame.

Electric versions of this tool are relatively inexpensive and work well on softwood frames. They are very fast and may seem a boon to the novice. But because of the guns' speed, mistakes are easier to make, and the staples they implant are difficult to remove without ripping the fabric. For the beginner, the upholsterer's hammer and tacks may be a better choice. In any case, tacks and hammer will be needed to pin the fabric to the frame before stapling.

Modern stuffing materials have also largely replaced the traditional horsehair, hog hair, dried moss and tow. Most new chairs and sofas owe their smooth contours to layers of cotton or polyester batting, foam rubber, polyurethane foam or rubberized hair. Sometimes, however, it is better to preserve the original horsehair or hog-hair stuffing of an old piece, for authenticity and because the stuffing is already shaped to the furniture contours.

Besides the tools shown here and the supplies listed in the chart, you will need other items, such as a knife, a mallet and white glue. Tailor's chalk is best for marking fabric cuts. Sturdy scissors—ideally, 10-inch shears with handles set at an angle to the blades—are used to cut fabric. And if you are rounding cushions by adding an extra layer of polyester batting, you will need spray adhesive for fastening the batting to the foam-rubber or polyurethane-foam stuffing.

Professional upholsterers usually wear a multipocketed carpenter's apron so that supplies are always close at hand. They also use padded sawhorses to raise pieces to a convenient height while they are being reupholstered.

Tools for Special Tasks

Tools for stripping fabric. A claw chisel, also called a tack lifter, has a V-shaped notch at its tip and is curved to give leverage for prying out tacks. The slotted tip of a staple remover is designed to reach under staples and lift them out. For very stubborn tacks and staples, the ripping chisel is held against the fastener and struck with a mallet to jar the fastener free.

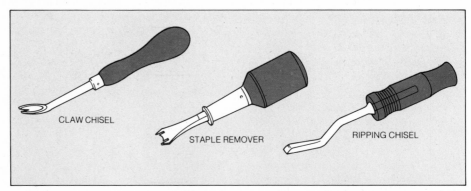

CLAW CHISEL

STAPLE REMOVER

RIPPING CHISEL

Tools for attaching fabric. In addition to an upholsterer's tack hammer, which has one magnetized end for picking up tacks, you will need upholstery pins and needles and a webbing stretcher. The stretcher's sharp spikes and corrugated rubber tread grip jute or linen webbing to pull it tight. Upholstery pins, sturdy enough to hold heavy materials, have pierced heads for easy removal. A 10-inch straight upholstery needle, pointed at both ends, goes through padding to attach buttons, gather tufting and anchor springs; a 3- or 4-inch curved upholstery needle is used for blindstitching from one side of the fabric and also for anchoring springs and stuffing. For large projects, requiring much tacking, an electric staple gun is useful though not essential.

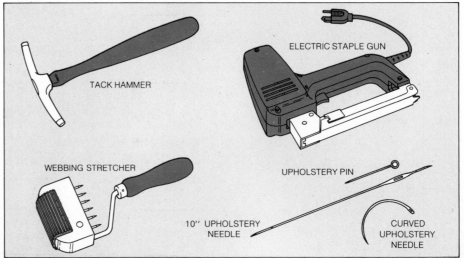

TACK HAMMER

ELECTRIC STAPLE GUN

WEBBING STRETCHER

UPHOLSTERY PIN

10" UPHOLSTERY NEEDLE

CURVED UPHOLSTERY NEEDLE

Hardware to Hold Coverings

Tacks and ornamental nails. Three useful tack sizes are No. 3, for one or two fabric layers; No. 6, for more than two layers; and No. 14, for burlap and webbing. The small, rounded gimp tack secures the decorative braid called gimp. Ornamental nails, available with brass, silver, colored and hammered heads, are used where the heads are to be exposed. Cardboard tack tape, either with or without embedded tacks, or metal tack strips are used where they can be concealed inside a fabric fold.

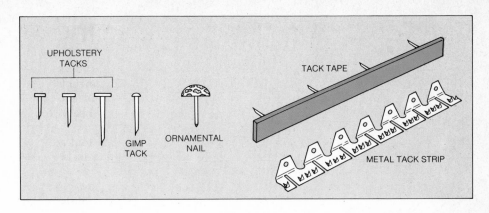

Supplies You Need and How to Use Them

Determining necessary supplies. This chart lists supplies needed to reupholster a chair or couch. The second column explains the use of each. Where a type, size or material is best suited for the task, it is listed in the third column.

Material	Use	Type recommended
Burlap	Separates springs from stuffing; covers webbing when no springs are used	10- to 12-ounce weight
Cambric	Covers the underside of a couch or chair, shielding it from dust	Glazed, black, tightly woven
Decking	Covers the chair seat under loose cushions	Denim, cotton duck or flannel
Edge roll	Prefabricated padding for front edge of chair seat	Burlap-covered, 1½ inches in diameter
Ornamental gimp and double welt	Covers tacks holding fabric to edge of frame	Available in many styles and colors to suit upholstery fabric
Padding	Covers wood-frame surfaces to cushion their edges; covers stuffing to shape it	One-inch-thick sheets of long-staple cotton, Dacron-polyester batting or sheets of high-density polyurethane foam
Stuffing	Covers springs and seat backs; fills cushions	Polyurethane foam or foam rubber in either bulk form or rolls; rubberized hair in rolls; occasionally, down for cushions
Spring twine	Ties down coil springs	Nylon or six-ply hemp
Stitching twine	Joins sections of cover fabric together, secures stuffing to springs and is used for miscellaneous hand sewing	Flax or linen
Webbing	Tacked across bottom frame to serve as a foundation for springs or padding	Generally tightly woven 3¼- to 4-inch-wide bands of jute or linen; a red stripe near the edge identifies the best quality. Occasionally rubber or steel webbing is used
Welt	Ready-made fabric-covered cord sewn into seams	Available in many colors and several sizes to suit upholstery fabrics
Welt cord	Soft cotton cord that is covered with fabric to make welt	For most purposes, ¼ or $^5/_{32}$ inches in diameter

Removing the Old Fabric and Readying the New

As mystifying as the whole process of reupholstering may seem, it really is nothing more than a methodical layer-by-layer unraveling of the planning and plotting that went into the piece originally. The top layer is the cover, which must be disassembled carefully and with a sharp eye for detail since the old cover may well be used as a cutting pattern for the new. Even more important, it provides valuable information on how the new cover should be assembled.

Rarely are two upholstery covers constructed in exactly the same way. One may have a number of machine-stitched seams; another may consist almost entirely of fabric fitted directly onto the frame, then tacked or stapled in place. As you remove the cover, note on paper which sections are tacked and to what, as well as which sections are sewed together and where. Pay particular attention to the location of welt (the decorative trim that outlines some seams), noting where it stops and starts. To record intricate details, professionals often draw sketches and take step-by-step snapshots.

Before beginning the actual stripping, take basic measurements to estimate the amount of upholstery fabric you will need. Working in an orderly fashion from the outside to the inside, measure the longest and the widest parts of the arm and back sections, as well as the overall dimensions of such elements as wing sections, seat front and arm fronts. On the insides of the arms and back, include the several extra inches of fabric that are tucked inside the seat.

When all these basic measurements are taken, make diagrams on graph paper, running vertical measurements vertically and keeping in mind that most upholstery fabrics are 54 inches wide. Add up the vertical inches on the diagrams and divide the total by 36 to translate the figure into yards.

To this basic yardage you will need to add extra fabric for welt, if you are making your own; usually a yard is enough, since one yard of 54-inch fabric will yield 18 yards of the 1½-inch bias strips that are needed for welt. You will also need additional yardage in order to match stripes or patterns, to center dominant design elements or to position napped fabrics.

One yard of extra fabric for every 5 yards of basic yardage is usually sufficient for these purposes.

Napped fabrics, such as corduroy or velvet, are always cut with the nap running in one direction—down toward the floor on the sides and back, to the front on the top of the seat cushion. To check the direction of the nap, run your hand over the fabric: The nap is down when the fabric feels smooth.

For the stripping process, you will need a hammer and a claw chisel or a staple remover to loosen tacked or stapled fabric from the frame, and a utility knife or single-edged razor blade to open seams. As you strip the fabric away, keep in mind your objectives: If you intend to use the old cover as a pattern when you cut the new, you will need to be more careful than if you plan to start with new measurements *(page 105)*.

In either event, label each piece as it is lifted from the chair or sofa. If the section contains a welted seam, leave it attached to the chair until you trace the outline of the welt onto the new fabric cut for that section *(page 106)*. Disturb the underlying padding as little as possible, and set aside any that falls off; it can often be reused, especially if supplemented with a layer of new cotton.

When all the fabric is removed, check the condition of the frame *(page 102)* and make whatever repairs are needed. This is also the time to renew the webbing and repair the seat if necessary *(page 112)*, and to refinish exposed wood on the arms and legs *(pages 81-95)*. That done, you can cut the new fabric, using the notes, sketches and diagrams previously made in the course of plotting fabric requirements and taking exact measurements from the chair frame. In cutting the fabric, as in making the diagrams, line up horizontal measurements with the crosswise grain of the fabric and vertical measurements with the lengthwise grain. Always work right side up, with the design of the fabric facing you.

For most sections of the cover, you will simply rough-cut a rectangle of fabric, which you will later pull and shape to the chair or sofa as the fabric is tacked or stapled to the frame. Sometimes these rough-cut sections are later contoured

more precisely. This is usually the case when parts of rough-cut sections are joined by corded welt, for which an accurate seam line must be established. Inner and outer arm sections, for example, are commonly rough-cut, but the seam that joins them is later carefully contoured so the welt can be inserted.

The choice of fabric for a reupholstery project is largely a matter of taste, but you will also want to consider practicality. One of the most popular fabrics for upholstery is an all-cotton drapery fabric; look for one with enough body to stand up to the rigors of stretching and tacking, plus the wearing effects of sitting. Regular upholstery material, usually a mixture of rayon, acetate, nylon and cotton, is somewhat sturdier. It is also thicker, however, and may be difficult for you to work with, especially if the fitting involves pleating and gathering or if you try to stitch through many layers with a home sewing machine.

Almost as strong as cotton is spun rayon, but be sure that it bears the label "spun rayon," not just "rayon"; ordinary rayon wears out quickly. A combination of cotton and linen is an elegant, lightweight upholstery fabric; corduroy will take much punishment, though it may be too thick for a home sewing machine. Also hard to work with are the plastics that imitate leather; they tend to be stiff and have little give.

Whenever possible, buy a fabric that has been treated with a protective, dirt-resistant finishing spray. The trade names for this finish, such as Scotchgard, are usually found on the bolt end or on hangtags attached to the fabric. If the fabric has not already been treated, you can spray the piece yourself after the upholstering has been completed.

Finally, to save money, you may want to cut some parts of the new cover from less expensive fabric. It is customary, for example, to make the decking (the seat cover under the cushion) from sturdy unbleached muslin. In addition, pull strips of the same muslin may be sewed to the parts of the inside arms and inside back coverings that are tucked inside the upholstery; these pull strips are used to pull the fabric taut against the frame of the piece for stapling or tacking.

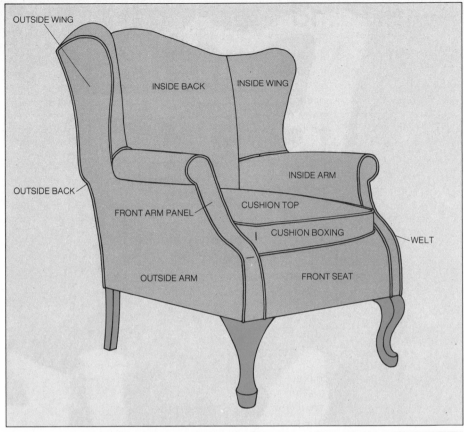

OUTSIDE WING

INSIDE BACK

INSIDE WING

OUTSIDE BACK

INSIDE ARM

FRONT ARM PANEL

CUSHION TOP

CUSHION BOXING

WELT

OUTSIDE ARM

FRONT SEAT

Complexities Simplified

The parts of an upholstery cover. The labels that identify the parts of the wing chair at left are standard terms used by professional upholsterers. Most fully upholstered furniture will have these same fabric sections, with the possible exception of the wings. Furniture that is more tailored will have additional pieces—called boxing—at the tops of the arms and chair back.

The upholstery pieces that surround you when you sit on the chair—called the inside sections—are tacked or stapled to the frame in a carefully planned sequence that conceals the hardware fasteners. Outside fabric pieces—the front seat, outside arm, outside wing and outside back—are blind-tacked (hooked onto hidden tacking strips) to adjacent fabric pieces. The curving front arm panels are attached to the inside and outside arm with a combination of machine sewing and blind tacking.

The corded welt that outlines the seams between some fabric sections is machine-stitched. The cushion sections—top, bottom and boxing—are sewed together, edged with welt, and used as a case to hold the stuffing. Hidden underneath the cushion in this illustration is a square of durable fabric that covers the deck, or top, of the chair seat; it is referred to as decking.

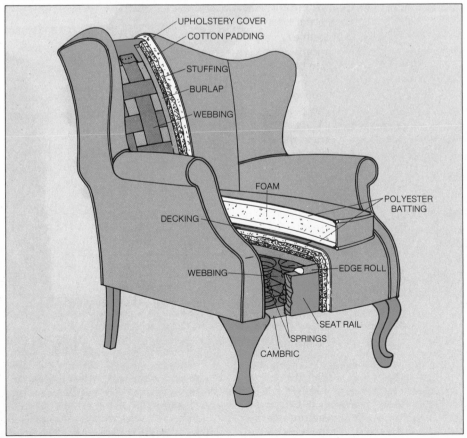

UPHOLSTERY COVER
COTTON PADDING
STUFFING
BURLAP
WEBBING
FOAM
POLYESTER BATTING
DECKING
WEBBING
EDGE ROLL
SEAT RAIL
SPRINGS
CAMBRIC

The chair's puffy interior. The inside of a chair is built up in layers designed to give both comfort and support. The bottom layer is a cambric dust cover, tacked to the bottom edges of the seat rails. Above that, interwoven strips of tightly stretched jute webbing are a foundation for coil springs. The springs are sewed to the webbing and tied together with twine to hold them in position. A layer of burlap is stretched above the springs and serves as a base for the chair's stuffing; a special burlap- or felt-covered padding strip, called an edge roll, cushions the top edge of the seat rail. Top layers of cotton padding define the final contours of the upholstery.

Although many older seat cushions contain springs, most modern cushions are stuffed with foam rubber or polyurethane foam and shaped with polyester batting. Many upholstered chairs, such as the one shown here, are built without springs in the chair back.

The chair's rigid skeleton. A typical frame for a piece of upholstered furniture is constructed of hardwood boards cut to size and assembled with conventional chair joints—usually mortise-and-tenon joints or butt joints strengthened with dowels. The horizontal rails and vertical posts frame the chair and provide the basic support. Corner blocks are added to reinforce the joints between seat rails. The other frame pieces—the arm boards, slats and braces—give shape to the upholstery and provide tacking surfaces for fastening the fabric. The post-and-rail construction of the wings is not essential to the chair's basic structure; the wings are a decorative addition designed to give shape to the seat back.

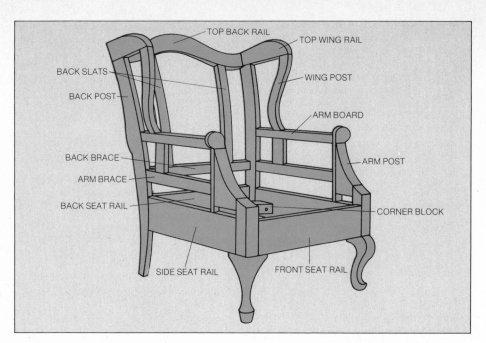

TOP BACK RAIL — TOP WING RAIL

BACK SLATS — WING POST

BACK POST

ARM BOARD

BACK BRACE — ARM POST

ARM BRACE

BACK SEAT RAIL — CORNER BLOCK

SIDE SEAT RAIL — FRONT SEAT RAIL

Step-by-Step Removal of the Old Covering

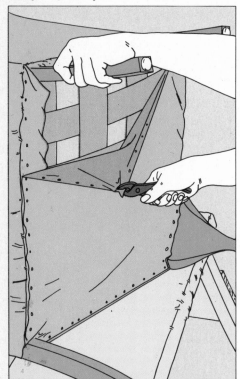

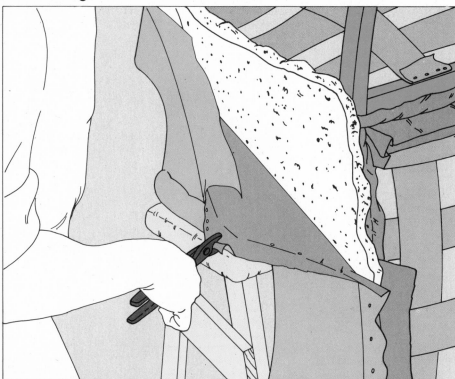

1 **Ripping off the cambric dust cover.** Place the chair on its back or its side atop two sawhorses, and use pliers to rip away the cambric from the bottom of the chair, exposing the webbing. To rip the cambric in a single motion, grasp an upper corner of the fabric with the pliers and pull it down in a diagonal line toward the opposite corner. Discard the old cambric, but leave the tacks embedded in the frame, to be removed later with a hammer and a claw chisel.

2 **Stripping the fabric.** With the chair in position upside down on the sawhorses, begin stripping fabric pieces from the outside of the frame. Use pliers for removing sections that have been tacked, again pulling downward in a diagonal line. For sections that have been hand-stitched onto the chair, use a knife or razor blade to cut the first few stitches. Then rip open the remainder of the seam, cutting the stitches when necessary to avoid tearing the fabric as you go. Leave in place temporarily any curved fabric pieces that are sewed together with welt; use these as a guide for locating the welt on the new piece (page 106).

If you intend to use the old fabric pieces as patterns for the new, label each piece with chalk as you remove it. Indicate where each piece was located on the chair (page 101), and mark the top of each piece with a T.

3 **Removing blind-tack tape.** When tack tape does not pull off with the fabric, use pliers to pull it away from the frame; always strip in a downward motion to minimize the danger of flying tacks. Discard the old tack tape. Leave in place any loose cotton padding, and set aside for later use any that falls from the chair.

If you plan to cut the new fabric according to measurements, stop at this point, with the inner fabric pieces still in place, and take exact measurements from the exposed portions of the frame (*page 105, Step 1*). If you plan to use the old fabric pieces as patterns for the new, skip the measuring step and continue stripping, turning the chair upright to remove the inside fabric pieces from the frame. Identify these pieces with chalked notations, as in Step 2.

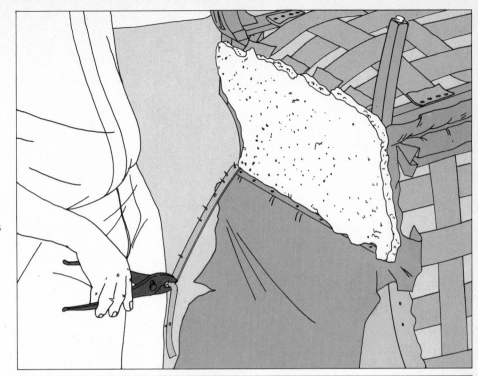

4 **Removing tacks and staples.** Using the appropriate tools, clear the frame of all fasteners. To remove any stubborn tacks, lay the bottom of a ripping-chisel blade (*page 98*) flat against the edge of the frame, with its tip wedged under the head of a tack. Strike the end of the handle squarely with a mallet to jar the tack out of the wood. For safety, point the chisel away from you; for ease in lifting the tack, point the chisel in the direction of the wood grain. To pry staples out, use a slotted staple remover (*page 98*).

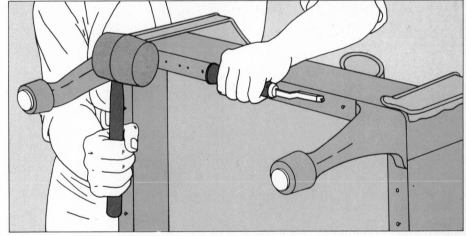

Using the Old Fabric Pieces as Patterns

1 **Flattening the pattern pieces.** Using a steam iron, smooth each piece of old upholstery removed from the chair. Use the pointed tip of the iron to flatten fabric edges that were folded under to fit around the frame or were joined into seams. Work on the right side first, then turn the piece over and iron the reverse side.

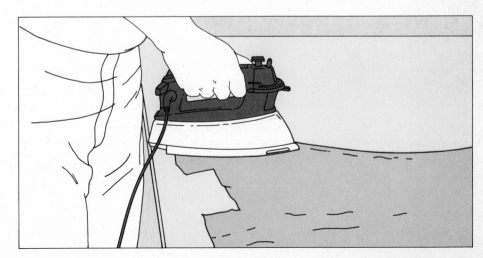

2 **Centering the pattern.** Unroll the new upholstery fabric, right side up, on a worktable or on the floor and lay an ironed pattern piece, also right side up, on it. Shift the pattern piece until the grain lines of pattern and new fabric are aligned, and until the pattern lies directly over the section of design that you want centered on the new piece. Pin the pattern piece for cutting, placing pins ½ inch from the pattern edges.

Continue pinning pattern pieces against the fabric, always lining up the grain and making sure that stripes or other designs match from piece to piece. If the new fabric has a nap, check its direction before centering the pattern *(page 100)*.

3 **Cutting out the new fabric.** Cut around the pinned pattern pieces, following their curves and angles exactly, but adding 2 inches all around to allow sufficient fabric for stretching, tacking and stitching. If the pattern is torn or is missing a corner, cut the new piece a little large, and square off its corners—this will leave room for adjustments when the piece is attached to the frame. As you unpin the old piece from the new, mark the top edge on the back of each new piece, and label its position on the chair.

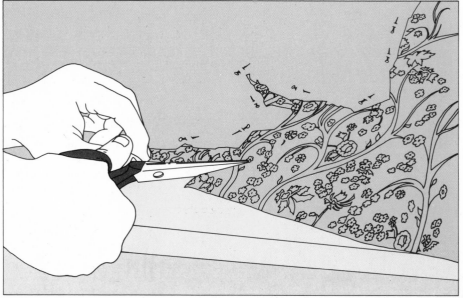

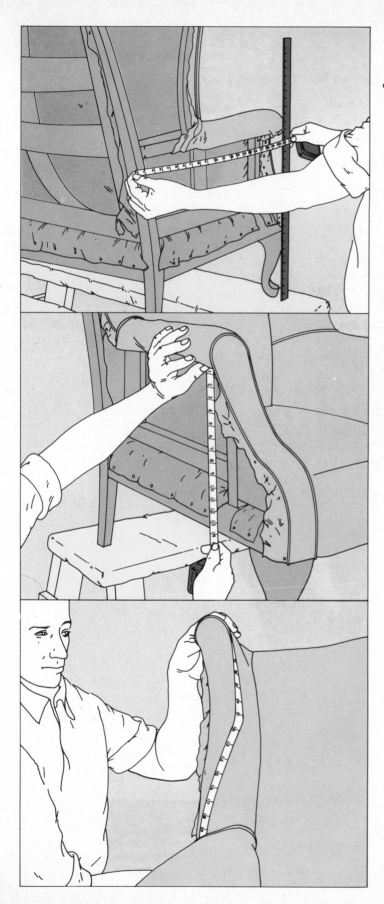

Rough-cutting New Fabric to Measurements

1 Measuring flat and curved surfaces. For a cover piece that will lie flat, measure the dimensions of the piece after the frame is bare. Measure between the points on the frame that are farthest apart, first horizontally, then vertically (*center left*). When there is a flat surface that is irregularly shaped, such as an outside chair arm (*top left*), prop a yardstick against the widest part on one side and measure across to the farthest point on the opposite side.

When a cover piece will lie over a curved surface, take the measurements for the piece before removing the old fabric. To measure the complex curve of a wing (*bottom left*), hold the tape measure against the seam at the highest point along the top of the wing, then carry it over the curve and across the rolled front edge, to the point where the wing rail meets the arm board.

For cover pieces that extend deep into a recess of the chair, as is the case with the inside arm or inside back, insert the measuring tape into the recess as far as it will go. Add 4 inches to the horizontal and vertical measurements for each piece, and note these measurements on the list to be used in cutting new fabric.

2 **Transferring measurements to fabric.** Working systematically from the largest piece to the smallest, measure the dimensions on the fabric with a yardstick. Mark the vertical dimensions first, centering the yardstick over the design element you want centered on each piece and being sure to hold the yardstick parallel to the selvage—the finished border of the fabric. Then, using these marks as guides, measure off the horizontal dimensions, with half on each side of the vertical center.

For the initial markings, you can use either chalk or pins, but when the outlines of the piece are established, rule them off with chalk lines, using the yardstick. Whenever possible, fit small pieces into fabric remaining along the margins.

Cutting Pieces of Fabric for Stitched Seams

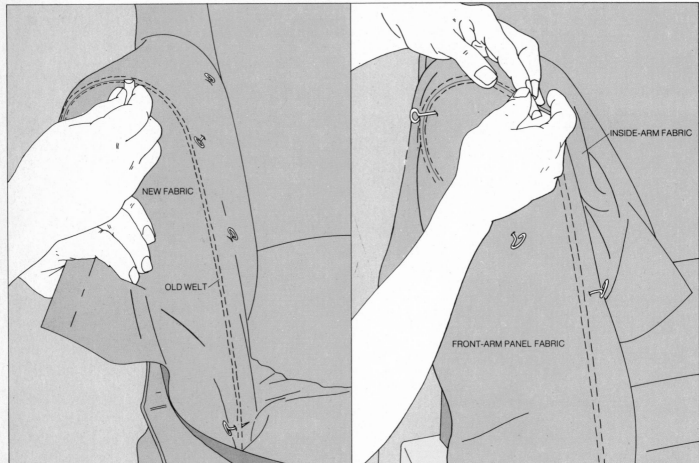

NEW FABRIC

OLD WELT

INSIDE-ARM FABRIC

FRONT-ARM PANEL FABRIC

1 **Tracing the welt line.** If two cover pieces are joined by a machine-stitched seam, mark the new fabric with an outline for the seam by using the existing welt as a guide. First, smooth one rough-cut section into place over the old cover (still on the chair—Step 2, page 102), tucking

it into any recesses, as on the inside chair arm above. Secure the piece with upholstery pins. Then pull the fabric over the welt, holding it snug with one hand while you trace the curve of the welt with chalk. Keep the chalk directly on top of the welt, to ensure a precise outline.

Unpin and fold back the first rough-cut section, exposing the welted seam that you have just traced onto the new fabric. Then smooth and pin the adjoining rough-cut section in place with its edges overlapping the welted seam; trace the outline of the welt on this section, too.

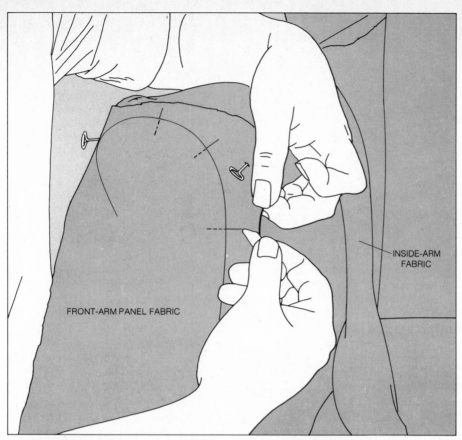

2 **Marking adjoining pieces for assembly.** Pin the two adjoining pieces into place, lining up their chalked seam lines with the welt. So that joining the pieces for stitching will be easier, mark them with perpendicular chalk lines through the seam at several points along its length. To align these marks, flip back the extra fabric at the edge of one section and make a chalk line across the welt; then hold your fingernail against this line, lift the other section, and make a matching mark across the welt.

INSIDE-ARM FABRIC

FRONT-ARM PANEL FABRIC

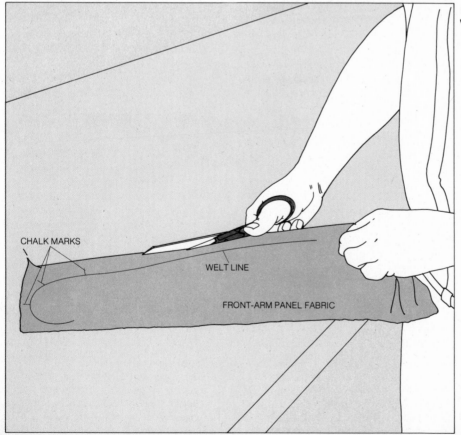

3 **Cutting the pieces to shape.** Unpin both fabric pieces and lay them flat on the worktable. Using the chalked outlines as guides, cut each piece to shape, leaving a ½-inch seam allowance along the section of seam to be joined by machine stitching. When you pin the seam in preparation for sewing (*page 118*), line up the perpendicular chalk marks to bring the sections of curve back into their original alignment.

After all the curved sections have been measured and the welt has been traced, strip the remaining upholstery pieces from the chair.

CHALK MARKS

WELT LINE

FRONT-ARM PANEL FABRIC

Firming the Inner Structure of Old Furniture

Styles in upholstered furniture come and go, but the notion of what makes a chair comfortable to sit on has not changed much since the introduction of stuffings in the 16th Century.

Mainly it is a matter of softness and springiness. The traditional method of achieving these qualities is with a succession of layers of various materials. They include springs or springy slats of metal or wood; cloth webbing to hold springs or to contribute springiness alone; matted horsehair or hog-hair stuffing to provide cushioning; and cotton padding to soften uncushioned wood parts and to smooth the surface under the covering.

For obvious reasons most of the layering involves the seat. If you lift the fabric cover of an upholstered side chair, for example, you may find a single layer of padding supported by webbing or a wood panel. You may also find a layer of some type of stuffing under the cotton padding. In armchairs and sofas, the number and composition of the layers depend to some extent on the vintage of the piece. In modern furniture, stuffing and padding or foam-rubber cushions are often supported by zigzag springs—flat, curvy strips of steel wire. And beneath the cushions of so-called Danish modern furniture you are likely to find straps of rubber webbing.

But the most conventional arrangement, tested by time and the weight of countless tired bodies, is the multilayered assembly of webbing, springs, stuffing and padding found in the comfortable armchair or sofa that occupies a place of honor in most American homes. This arrangement usually consists of nine or more coil springs tied together and sewed to supporting crisscross strips of jute webbing. In some modern constructions, the jute webbing itself is reinforced with several strips of flat steel webbing that span the underside of the chair or sofa frame.

Under the webbing is a protective cover of cambric and above the springs is a layer of burlap, on which rests the stuffing. The stuffing is topped by padding, and the seat is finished off with a covering of muslin or denim, called decking, on which the cushion rests.

Such a seat is used to illustrate the upholstery repair techniques that follow. The techniques are standard and are easily modified to suit the structure of any chair or sofa, as well as the different configurations that may underlie various parts. Springs, for example, may or may not be found in the back of a chair and are almost never present in the arms. Here, the support normally provided by the webbing may instead be a panel of stretched burlap.

The first step in restructuring a seat is to check the condition of the webbing. Look underneath the chair for sagging, which indicates that the webbing has stretched. Press up against the cambric covering; if the surface yields easily, the webbing has lost its tension. Then turn the chair upside down and remove the cambric covering for a closer look at the webbing itself, which may simply be slack or may have begun to fray or even come loose along the wood frame.

It is not always necessary to replace worn or loose webbing; sometimes you can simply reinforce the existing webbing by adding new strips over it. On the other hand, if further inspection shows that the frame needs structural repairs or the springs need retying *(pages 114-115)*, or if you are planning to put a new cover on the chair, it is better to remove loose webbing and replace it with new.

A chair or sofa may also contain steel webbing strips beneath the jute webbing. If steel webbing has sagged it can be restretched with a special tool that you may be able to borrow or rent from a professional upholsterer.

To reinforce old jute webbing or replace it with new, you will need a roll of webbing that matches the width of the original, and a supply of No. 14 upholstery tacks. You will also need a webbing stretcher, an upholsterer's tack hammer and, to sew new webbing to the springs, a 4-inch light-gauge curved needle and nylon stitching twine. To hold tacks at the ready, you may find it useful to make a tack holder by sawing several 1-inch-deep cuts the length of a scrap of 2-by-4 and lining up tacks, heads up, in the cuts.

Before tacking new webbing to the frame, fill in small cracks and holes left by previous repairs, using white glue or wood putty. If the edge of the frame has been weakened by too many tack holes, you can sometimes attach the new webbing to the side of the frame, leaving the ends unfolded in order to avoid bulges under the final fabric cover.

When you stretch webbing, certain general rules apply. Webbing on a seat is always stretched first from back to front; on the back of a chair it is stretched from bottom to top. The first strip is always placed in the center of the frame, with additional strips placed alternately on either side. When all the strips in one direction are attached, perpendicular strips are woven through them, again beginning in the center and working outward on alternate sides.

A New Layer of Webbing for Reinforcement

1 Reanchoring loose springs. Clip away any bits of loose or broken twine anchoring the springs to the existing webbing, then reattach the affected springs to the webbing with a pattern of stitches that forms a square over two intersecting strips of webbing. Using a 4-inch curved needle you have threaded with a 3-foot length of nylon stitching twine, make the first of four stitches at one corner of the intersecting strips, being sure to plot this first stitch so that the last stitch will be as close as possible to the next coil that requires sewing. Push the point of the needle down through the webbing on the inside of the coil (*top left*), and bring it up again through the webbing outside the coil (*top right*). Tie a slipknot in the twine (*bottom left*), and pull the knot down until it rests against the webbing.

Take the second stitch in the square at the adjacent corner, again pushing the needle down through the webbing inside the coil and bringing it up outside the coil; lock this stitch by drawing the needle underneath the twine carried from the first stitch (*bottom right*). Complete the third and fourth stitches in the same fashion, then move on to the next loose coil. If the two coils are adjacent, do not cut the twine; if they are some distance from each other, cut the twine and tie a knot. Continue until all the springs are firmly attached to the webbing.

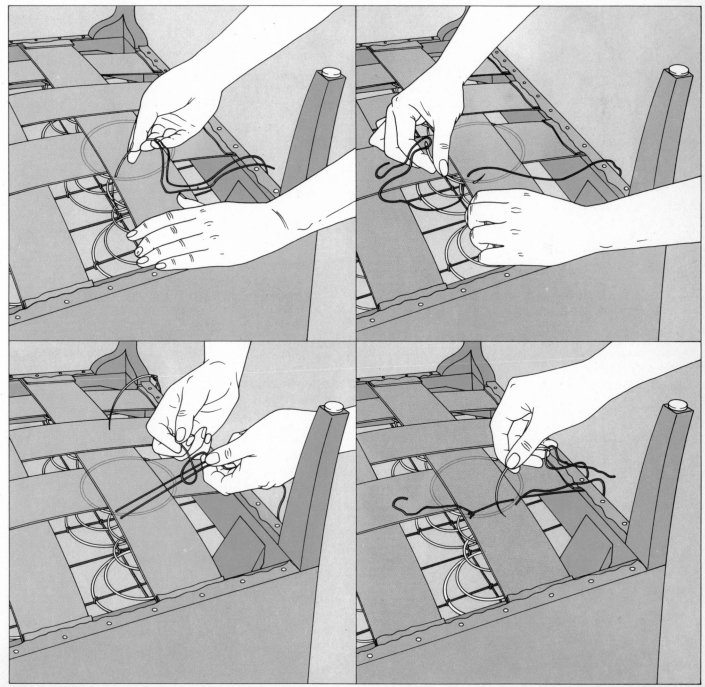

2 **Starting new webbing.** Unroll new webbing over the center strip of the existing webbing and fasten it to the back seat rail with five No. 14 upholstery tacks driven in a staggered pattern; allow an overlap of 1 inch. If the folded edge of the existing webbing falls slightly in from the edge of the seat rail, try to place some of the tacks in that narrow strip of wood.

3 **Stretching new webbing.** Unroll a length of webbing that will reach across the chair frame and, holding the webbing stretcher at a 45° angle against the front seat rail, pull the strip down over the teeth of the stretcher. Push down on the stretcher handle until it is horizontal.

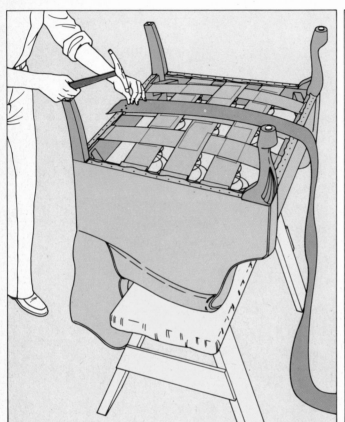

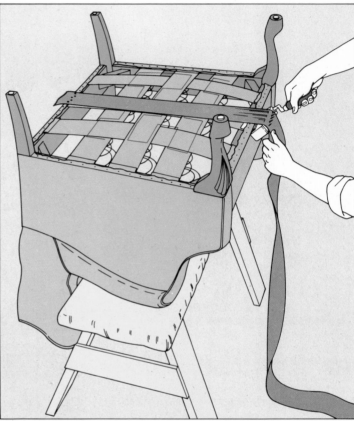

4 **Tacking stretched webbing.** As you hold the stretcher horizontal with one hand, use the magnetic end of the hammer to pick up a tack. Position the hammer about 6 inches above the center of the webbing strip and, with a sharp blow, drive the tack down through the webbing, partway into the rail. Flip the hammer and, with the nonmagnetic end, drive the tack all the way into the wood. Tack both edges of the strip in the same way, then remove the stretcher and drive in two intermediate tacks. Cut the webbing from the roll, leaving a 1-inch overlap.

Add the remaining back-to-front webbing strips, then interweave them with side-to-side strips, stretching and tacking each to the rail, as before, leaving a 1-inch overlap. When all of the new strips are attached, fold over and fasten down the overlapping ends with five additional tacks.

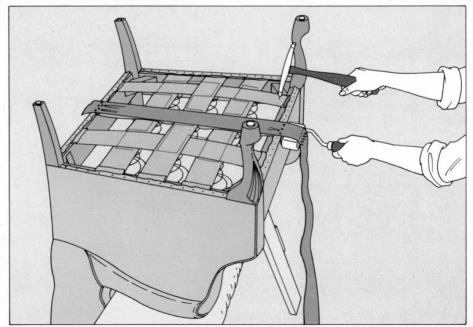

Repairs for Back and Arm Supports

Restretching loose back webbing. After freeing the top end of the center webbing strip on the back with a ripping chisel and mallet, fasten an 8-inch extension to the original webbing with two upholstery pins, overlapping the ends of the strips ½ inch. Pull the extension across the top of the rail and onto the stretcher teeth, then push the stretcher flush with the back. Retack the original webbing to the inside face of the rail. Remove the extension and use it to restretch the remaining strips of webbing. Fold the loose ends over and tack them in place.

Tightening sagging burlap on an arm. If all of the old upholstery is being replaced and the frame is bared, you can tighten burlap by removing it from the frame and retacking it. First, attach the top edge of the burlap to the inside face of the arm board with tacks spaced at 2-inch intervals. Then pull the burlap taut and tack its bottom edge to the inside face of the arm brace. Finally, stretch and tack the side edges to the arm post and the arm slat.

Once the new upholstery has been added to the inside of the frame, place a layer of padding over the burlap and hold it in this position by stretching and tacking a single strip of webbing across it and the frame (*inset*).

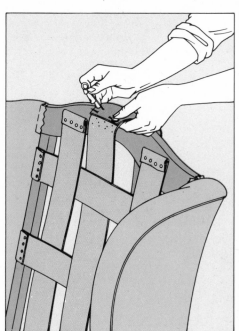

Replacing Worn-out Rubber Webbing

Fastening new end clips. Slide the old strips of rubber webbing out of the grooves on the seat rails and use them to cut out new rubber strips, ½ inch shorter. Fasten new clips to both ends of the new strips by pinching the jaws of the clips around the webbing with pliers (*inset*). Slide the clips back into the grooves in the frame.

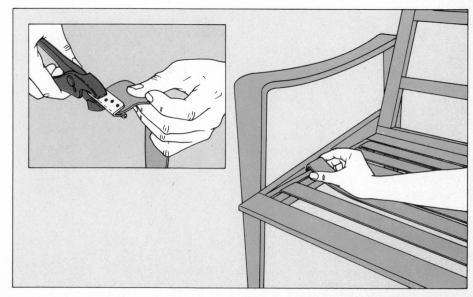

Putting Bounce Back in Springs

The coiled wire springs that give upholstered seats their bounce rarely wear out. It is the webbing that supports the springs, the thread that anchors them to the webbing and the twine that ties them to one another that break, stretch or fray.

If the only problem is stretched or frayed webbing, or broken thread, you can reinforce the bottom of the seat without actually exposing the springs. But if the springs are popping through the fabric, either above or below, or if they are so loosely joined to one another that they are easily pushed out of alignment, it is time to restructure the entire seat. This means taking apart all the old layers from top to bottom—the burlap, the springs and twine, the webbing, the cambric—and installing a new support system for the old springs.

Before you tear the seat apart, remove the cambric and mark the positions of the old webbing strips on the bottom edges of the seat rails with chalk; the marks will serve as a guide for installing new webbing. Then, working from the top of the seat, clip the stitches that anchor the burlap to the springs and strip off the burlap, using a claw chisel and mallet to pry out the old tacks from the seat rail. Next, cut the twine that fastens the springs together at the top, as well as the stitches that anchor the bottom of the springs to the webbing. Then take out the springs and remove the webbing.

The springs that you find inside the seat of a well-made chair or sofa will be of 9- to 11-gauge wire. They will have a double-helical shape, with wide coils at the ends and narrow coils in the middle.

If the chair or sofa has been comfortable, there is no need to replace springs. But if you want either a softer or a firmer seat, buy new springs of the same height as the old ones, but with more or less springiness. Double-helical springs are rated as hard, medium or soft: The smaller the waist coil—the narrowest coil in the middle of the spring—the harder the spring. No matter which degree of firmness you choose, look for springs with at least seven coils; springs with fewer coils are weaker and less efficient.

If you find that the seat has conical springs, each with a large coil at the top tapering down to a small coil at the bottom, you may want to replace them with double-helical springs. Conical springs are very rigid and cannot be attached to regular jute webbing. They must be mounted on metal bars and arranged as a single unit to fit over the seat frame.

You may also find cylindrical coil springs in the chair back or cushions and, occasionally, inside arms. These springs are generally shaped of lighter-gauge wire and are encased in burlap, muslin or foam rubber to form a single unit. Since they are rarely defective, such spring units can be reused just as you find them.

Restructuring a coil-spring seat takes time but does not call for any special expertise. First you stretch a new layer of jute webbing across the bottom of the seat (page 110). Then stitch the bottom coil of the springs to the webbing with nylon stitching twine, using a 10-inch heavy-gauge double-pointed needle. Nylon is preferable to natural-fiber stitching twines because it is stronger. Finally, you tie together the spring tops, using seat-spring twine of 6-cord hemp or flax; this twine is sold in 8-ounce balls.

In some modern upholstered furniture you may find flat zigzag-shaped springs instead of coil springs. Such springs are fastened to the frame with metal clips and always run across the frame in one direction only—back to front on the seat, bottom to top on the chair back. On a seat, the spring strips are slightly longer than the frame and arc upward to give support with resilience.

Zigzag springs do not require webbing and they are sometimes referred to as sagless springs. They are generally fastened to one another with metal connectors instead of twine. However, if such springs begin to slip from side to side because their connectors are broken or lost, the simplest remedy is to tie them together with spring twine (page 115).

Sewing the Springs to New Webbing

1 **Anchoring the first spring.** Center the first spring over the intersection of the front and center strips of webbing; if the spring is interlocked at one end, place that end up. Plot four equally spaced stitches around the bottom coil so the last stitch will fall at the back of the coil. For the first stitch, push a double-pointed needle that is threaded with nylon stitching twine straight down through the webbing just inside the coil *(top left)*. Bring the needle up through the webbing on the outside of the coil *(top right)* and pull the twine through this stitch, leaving a 1-foot end.

Secure the first stitch with a slipknot, doubling the loose end over the length of twine and back through the loop in the loose end *(bottom left)*. Tighten the knot against the coil *(bottom right)*, then push the needle down, outside the coil, through the original hole in the webbing.

Move 90 degrees around the coil and make a second stitch, pushing the needle up through the webbing inside the coil and back down outside the coil. Then repeat this procedure to complete the third stitch. Neither the second nor the third stitch is secured with a slipknot.

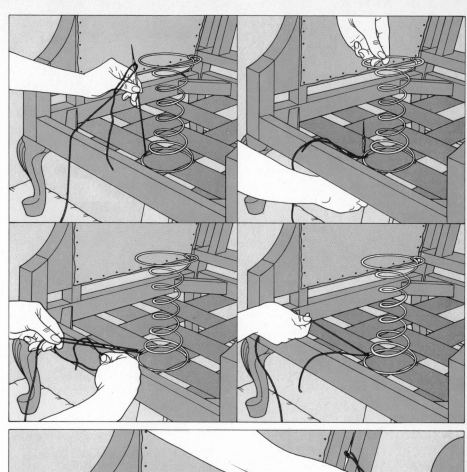

2 **Running stitches between springs.** For the fourth stitch on the first spring, reverse the procedure that you used for the second and third stitches: Push the needle up through the webbing outside the coil, then down through the webbing inside the coil *(top)*. Place a second spring behind the first, again at the intersection of two webbing strips. At the point where this coil is nearest the first, bring the needle up through the webbing on the inside of the coil *(bottom)* and down through the webbing on the outside.

Complete the second and third stitches, pushing the needle up on the inside and down on the outside of the coil. Complete the fourth stitch as before, pushing the needle up on the outside and down on the inside, but with this stitch in place, move on to a third spring placed to the side of the second spring, adjacent to this stitch.

When your stitching takes you into a corner *(inset)*, fasten off the twine by using the needle to draw the twine underneath the last stitch you made; then remove the needle, pull the twine taut and tie a knot. Continue anchoring springs at every intersection of the webbing strips until all the intersections are covered.

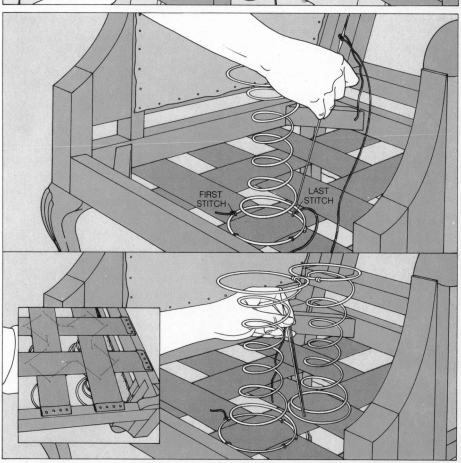

Tying Springs in Place with Lengths of Twine

1 **Anchoring the twine.** For each row of springs, front to back and side to side, cut a length of spring twine 1½ times the distance between the rails, and anchor the twine to the rails with pairs of upholstery tacks. Along each of the four rails and in line with the center of each row of springs, drive a No. 14 tack halfway into the top edge of the frame. Then loop one end of the first length of twine around the middle tack on the back rail and drive the tack all the way into the wood *(top)*. Drive a second tack halfway into the rail ⅛ inch away from the first tack; loop the twine in the opposite direction around this tack, forming a figure 8 *(bottom)*. Then drive the second tack all the way into the wood *(inset)*.

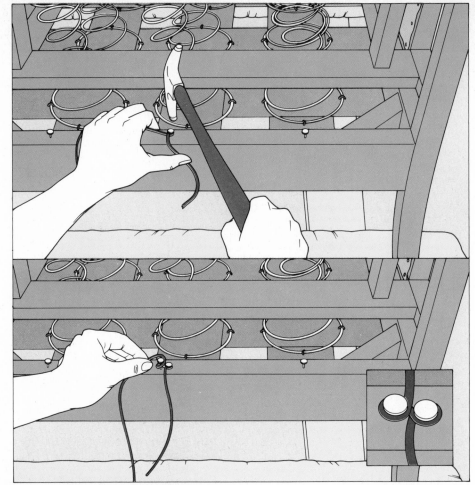

2 **Tying the coils.** Standing at the front of the frame, draw the anchored twine up under the back brace to the second coil from the top on the back spring. Pass the twine under this coil, pull the twine taut and hold it against the coil with your thumb to maintain tension while you tie a simple knot around the coil *(inset)*.

Draw the twine across this same spring and with your thumb hold it taut against the underside of the top coil while you tie a knot around that coil. Continue working from the back to the front, tying down the rest of the springs in the center row. At each spring, knot the twine around both sides of the top coil until you get to the front spring; at that point, tie the second knot against the second coil from the top.

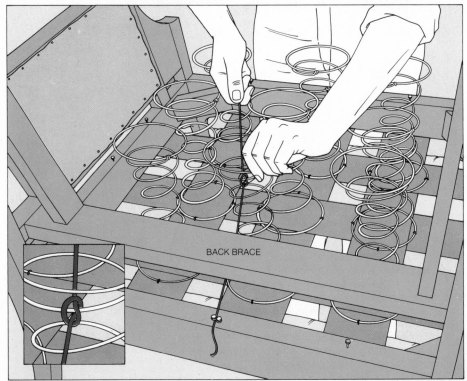

BACK BRACE

3 **Securing the twine.** At the end of the row, push the front spring down firmly and loop the twine on the center tack of that rail. Pull the twine tight and drive the tack into the wood. Add a second tack and loop the twine in a figure 8.

Tie down the rows of springs on either side of the center row in the same fashion, alternating sides until all the rows running back to front have been tied. Then tie the side-to-side rows, again beginning with the center row and working out on alternate sides (*inset*).

Cut a secondary set of cords, but this time cut one cord fewer of each length. Drive tacks halfway into the frame around all four sides, midway between those used to anchor the existing twine.

4 **Tying the secondary cords.** Starting with an inner cord on the back rail, anchor the first end as in Step 1, then draw the cord under the back brace and, knotting as in Step 2, tie the cord to each piece of twine it crosses. Anchor the cord end on the opposite rail. Tie all back-to-front cords first, then side-to-side cords.

Cut cords that are 1½ times the length of each diagonal row. Anchor and tie these cords as in Step 2, placing the first and last knot in each row one coil from the top (*inset*). Start with the center diagonals and work toward the corners, first doing all the rows in one direction, then crossing them with rows running the other way. On the corner springs, tie both of the knots on the second coil from the top.

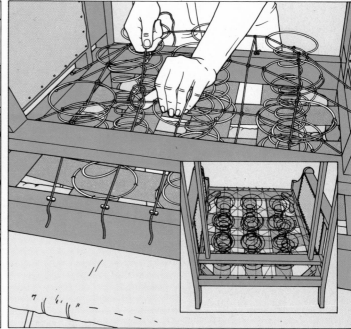

A Fix for Zigzag Springs

Tying zigzag springs. To secure zigzag springs that slip out of line, tie them with cords of spring twine running between the side rails. Space the cords 6 to 8 inches apart. Anchor the cord ends and tie the knots as for coil springs.

To tighten metal spring clips that have worked loose from the rails, ease the spring out of the clips, keeping a firm hold on the spring to prevent it from snapping out of control. Release the relaxed spring, then remove the tacks anchoring the loosened clip, fill the holes with white glue and allow the glue to dry. Reposition the clip at a spot free of tack holes but as close as possible to its original position. Refasten the clip, then move the matching clip on the opposite rail so that it is in line with this new position. Slip the spring ends back into their clips.

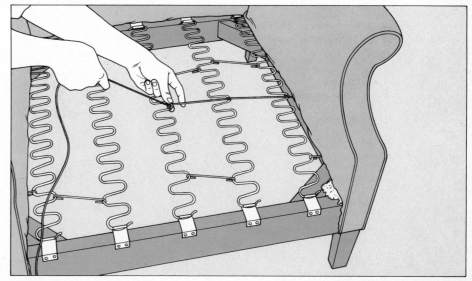

Stuffing for Softness and Shape

Burlap and stuffing top off the springs in upholstered seats and constitute the complete inner structure of most chair backs and arms. The burlap provides a support for the stuffing and keeps it from falling down into the springs. Stuffing gives the furniture softness and shape.

The standard burlap used weighs at least 10 ounces per square yard. It is stretched by hand over the area to be covered and fastened to the frame with No. 14 tacks. When stretched over springs, the burlap is sewed to the top coil of each spring with a 4-inch light-gauge curved needle and nylon stitching twine. As a finishing touch, a burlap-encased cylinder of either cotton or felt, called an edge roll, is tacked along the edge of the front seat rail to pad and shape the front edge of the seat.

Stuffing materials are available in bulk form or in prefabricated sheets. The common loose stuffings are horsehair, cattle hair or hog hair and other natural substances such as moss, palm fiber, cocoa fiber, sisal and tow. Hair is preferable to fiber stuffings—it is more resilient, cleaner and longer lasting. In fact, most hair stuffing lasts indefinitely, and seldom must be replaced when you reupholster.

If you do need new stuffing, the most convenient form is rubberized hair, which is sold in sheets or rolls and is easy to use because it forms a smooth, symmetrical surface without the coaxing and rearranging needed for loose stuffings. This preshaped material is more expensive than loose stuffing, but its excellent resilience and timesaving qualities make it the choice of many professionals.

Adding a Layer of Burlap over the Springs

1 **Slitting the burlap for a neat fit.** Cut a rectangle of burlap 6 inches longer and wider than the seat frame and lay the burlap over the springs, folding the 6-inch overlap back toward the center of the seat. Make a diagonal cut from the back corners of the burlap to the fold so that the burlap will fit around the back posts when it is pulled down and tacked to the back and side seat rails. Make similar diagonal cuts at the arm posts in front, and a perpendicular cut to any other vertical section of frame that the burlap must pass around.

BACK POST

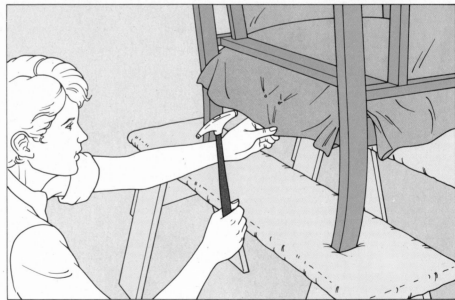

2 **Tacking the burlap edges.** Draw the overlapping edge of burlap down between the back brace and back rail and fasten it to the outer face of the rail with No. 14 tacks at 4-inch intervals. Then pull the burlap taut over the springs and tack the front edge to the front rail. Place the first tack at the center of this rail, then tack down the two corners and gradually fill in the intervening space, stretching and smoothing the burlap as you go. Repeat this procedure to stretch and tack the sides.

Stretch and tack rectangular pieces of burlap to the inside of the arms, wings and back of the chair, but do not pull these coverings over the frame. Instead, tack them to the inside faces of the frame. Trim away the excess burlap, leaving a ½-inch edge beyond the tacks.

3 Sewing the burlap to the springs. To anchor the burlap to the springs, stitch it to the top coil of each spring at three places. Begin at a corner spring and, using a curved needle threaded with nylon twine, stitch down through the burlap on the outside of the coil and back up inside the coil. Tie a slipknot *(page 113, Step.1)* to anchor the first stitch. Plan the positions of the second and third stitches so that the third stitch will be close to an adjacent spring *(inset)*. Lock each of these stitches in turn by drawing the needle back under the twine running from the previous stitch. Move on to the next coil. When you reach the end of a length of twine, tie it off with a slipknot and rethread the needle.

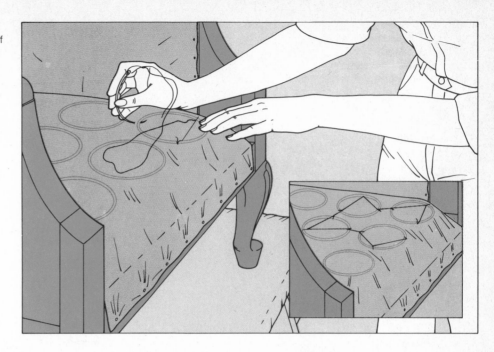

Padding to Cushion the Front Seat Rail

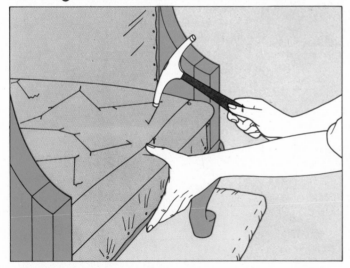

Tacking on the edge roll. Measure and cut a section of edge roll the same length as the front seat rail; hold it in position over the burlap and tack through the seam allowance into the top edge of the seat rail. Use No. 14 tacks and space them at 4-inch intervals along the rail.

Stitching a Layer of Stuffing to the Burlap

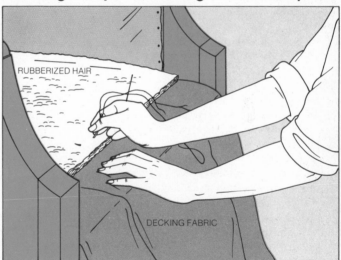

RUBBERIZED HAIR

DECKING FABRIC

Stitching down new stuffing. Cut a slab of rubberized hair to fit the area bounded by the inside edges of the side seat rails, the inside edge of the back seat rail and the line where the decking will be sewed to the burlap *(page 127, Step 1)*. Stitch the rubberized hair in place with nylon twine, guiding the curved needle down through the stuffing and burlap and under the outer curve of the top coil of a spring. Work around the perimeter of the stuffing and make one stitch per spring. Sew stuffing to the outer ends of zigzag springs in the same way.

Cut similar slabs of rubberized hair for the inside back, arms and wings, shaping each piece to fit between the inside edges of its frame. Stitch the perimeter of the stuffing to the burlap pieces already attached to the frame.

Using a Home Sewing Machine for Upholstering

A home sewing machine that is powerful enough to stitch through four thicknesses of light- to medium-weight upholstery fabric will perform all the machine stitching needed for reupholstering a chair or sofa. This stitching includes only a few seams: one to join the deck under the cushion to the seat front *(page 127);* three to join the pull strips used to stretch fabric against the inner arms and back *(pages 129 and 131);* and the seams used to shape the cushion.

With a home sewing machine that has a zipper foot, you can also attach the welt that outlines various pieces of upholstery and strengthens the edges. You can also, if you like, make the welt instead of buying it, by stitching bias strips of fabric over lengths of cotton cord—some home machines have a cording attachment that makes this job even easier.

For the extra strength needed in upholstery, and to help the covers withstand hard wear, use special upholstery thread and heavier-than-average needles. The strongest thread, nylon No. 69, has the advantage of being thin; but 16-gauge, 4-ply cotton thread, commonly known as 16-4, will also serve. The best needle size is 16 or 18. Generally the density of the fabric calls for a fairly long stitch, 12 or even 8 stitches per inch, but you should shorten the stitch length around curves and at corners to provide extra strength. You can also stitch each seam twice, for additional reinforcement.

Seams on upholstery are customarily stitched ½ inch from the edge of the fabric. To maintain this distance as you guide the fabric under the needle, a seam gauge is handy. Many machines have special attachments for this purpose; if your machine does not, a strip of masking tape placed on the throat plate of the machine, ½ inch away from the needle, works just as well.

After stitching the seam that joins deck to seat front and the one that joins pull strips to arms and back, spread the seams open and press them to lie flat. When the seam joins many layers of fabric, the seam allowance should be graded after stitching, to reduce bulk. To grade a seam, cut each layer of the seam allowance a slightly different width, graduating from ½ inch on the bottom layer to ¼ inch on the layer at the top.

Sewing a Straight Seam

1 **Using a seam gauge.** With the right sides of fabric together, secure the seam with pins placed at right angles to the seam line, a technique known as pin basting. Then align the outer edges of the fabric against the seam gauge.

2 **Backstitching to secure a seam.** Beginning about ½ inch from one end of the seam, and with the machine set to reverse, stitch backward to the top of the seam, then forward for the length of the seam. Guide the fabric with your hands, butting its outer edges against the seam gauge. When you reach the other end of the seam, backstitch again for about ½ inch.

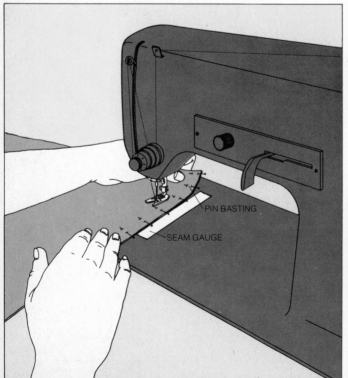

PIN BASTING

SEAM GAUGE

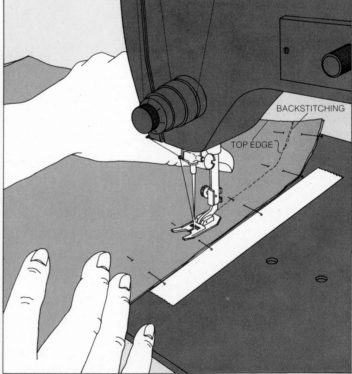

BACKSTITCHING

TOP EDGE

Making Welt from Bias Strips

1 **Finding the bias.** On a flat surface, fold the fabric diagonally, so that the lengthwise grain of the bottom layer parallels the crosswise grain of the folded-over portion. Press along the diagonal fold with an iron, then spread open the fabric. Using the fold line as a guide, draw parallel lines, 1½ inches apart, on the wrong side of the fabric, using a straightedge and either tailor's chalk or marking pencil. Then cut along these lines in order to make the bias strips.

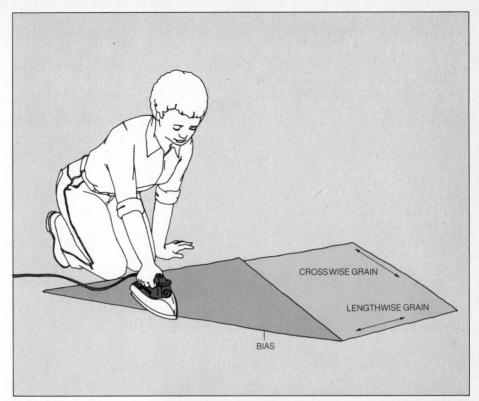

CROSSWISE GRAIN

LENGTHWISE GRAIN

BIAS

2 **Joining bias strips.** Pin-baste the end of one bias strip at right angles to another, right sides facing, and double-stitch them together, using the seam gauge as a guide. Press the seam open and clip off corners of seam allowance that protrude beyond the edges of each strip (*inset*). Continue adding strips in the same way, creating a single length of bias strip. Lay welt cord along the middle of the strip, on the wrong side of the fabric, in such a way that about an inch of cord extends beyond each end of the strip. After folding the fabric over the cord, align the edges and pin-baste them together.

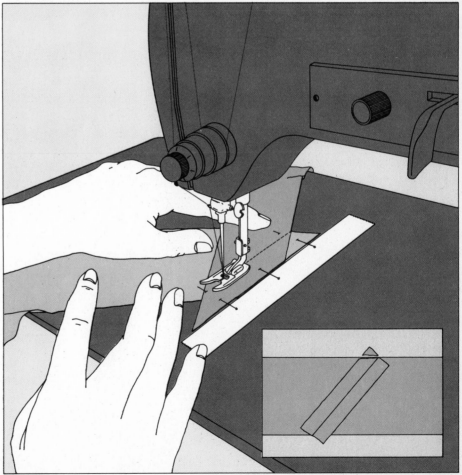

3 **Covering cord.** If you have a cording attachment for your machine, follow the manufacturer's instructions. Otherwise use the zipper foot to sew through the folded welt, close to but not directly against the cord inside it. Guide the strip with your hands to keep the stitching line straight. If the finished seam allowance is uneven, trim it so that it is an even ½ inch.

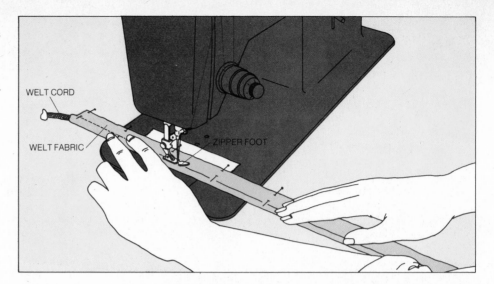

Attaching Welt to Fabric

Stitching welt in place. Pin-baste welt to the right side of the upholstery fabric, keeping the seam allowances aligned, and stitch with a zipper foot just inside the welt seam line. If a second piece of upholstery fabric is being joined to the first, pin-baste the two pieces together, right sides facing, with the welt sandwiched between them and seam allowances aligned. Turn the pieces so that the previously stitched seam is visible and, using the zipper foot, sew through all layers of fabric, between the seam line and the cord (*inset*). Grade the seams.

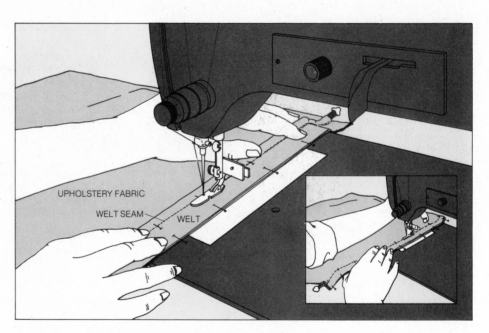

Special Techniques for Applying Welt

Attaching welt to curved and squared seams. On a curved seam (*near right*), anchor the welt with a pin just short of the curve, keeping seam allowances aligned. Pull and pin the welt around the curve, clipping several V-shaped notches in the welt seam allowance to permit the welt to lie flat. Stitch with a zipper foot as for a straight seam, but shorten the stitch length along the curve. To turn a sharp corner (*far right*), pin welt to the fabric to within 1 inch of the corner, then notch the seam allowance of the welt at the corner; pin and stitch.

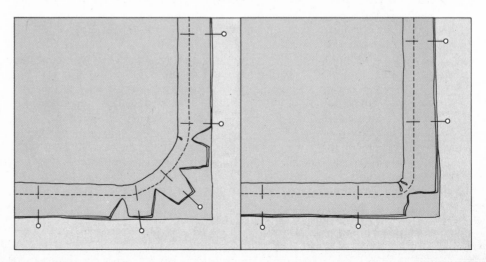

Rejuvenating a Loose Cushion

The loose cushion that covers the seat of most upholstered furniture is commonly made of identical top and bottom pieces, separated by a boxing strip the height of the cushion. Generally the cushion is square, as shown here, but sometimes the back is rounded to fit the chair.

Inside the cushion you will usually find a stuffing of polyurethane foam or foam rubber. Older cushions may be filled with rubberized hair, moss or tow; some even contain springs. In expensive furniture and some antiques, the cushion may be filled with down, encased in an inner cover of downproof ticking.

Restoring a loose cushion usually means simply replacing the cover, although you may want to discard the stuffing and springs of an old cushion and substitute a slab of foam. If the cushion is filled with down that has matted with age, you may be able to revive it. Sometimes you can do so by pinning the cushion on a clothesline and beating it with a broom. Twirling it in a clothes dryer set on low heat may also restore it—and a clean sneaker dropped into the dryer with it will serve as a beater.

In addition, you can revive a down cushion by adding more down, although you must do this with care, using a funnel, to avoid creating a blizzard of tiny feathers. If all the down must be removed, either for cleaning or to replace the ticking, put the job in the hands of a professional; large quantities of down are difficult to handle.

Fashioning a new cover for a cushion involves cutting the pieces, machine-stitching the seams and welt, and inserting a zipper. The easiest way to ensure a perfect fit is to use the old top and bottom pieces as patterns for the new. When this is not possible, lay a rough-cut piece of fabric on the chair deck and trace the outline onto it with a piece of tailor's chalk. If the fabric has a dominant design element, such as a large rose, center it on the cushion. When all the seam lines have been marked, cut the fabric ½ inch outside the chalk line.

For the boxing, cut three strips on the lengthwise grain of the fabric, the height of the cushion plus an allowance for ½-inch seams all around. Cut one strip long enough to cover the combined length of the front and the two sides (this strip will later be recut). Each of the other two strips should be the length of the back, plus 8 inches.

If the cushion has a rounded back, cut one boxing strip the length of the front plus 5 inches, and two strips of back boxing 1 inch longer than the zipper length. (The zipper is usually about half the length of the entire curved edge.) Cut two more boxing strips long enough to span the space between the back and front boxings, plus 3 inches.

To make it easier to join the pieces, locate the center front and back of the top and bottom pieces by folding them in half and marking the fold line with tailor's chalk. Similarly mark the center top and bottom of the back boxing strip.

Apart from the standard reupholstery supplies *(pages 98 and 99)*, you will need an upholstery zipper—stronger than a dressmaking zipper—as long as the back boxing strips. This zipper will lap several inches onto the sides, to make it easier to insert the stuffing. If you are adding new stuffing, you will also need a piece of polyurethane foam or foam rubber.

Polyurethane foam, also called polyfoam, is available in many grades and should be judged by its density and compressibility: The denser and heavier it feels, the longer it will last. Polyfoam with a density of 1.5 pounds per cubic foot and a compressibility of 35 pounds is ideal; it can be found at upholstery-supply shops or in stores that specialize in foam. If you are using foam rubber, choose a medium density. The standard cushion thicknesses in both of these foams are 3 and 4 inches.

If possible have the supplier machine-cut the foam to the desired size, since the result will be more even. If you must cut the foam yourself, an electric carving knife is the best tool. A serrated bread knife may also be used.

To round the contours of the cushion, you may want to add a layer of polyester batting to the top and bottom of the foam; glue it on with aerosol adhesive. Layers of the same batting can also be used to refurbish the contours of an old cushion or can be stuffed into the corners of a cushion whose foam slab is somewhat too small.

Anatomy of a Box Cushion

Creating the boxing strips. In this square cushion, the long front boxing strip has been cut into three pieces—one piece 5 inches longer than the cushion front, the remainder cut into two even lengths for the boxing at the sides. The two back boxing strips have been folded in half lengthwise, right side out, and each stitched ¼ inch in from the open edges, creating two double-thick back strips to hold the zipper along the folds. The edges of the cushion have been outlined with lengths of welt, cut 2 inches longer than the measure of the cushion's perimeter.

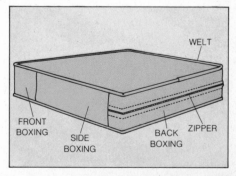

Circling a Cushion with Welt

Joining welt ends. Pin-baste the welt to the
cushion top (*page 120*), beginning at the center
back and clipping the fabric at the corners so
that the welt lies flat. Open the stitching at one
end of the welt and cut the exposed cord so it
butts against the covered cord at the other end of
the welt. Trim the opened welt cover ½ inch
longer than the exposed cord, fold under ¼ inch
of the fabric, and lap it over the other end of the
welt. Pin the joint to the cushion top, then saw
the welt in place with a zipper foot. Repeat this
procedure for the cushion bottom.

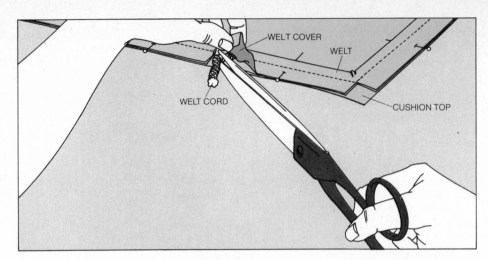

Installing an Access Zipper

1 Setting the zipper in boxing strips. Line up
one end of both back boxing strips with the top of
the zipper tape, folded edges against the edge
of the zipper teeth; pin the zipper tape in place,
open the zipper and machine-stitch along one
folded edge, ¼ inch from the fold. Begin stitching
at the top of the zipper, closing the zipper as you
near its base. At the base, pivot and stitch
across the zipper tape; then pivot again and stitch
along the other folded edge, ¼ inch from the
fold. With the zipper still closed, pivot and stitch
across its top, just above the glider.

2 Attaching back boxing to side boxing. Pin the
back boxing to the side boxing strips, right
sides together (*below, left*), and stitch ½-inch
seams. Then, with the boxing right side out,
fold 2 inches of one side boxing over the glider
end of the zipper, creating a pocket. Pin the
pocket edges to the back boxing and stitch along
the seam lines to hold the pocket in place.

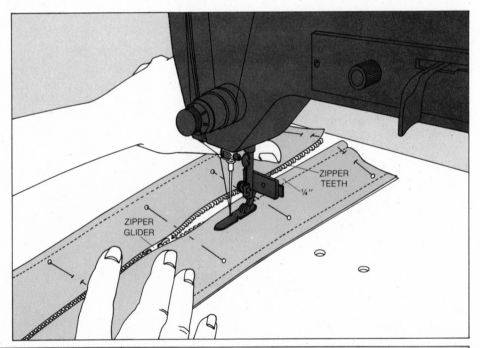

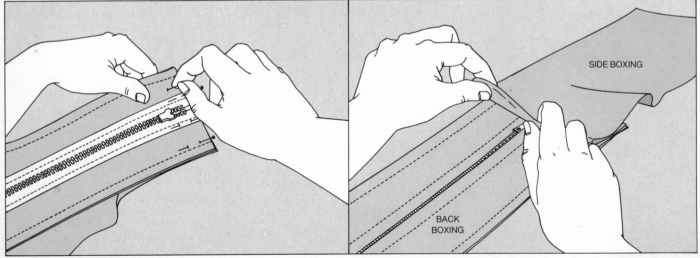

Attaching Boxing to Top and Bottom

1 **Pinning boxing to the cushion top.** Pin the back boxing strip to the cushion top, right sides together. Begin at the center back and work out to the ends of the strip, clipping the boxing for a smooth fit at the corners. Then pin the front boxing strip to the cushion top, beginning at the center front and again clipping the boxing at the corners for a smooth fit.

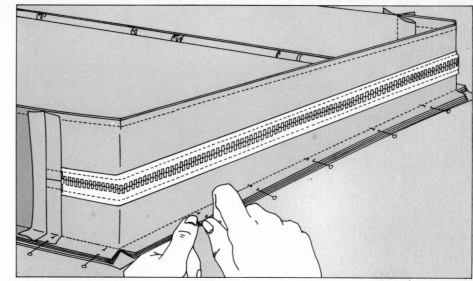

2 **Joining front and back boxing strips.** Pin together the front and back boxing strips along the side of the cushion, taking up in the seam any excess boxing fabric so the boxing fits smoothly around the cushion. Stitch the seam that joins the two boxing strips, then stitch the boxing to the cushion top, ½ inch from the edge. Pin and stitch boxing to the bottom in the same fashion.

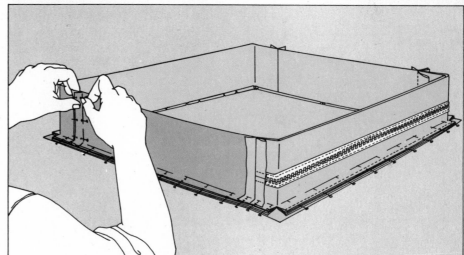

Stuffing the Cushion

Creating rounded contours. Using an aerosol adhesive suitable for polyurethane or foam rubber, coat the top of the foam and lay a sheet of polyester batting on top; press the sheet into place and trim it with scissors to fit the block. Repeat on the bottom. Slide the cushion into the cover, compressing the foam and reaching inside to push it into the corners. Close the zipper.

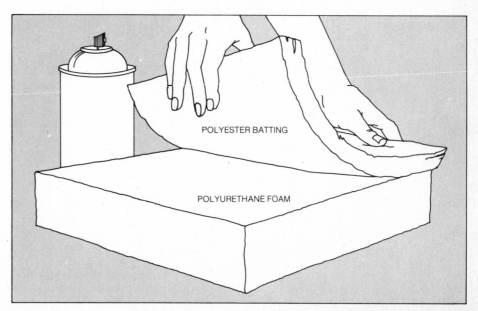

Attaching a New Cover to Finish the Project

The fabric that covers an upholstered chair or sofa is a true cover-up—outwardly it appears to be almost as seamless as skin, with few visible signs of construction. Yet actually the pieces of fabric have been joined to each other in a special overlapping order that simplifies the fitting task and minimizes the chance of error. One basic rule governs the job from beginning to end: Work from the inside of the chair to the outside, first attaching the inside cover pieces to the wooden frame, then covering their raw edges with the outside pieces.

Although there are hundreds of furniture styles, you can cover almost any chair or sofa by following the procedures used for the wing chair shown on these pages. For sofas, the sections of fabric simply are larger. On antiques, the procedures are actually easier because there are fewer upholstered parts and more "show wood"—sections of exposed and finished wood. Many modern chairs are not really upholstered at all: They are an assemblage of cushions screwed to an exposed frame, and you can simply remove the cushions and make new covers for them *(pages 121-123)*.

When professionals re-cover a chair or sofa, they usually try to duplicate the techniques used in the original covering.

As they remove the pieces of fabric *(pages 102-103)*, they note how each piece was trimmed and fitted around curves and frame parts, and where it was fastened. You need not, however, duplicate precisely the fastening techniques used originally, many of which may have been superseded by newer methods and even by new hardware.

The easiest way to join two pieces of upholstery fabric is to tack one piece directly to the frame and then fasten the other piece over it, using a technique known as blind tacking *(below and opposite, top)*, so called because the tacks are hidden by a fold of fabric. Where this is impossible because there is no wood beneath the joint, the two pieces must be sewed together—by machine if possible *(pages 118-120)*, by hand if necessary.

To hand-sew two pieces, upholsterers use a nearly invisible stitch called a blind stitch *(opposite, bottom)*, which buries almost all of the thread beneath the fabric. In some instances, as on the front of a chair arm *(page 129)*, where stitching produces a neater joint than blind tacking, upholsterers prefer to machine-sew as much of the seam as possible, then to finish the remainder by hand.

Ordinarily the new cover will be attached directly over a layer of cotton

padding. But in stripping an antique chair, you may find an undercover of muslin; decades ago most fine pieces were covered first with muslin, then with fabric of the buyer's choice. If the stuffing and frame of an old chair are in good condition, you can leave most of the muslin in place, but you may have to remove some of it to expose frame parts that the new cover will be attached to. These critical parts include the framing at the bottom of the chair and the outer faces of the arms, back and wings.

On all of these surfaces, you will have to remove the muslin undercover if the shape of the wooden framing members is not apparent. You may also have to untack the muslin cover if it obstructs the gaps in the frame through which you must pull the new fabric; usually you can retack the muslin to a part of the frame where it will not be in the way.

Professional upholsterers rarely discard existing padding when re-covering a chair. Rather, just before fastening the new cover, they add a layer of cotton padding over the old. This new padding does not need to be shaped; the cover will shape it. Since padding is inexpensive and can only improve the resiliency of what lies beneath it, use it anywhere the old padding seems thin or worn.

Techniques for Achieving a Snug Fabric Fit

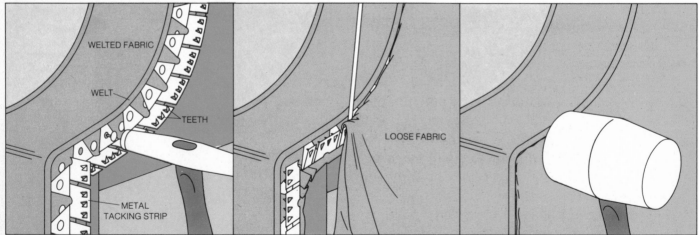

Blind tacking along a curve. Most seams on a chair or sofa are made by blind tacking the raw edge of one piece of fabric over the welted edge of a piece already in place. For blind-tacking along a curve, tack a length of flexible,

L-shaped metal tacking strip to the frame, setting the base of the L against the welt, with the toothed half of the strip facing out *(left)*. Fold the toothed half toward the tacked half, leaving a ¼-inch gap. Tuck the raw edge of the loose

fabric into this gap with a 10-inch straight needle *(center)*. Then hammer the tacking strip shut with a soft rubber mallet *(right)*. The teeth in the tacking strip will fasten the fabric against the welt, and the tacking strip will be invisible.

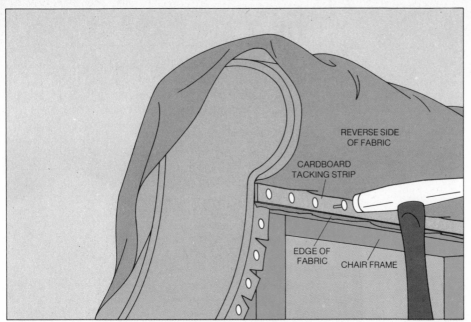

Blind tacking along a straight line. To blind-tack along a straight line, use a cardboard tacking strip. Position the loose fabric, wrong side out, against the welted fabric, aligning the raw edges. Hold the tacking strip against the corded welt and fasten the tacking strip to the frame, tacking through both layers of fabric. Then fold the loose fabric down over the tacking strip, so that the strip is hidden from view.

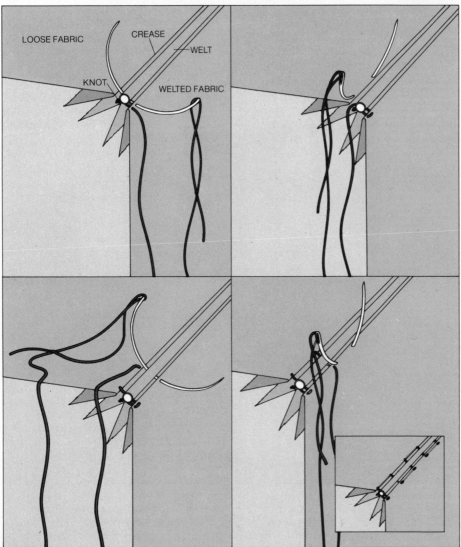

Blindstitching. Where a loose piece of fabric cannot be blind-tacked to a welted piece, you can sew it by hand with a blind stitch, using a curved upholsterer's needle. To make a blind stitch, first crease the loose fabric along its seam line, then cut a length of thread twice the length of the seam to be sewed. Tie a knot in one end of the thread, and hide the knot by stitching through the corded welt, close to the cording, bringing the needle up through the welted fabric, close to the welt. To make the first stitch, push the needle back through the welted fabric and corded welt (*upper left*), and carry the stitch inside the crease of the loose fabric, bringing it up ½ inch farther along (*upper right*).

Return the needle to the welted fabric by passing it through the corded welt (*lower left*). Then carry the stitch inside the welted fabric, bringing it back out ½ inch farther along (*lower right.*) Pull the thread tight to draw the pieces together, and repeat the stitch (*inset*), forming a pattern of crenelated stitches against the welt. To anchor the thread at the end of the seam, blindstitch backward about 2 inches, and use scissors to cut the thread off close to the welt.

Fitting the fabric to curves. If fabric must lap over an outside curve, relieve pressure on the fabric by slashing the edges at 1-inch intervals, cutting to within ¼ inch of the visible edge.

Where fabric must lap over an inside curve, fold the fabric edges into ½-inch pleats. To keep pleats even, put the first one at the middle of the curve, and work out toward the ends.

Fitting around exposed corner framing. Fold the fabric diagonally back from the corner of the frame, leaving about ⅜ inch between the corner of the frame and the fold line. Cut from the corner of the fabric in as far as the fold line. Then unfold the fabric, tuck the triangular sections under so that they fit against both sides of the frame (*inset*), and secure the fabric to the underside of the frame with tacks.

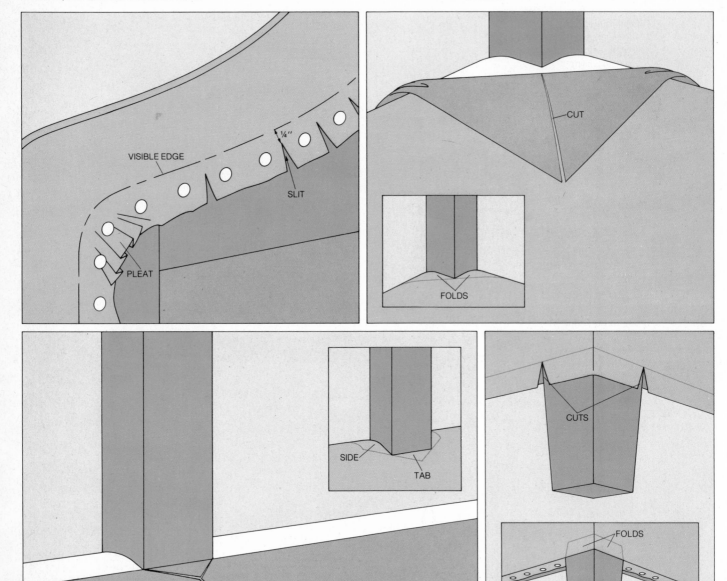

Fitting around three sides of a post. Fold the fabric back, parallel to the inner side of the frame, leaving a narrow space between the frame and the fold line. Make a Y-shaped cut that reaches the corners of the frame; the throat of the Y should be about 1 inch from

the frame. Fold under the tab at the top of the Y (*inset*), aligning it with the inner side of the frame. Then fold the two sides of the Y under, fitting them neatly against the remaining two sides of the frame. Finally, tack the bottom edge of the fabric to the underside of the frame.

Fitting fabric around a leg. Cut into the seam allowance of the fabric at the corners where the leg meets the frame, ending the cuts at the bottom of the frame. Fold the fabric under at the top of the leg (*inset*); tack it securely to the underside of the frame to hold the folds in place.

Attaching the Cover Fabric

1 **Sewing the decking to the seat.** Machine-stitch the decking—the rough fabric under the seat cushion—to the front seat cover (*page 118*). Then hand-sew the joined pieces to the burlap-covered seat along the seam line, positioning the seam 5 inches behind the edge roll (the padding at the front of the seat). Pin the decking to the burlap with upholsterer's pins, then fold back the front seat cover to expose the seam allowance. Hand-sew the seam allowance to the burlap with 1-inch stitches, using a curved upholsterer's needle and nylon stitching twine.

Return the front seat cover to its place, then fold the decking forward, along the seam line. Sew a piece of rubberized hair to the burlap behind the seam (*page 117*), and cover the hair with cotton padding. Fold the decking back.

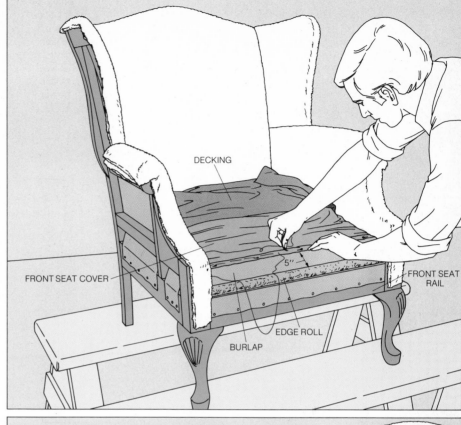

DECKING

FRONT SEAT COVER

FRONT SEAT RAIL

5"

BURLAP

EDGE ROLL

2 **Tacking the decking to the frame.** Slit the rear corners of the decking (*opposite, top right*) so that you can fit it around the back posts of the chair frame, and pull the decking through the back and sides of the frame—between the seat and the back and arm braces. Holding the decking taut, drive tacks halfway in at the middle of the back seat rail and the middle of each side seat rail. Then, working from the middle to the end of each rail, tack the decking permanently to the rails at 1-inch intervals.

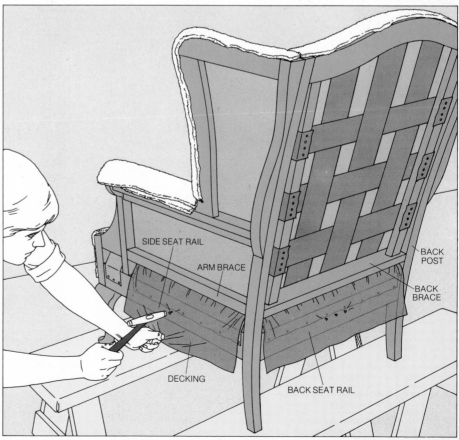

SIDE SEAT RAIL

ARM BRACE

BACK POST

BACK BRACE

DECKING

BACK SEAT RAIL

3 **Padding over the edge roll.** Again fold back the front seat cover along the seam line, and cut a piece of cotton padding to fit between the edge roll and the seam. Lay the padding loosely in place. Then cut a second, larger piece of padding (*inset*) to extend from the seam, over the edge roll, down to the bottom edge of the front seat rail. Tack this second piece of padding to the front seat rail, leaving it loose at the top, at the seam.

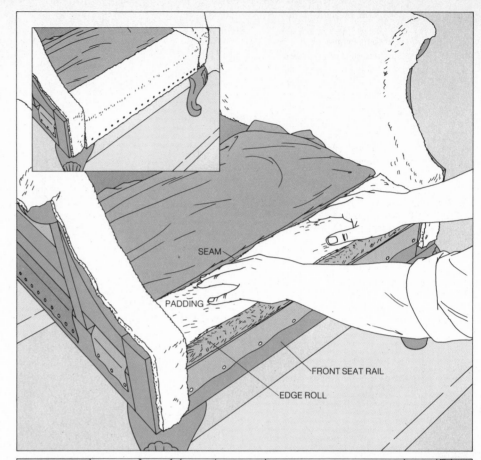

SEAM

PADDING

FRONT SEAT RAIL

EDGE ROLL

4 **Covering the front of the seat.** Pull the front seat cover down over the two layers of cotton padding and the edge roll; hold it taut and tack it temporarily to the underside of the front seat rail. Then pull at the sides of the cover, slit it to fit around the arm posts (*page 126*), and tack it temporarily to the outsides of the arm posts and to the side seat rails (*inset*). Cut and fold the cover so that it fits neatly around the front legs (*page 126*), and then tack it permanently to the lower edge of the front seat rail and to the arm posts and side seat rails.

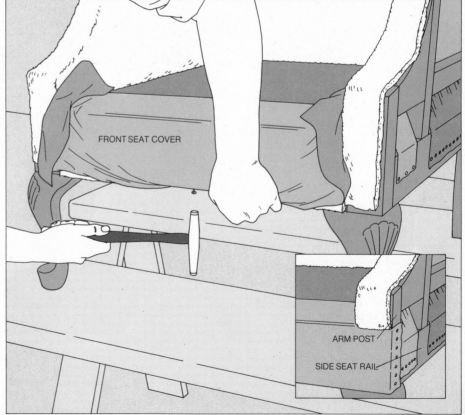

FRONT SEAT COVER

ARM POST

SIDE SEAT RAIL

5 Covering the inside arm. Machine-stitch an inside arm cover to the inside edge of a front arm cover, with welt already attached (*pages 106 and 107*); leave the unwelted outer edge of the front arm cover loose. Place the joined pieces on the chair (*inset*) and pull the top of the inside arm cover over the arm, tacking it temporarily to the outside of the arm board. Pull the back edge of the inside arm cover through to the back of the frame, at the gap between the back slat and the back post, and tack it temporarily to the back post. Then slit the bottom edge of the cover to fit through the arm frame, pull it down through the gap between the seat and the arm frame and tack it temporarily to the outside of the side seat rail, over the front seat cover and the decking.

Adjust the cover to fit smoothly over the arm stuffing, slitting it at the edges to eliminate wrinkles and bunching. Tack the cover permanently to the chair frame at 1-inch intervals.

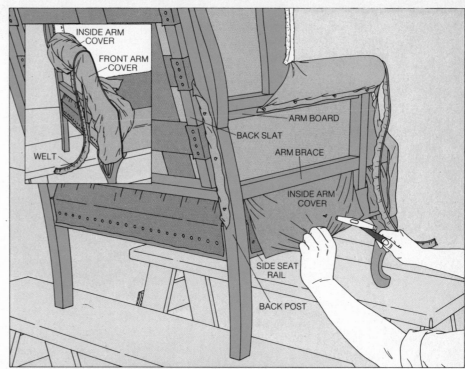

6 Fitting the front arm cover. Attach the bottom inside edge of the front arm cover to the arm post by folding back the cover and tacking the welted seam allowance to the post; place the last tack about 1 inch above the top of the chair leg. Then draw the cover tightly over the stuffing, tacking it temporarily to the outside of the arm post to hold it in place. Using scissors, slit and pleat the fabric to fit neatly around the curve of the arm post, and tack it permanently to the post at 1-inch intervals down to within 1 inch of the top of the chair leg.

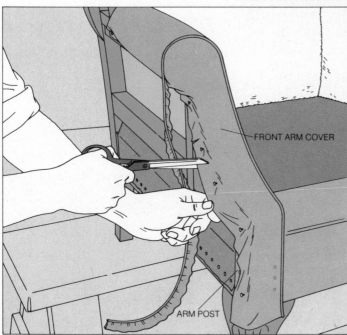

7 Fastening the arm welt. Hold the loose end of the welt against the curve of the front arm cover, checking that the previously stitched seam matches the curve of the upper arm; if it does not, open the seam with a razor blade where it does not fit. Then tack the welt to the outside of the arm post down to within 1 inch of the top of the chair leg, clipping and folding it for a neat fit. Finally, finish fastening the inside arm cover—still loose along the sharp curve at the top of the arm—by blind-stitching it (*page 125*) against the welt of the front arm cover.

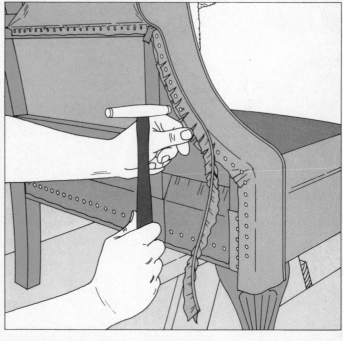

8 **Ending the welt.** Grasp the end of the cord inside one end of the welt, and slide the fabric back to expose more of the cord. Snip off the end of the cord even with the top of the chair leg and pull the excess fabric back over the end. Repeat at the other end of the welt. Then fold the fabric under, even with the top of the leg, and tack it to the arm post just above the leg.

Following Steps 5 through 8, attach the inside arm cover, front arm cover and welt to the opposite chair arm in the same way.

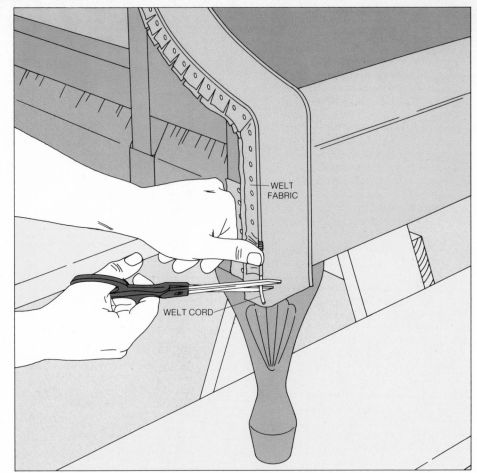

9 **Covering the inside wing.** Place an inside wing cover against a wing, centering the dominant design element if there is one, and mark the line where the bottom of the wing meets the arm; machine-stitch welt along this line (*page 120*). Begin to fit the cover at the top of the wing, temporarily anchoring the bottom by tacking the welted bottom edge to the outside of the wing frame. First, make a large V cut at the top rear corner, where the top back rail meets the back post. Pull the upper edge of the V-cut fabric over the top back rail and tack it to the rail temporarily (*inset*). Pull the lower edge through the gap between the back post and back slat, and tack it temporarily to the back post.

Lap the fabric over the top of the wing and, holding it taut against the stuffing, pleat it so it fits around the sharp curve along the front of the wing top; drive tacks permanently through the pleats into the top wing rail and into the wing post. Then slash the fabric to fit along the gentler curves at the top and front of the wing, and tack it temporarily. After adjusting the fabric to eliminate wrinkles and bunching, tack it permanently to the front, back and top of the wing frame at 1-inch intervals. Blind-stitch (*page 125*) the welted bottom edge to the inside arm. Attach the cover for the other inside wing in the same way.

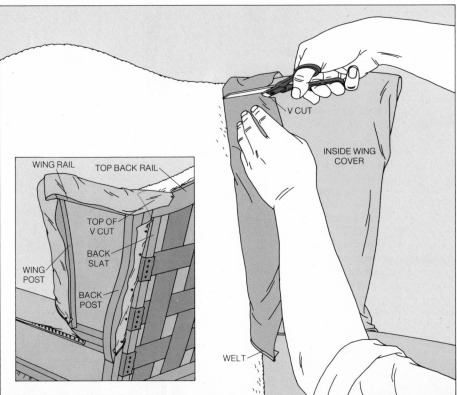

10 **Covering the inside back.** Lay the cover for the inside back over the stuffing, centering the dominant design element if there is one, and make four V cuts in the corners of the cover—two at the top, where the top back rail meets the back posts, and two at the bottom, where the back posts meet the back brace. Pull the cover over the top of the back and through the gaps in the sides and bottom of the frame *(inset)*. Temporarily tack the cover to the outside of the top back rail for several inches along the middle of the rail. Pull the sides of the cover over the back posts and tack them temporarily at the middle of the posts. Pull the bottom edge downward and tack it temporarily to the back seat rail at the middle. Starting from the midpoint of each post or rail, tack the cover permanently to the frame at 1-inch intervals. If you want buttons on the back, attach them now *(page 133)*.

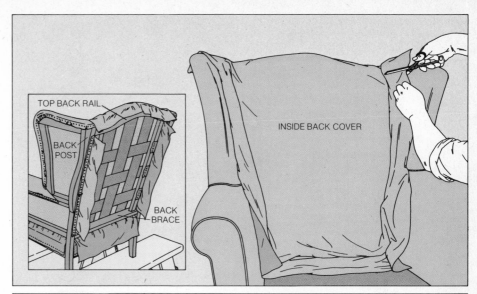

11 **Tacking on the wing welt.** Cut a length of welt —called the wing welt—to fit the outer edge of the two wings and the back, adding 2 inches at each end for finishing. Slide back the fabric at each end, and clip the cord to fit the exact measurement of the wing welt. Tack one end of the welt to the underside of the arm board just below the wing, to hide the raw end. Then tack the welt to the entire edge of the combined wings and back, placing the tacks at 1-inch intervals and clipping or pleating the welt seam allowance to fit around curves. Hide the end of the welt under the opposite arm board as at the beginning of the tacking operation.

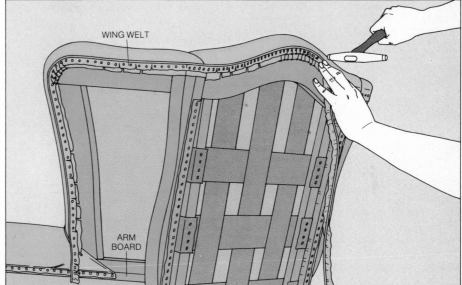

12 **Fastening the outside wing cover.** Tack a length of metal tacking strip to the outside of the wing frame, beginning at the bottom of the wing post, following the line of the wing welt, and ending at the upper rear corner of the wing. Then tack a piece of burlap over the outside wing, doubling the edges of the burlap to keep it from tearing, and tack a layer of cotton padding over the burlap. Place the outside wing cover over the wing, and tack it temporarily over the back post and under the arm board. Blind-tack the cover to the frame at the front and top of the wing *(page 124)*, and tack it directly to the frame along the back and bottom of the wing *(inset)*, placing the tacks at 1-inch intervals. Attach the opposite outside wing cover in the same way.

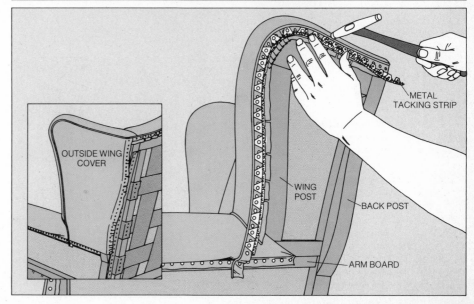

13 **Fitting the outside arm cover.** After turning the chair on its side, fasten a metal tacking strip along the welt that outlines the front of the outside arm. Cover the entire outside arm with burlap and cotton padding, as in Step 12, page 131. Place the outside arm cover on the chair, matching its pattern to that of the outside wing cover so that the two appear to be one continuous piece of fabric. With a row of pins, mark the seam line where the inside and outside arm covers join. Then carefully fold the outside arm cover up over the inside arm cover, using the row of pins to align their common seam. Using a cardboard tacking strip, blind-tack the outside arm cover in place on this seam line, driving the tacks into the side of the arm board *(inset)*.

Temporarily tack the back and bottom edges of the cover to their respective sections of frame —the rear of the back post and the lower edge of the side seat rail. Then, using the metal tacking strip, blind-tack the front edge against the welt, and cut and fold the bottom edge of the cover to fit around the front and back legs *(page 126)*. Finally, fasten the back and bottom edges permanently with tacks at 1-inch intervals.

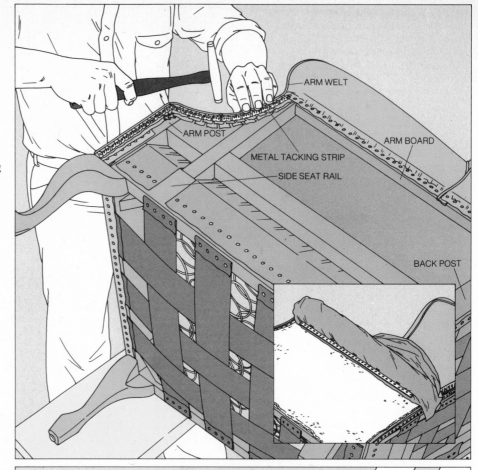

ARM WELT

ARM POST

METAL TACKING STRIP

SIDE SEAT RAIL

ARM BOARD

BACK POST

14 **Covering the outside back.** After resting the chair on its arms, tack two vertical strips of welt down the full length of the back (one on each side) and finish off their ends, top and bottom, as in Step 8, page 130. Outline the top and sides of the back with a continuous length of metal tacking strip. Cover the entire back with burlap and cotton padding. Using the metal tacking strip, blind-tack the cover to the back, centering the dominant design if there is one. Then tack the bottom edge of the cover to the underside of the back seat rail at 1-inch intervals, folding and fitting the cover at the rear legs *(page 126)*.

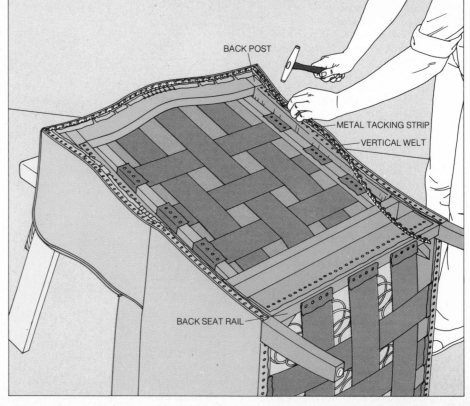

BACK POST

METAL TACKING STRIP

VERTICAL WELT

BACK SEAT RAIL

15 **Covering the bottom with cambric.** Turn the chair upside down and cut a piece of cambric that is ½ inch wider than the outer dimensions of the bottom of the chair frame. Fold under ¾ inch on all four sides of the cambric, and tack it temporarily to the frame at the midpoints of the seat rails at the front, sides and back; leave ¼ inch between the fold line and the edge of each rail. Then, working out from the middle to the end of each rail, tack the cambric permanently to the frame at 1-inch intervals, fitting it around the legs as shown on page 126.

Attach any remaining finishing decorations, such as braid or decorative tacks (*below*). Make a seat cushion, as described on pages 121-123.

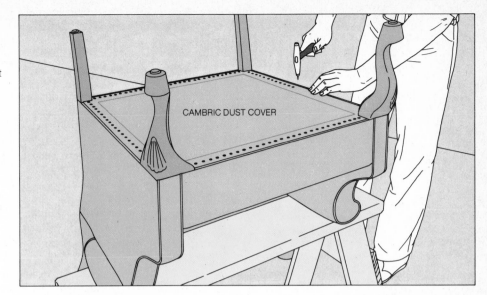

CAMBRIC DUST COVER

Finishing Touches for Alternate Styles

Hiding a raw edge. If fabric is tacked to the outside instead of the underside of the frame, conceal the tacks with gimp—ornamental trim— or with decorative nails or both. To fasten gimp, spread a bead of white glue along the fabric edge and hold the gimp in place for several minutes, until the glue dries. To hold the gimp more securely, you may also tack it to the frame with small gimp tacks 1 inch apart. If the gimp tacks are too conspicuous, hide them by placing broad-headed decorative nails next to them (*inset*). To hide exposed tacks with decorative nails alone, cover the edge with a continuous row of nails, heads touching.

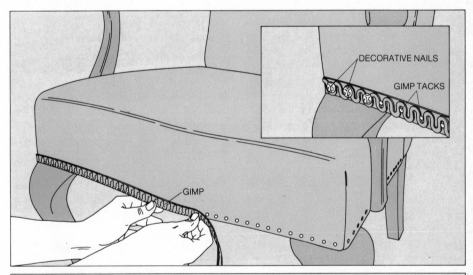

DECORATIVE NAILS

GIMP TACKS

GIMP

Attaching buttons. If you use buttons, fasten them to the inside back cover (*Step 10*) before attaching the outside cover. Using chalk, mark locations for the buttons on the inside cover of the chair back. For each button cut a length of nylon stitching twine about 18 inches long, and thread the twine through the eye on the back of the button. Then bring the two ends of the twine together, and thread them through the eye of a 10-inch straight needle. Push the needle through the inside cover of the chair back at a mark, and pull it through to the outside.

From the rear, fasten the button twine to the webbing of the chair back with a knot made with the two ends of the twine; insert a wad of cotton padding into the knot (*inset*) before tightening it. Secure the twine with two additional knots.

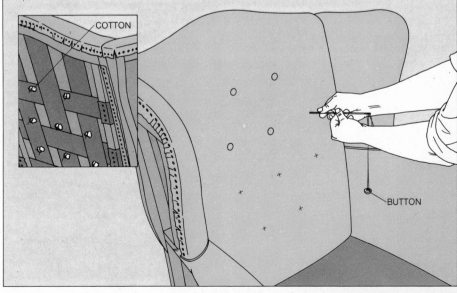

COTTON

BUTTON

Picture Credits

The sources for the illustrations in this book are shown below. The drawings were created by Jack Arthur, Laszlo Bodrogi, Roger C. Essley, Charles Forsythe, Dick Lee, John Martinez, Joan S. McGurren and W. F. McWilliam. Credits for the illustrations from left to right are separated by semicolons, from top to bottom by dashes.

Cover: Fil Hunter. 6: Fil Hunter. 8, 9: Forte, Inc. 10-17: Frederic F. Bigio from B-C Graphics. 18-25: John Massey. 26-31: Walter Hilmers Jr. from HJ Commercial Art. 33: Michael Dunne, London. 34: Andrejs Legzdins, Stockholm. 35: Robert Perron, courtesy of Arthur Ferber, designer; Michael Dunne, London. 36: Jaime Ardiles-Arce, courtesy Juan Montoya/ Design Corporation. 37: Charles Nesbit, courtesy Design Coalition, Alan Buchsbaum, architect—Bradley Olman, courtesy Ward Bennett, designer. 38: Carla de Benedetti, courtesy Achille Castiglioni, architect, Milan; Michael Dunne, London, courtesy Andrew Usiskin/Redington Design Co., Ltd. 39: Robert Perron, courtesy Gordon Thorne. 40: Fil Hunter. 42- 45: Elsie J. Hennig. 46-49: John Massey. 50-55: William J. Hennessy Jr. 56, 57: John Massey. 58-63: Eduino J. Pereira. 64, 65: Forte, Inc. 67-71: Eduino J. Pereira. 72-75: Terry Atkinson. 76-79: Walter Hilmers Jr. from HJ Commercial Art. 80: Fil Hunter. 85-90: Frederic F. Bigio from B-C Graphics. 94, 95: Walter Hilmers Jr. from HJ Commercial Art. 96: Fil Hunter. 98, 99: Frederic F. Bigio from B-C Graphics. 101-107: Snowden Associates, Inc. 109-117: Frederic F. Bigio from B-C Graphics. 118-120: Forte, Inc. 121-123: Melissa B. Pooré. 124-133: John Massey.

Acknowledgments

The index/glossary for this book was prepared by Louise Hedberg. The editors also wish to thank the following: Walter Angst, Chief Conservator, Conservation Analytical Laboratory, Smithsonian Institution, Washington, D.C.; Henry Barrow, Glen Echo, Md.; Ward Bennett, New York, N.Y.; John Bertalan, Chief of Conservation, Department of Collections, Colonial Williamsburg, Williamsburg, Va.; Jack and Caroline Blevins, Annandale, Va.; Alan Buchsbaum, Architect, New York, N.Y.; C. S. Osborne Co., Harrison, N.J.; Charles Carson, Carson's Furniture Refinishing and Repair, Lorton, Va.; Achille Castiglioni, Architect, Milan, Italy; James Clark, M. C. G. Limited, Washington, D.C.; Sid Diamond, Sid Diamond Display Corporation, New York, N.Y.; Thomas Doyle and Harold J. Tyson, Wood Hobby Shop, Bolling Air Force Base, Washington, D.C.; Arthur Ferber, New York, N.Y.; Hugo Henth, Brown Jordan Company, Suffolk, Va.; Carolyn Jones and Dot Vann, Miss B's Antiques, Ltd., Washington, D.C.; Andrejs Legzdins, Architect, Hägersten, Sweden; Roghilo Mandez, Market Place Interiors, Alexandria, Va.; Maurice Miller, Miller's Upholstery Shop, Washington, D.C.; Juan Montoya, Design Corporation, New York, N.Y.; Hillel Nachbi, Centennial Antiques and Restoration, Washington, D.C.; Bill Shotwell, Restorations Unlimited, Fairfax, Va.; David Termini, Silver Spring, Md.; Gordon Thorne, Artist, Thorne's Market, Northampton, Mass.; Andrew Usiskin, The Redington Design Company Limited, Hampstead, England; Bill Whitman, The Strip Joint, Alexandria, Va.; Norval Wilson, Bowie, Md. The editors are indebted to Carol Corner, Eduardo D. Cortez, Kathryn G. Heavey, James Koenig, Diane Odgen and Ania Savage, writers, for their help with the preparation of this book.

Index/Glossary

Included in this index are definitions of some of the technical terms used in this book. Page references in italics indicate an illustration of the subject mentioned.

Amalgamation: *process by which old finish is dissolved and respread after application of proper solvent.* Restoring damaged surface, 82, 84

Antique: repairs and value of, 41; restoring professionally, 7

Apron: in cabinet, 26; in table, *18, 19, 20, 21*

Bedframe: correcting warped rails, *25;* reinforcing side rails, 22, *24;* replacing fasteners for joints, *22-24*

Bentwood furniture: gluing a split, *56-57;* reinforcing split with dowels, *57*

Bleach: neutralizing, 90; removing stains with, 90; on wood, 90

Blind tacking: *method of attaching pieces of fabric with hidden tacking strips.* On upholstered chair, 101, *124-125*

Bracing blocks: *supports for glued breaks.* Hardwood for, 50; hidden, *54;* mortised, *53-54*

Burlap: *material in upholstered seat that supports stuffing.* Fitting to chair, *116;* sewing to springs, *117;* tacking to chair, *131, 132;* tightening on an arm, *111;* in upholstered furniture, 99, *101,* 108

Burn, in wood, patching area with wax stick, 82, 83, *85*

Butt joint, reinforced with dowels, *18, 19, 20*

C clamps, *18, 19, 28, 43, 44, 50, 52, 53, 54;* padding, *18, 19;* placing, 50

Cabinet: joints, *26;* replacing faulty casters, 26, *30-31;* warped door, 26, *29*

Cambric: *dust cover on underside of upholstered chair or couch.* Adding, *133;* on chair, *101,* 108; material for, 99; removing, 102

Cane seats: restoring with prewoven cane, 66, 67, *71;* weaving cane by hand, 66, 67, *72-75*

Casters: replacing broken or bent, 26, *30-31*

Caul clamp, *55*

Chair: cutting a new arm, *63;* duplicating legs, *61-63;* frame, *8, 13, 17;* mending broken leg, *51-52;* platform, *8, 13, 16-17;* reassembling, *16-17;* refitting and

replacing joints, *13-16;* regluing joints in, *8, 9, 10-12, 16-17;* replacing rocking-chair runner, *59-60;* shaping curved rail, *61;* taking apart, *13*

Chair seats, woven: finishes, 66; supplies, 66, 67; using prewoven cane, 66, 67, *71;* weaving cane by hand, 66, 67, *72-75;* wrapping fiber rush, 66, 67, *69-70*

Clamping: bentwood, *57;* C clamps, *18, 19, 28, 43, 44, 50, 52, 53, 54;* caul clamp, *55;* cracked tabletop, *55;* glued breaks, 9, 18, 50; pipe clamp, *18, 19, 20,* 50, 52, *53, 54, 55;* web clamp, *8, 11, 16, 17*

Cushions, box, *101;* adding batting, 98, *121, 123;* buying new foam, 121; covering, *121-123;* reviving down, 121; welt on, *121, 122;* zipper, *122*

Decking: *rough fabric under seat cushions.* Attaching, *127;* material for, 99, 100; sewing seams, *118;* in upholstered furniture, *101,* 108, *117*

Denatured alcohol: amalgamation, 82, 84; solvent for shellac finish, 83

Door, cabinet: planing edges, 29, *30;* throwing hinges, 26, 29; warped, 26, *29*

Dovetail joint, 6, 27

Dowel: broken, *15;* hardwood for, 50; measuring, *58;* mending bentwood, 56, *57;* mending breaks with, 50, *51-53*

Dowel joint: pinning, *10, 11, 12;* refitting, *13-14;* regluing loose, *8, 10-11*

Doweling jig, *18, 20, 31, 51*

Drawer: drawer-glide buttons, 26; regluing joints, 26, 27; replacing guides, 26, *28;* reshoeing, 26, *28*

Drop-leaf table, wedging, *18, 21*

Duplicating broken or missing parts: cabriole leg, *61-62;* chair arm, *63;* curved chair rail, *61;* measuring for pattern, *58-59;* replacing tapered leg, *62-63;* rocking-chair runner, *59-60;* shaping piece on lathe, *64-65*

Edge roll: *prefabricated cylinder that shapes and pads front edge of seat.* Attaching, *117;* on chair, 99, *101,* 116; padding, *128*

Enamel finish, 82, 83

Extension table, lubricating tracks, 21

Fabric, upholstery: choosing, 100; and home sewing machine, 98, *118-120;* making pattern pieces from old cover, 100, *102, 103-104;* rough-cutting to measurements, 100, *103, 105-106;* sewing supplies, 118; welt, 118, *119-*

120. See Reupholstery

Fiber-rush seat, wrapping, 66, 67, *69-70*

Finish, repairing damage to: blemishes, 82; burns and chips, 82; cleaning surface, 82; restoring surface, 84; scratches, 82; silicone haze, 82, 84; spot repairs, 82, *chart* 83; stripping, *86-87;* white haze, 82, 84; white rings, 82, 83

Finishes, wood: amalgamating, 82, 84; applying, *94-95;* chemically reactive, 82; choosing, 81, 92-93; cleaning, 82; clear, 92-93; identifying, 82; penetrating, 81; solvent-release, 82; surface-coating, 81

Foam rubber, in cushions, 121

Frame: of cabinet, 26; measuring chair for new cover, *105;* of upholstered chair, *102*

Furniture dye, covering scratch with, 83

Furniture polish: covering scratches, 83; restoring surface with, 84

Gimp: *decorative braid.* Attaching, 133; tack, 99

Glue, types of, 9

Glue injector: *syringe for applying glue in tight spots.* Using, *10,* 12, 18, 46, 47, 55

Gluing: bentwood, *56-57;* bonding, 9, 50; with braces, 50, *53-54;* breaks, 50; chair joints, *8, 10-12, 16-17;* clamping glued breaks, 9, 18, 50; cracked tabletop, *55;* with dowels, 50, *51-53;* drawer joints, 26, 27; patching wood, *43;* rebuilt corner, *44;* table joints, *18, 19-20;* veneer, 40, 46, 47, *48-49. See also* Joints

Grave: *depression left when damaged section of finish is removed to permit patching.* In solid wood, 42, *43;* in veneer, 40, *48-49*

High tech: *decorating style that uses adaptations of industrial equipment and materials for home furnishings.* Examples, 32, *33-39*

Joints: cabinet, *26;* dado-and-rabbet, *26, 27;* dovetail, 6, 27; dowel, *8, 10-11, 13-14, 15;* drawer, 26, 27; fasteners for, in bedframe, *22-24;* lap, *19;* mortise-and-tenon, *8, 10, 11-12, 16, 19;* refitting, *13-14, 16;* regluing chair, *8, 10-12, 16-17;* repairing in table, *18-21;* shrink, *10*

Lacquer: amalgamating, 82, 84; on cane seat, 66; finish, 81, 82, 92-93; restoring